THE SOLDIERS' WALL

A GLIMPSE INTO THEIR WORLD

THE SOLDIERS' WALL

A GLIMPSE INTO THEIR WORLD

LYRIS MITCHELL

First published 2013

National Library of Australia Cataloguing-in-Publication entry:

Author:	Mitchell, Lyris.
Title:	The soldiers' wall / Lyris Mitchell.
ISBN:	9781922109606 (pbk.)
Subjects:	World War II Soldier Signatures Wall (Brisbane, Qld.)
	World War, 1939-1945--Graffiti.
	Graffiti--Queensland--Brisbane.
	World War, 1939-1945--Queensland--Brisbane--History.
	Soldiers--Queensland--Brisbane.
	Brisbane (Qld.)--Social life and customs--1922-1945.
	Brisbane (Qld.)--History--1939-1945.
Dewey Number:	940.539431

Typeset in Cambria 10pt.

Cover Design: Boolarong Press

Images: *Soldiers' Wall* (Lyris Mitchell) and *Brisbane, December 1939: AIF Infantry procession in Queen Street with the Treasury Building in the background.* (John Oxley Library, State Library of Queensland)

Published by Boolarong Press, Salisbury, Brisbane, Australia.

Printed and bound by Watson Ferguson & Company, Salisbury, Brisbane, Australia.

DEDICATED TO AUSTRALIA'S WARTIME GENERATION

FOREWORD

City Hall is known as the 'People's Place'. From its official opening in 1930, this grand building has served the City of Brisbane and provided a unique meeting place for both residents and visitors.

You can imagine my surprise when, in October 2008, a workman discovered pencilled names and numbers on a wall while renovating part of the basement in the Red Cross rooms. What made it especially exciting was that it was just prior to the 70th Anniversary of World War II.

As a City Hall tour guide, Lyris Mitchell was passionate about this historic find. In her spare time, she embarked on a quest to painstakingly document and research more than 150 signatures that were found on what is now known as *The Soldiers' Wall*. I am proud to advise that Lyris was awarded a special commendation in 2009 by the then Lord Mayor of Brisbane, Campbell Newman, for her dedication and hard work.

I am sure you can appreciate the significant historic importance of this artefact. The wall has attracted the attention of the public, including veterans, and is particularly moving for the relatives of wall signatories.

As Lord Mayor, it is a great honour for me to acknowledge the hard work Lyris has undertaken. The wall is a very special find that further connects us to those who played a part in World War II and which now forms part of our historical fabric.

I trust you will enjoy reading this fascinating history behind *The Soldiers' Wall*.

Yours sincerely

Graham Quirk

LORD MAYOR

FOREWORD

PREFACE

This book has been written to provide an historical record of the Heritage listed World War II Soldiers' Signatures Wall, which is located in the basement of Brisbane's City Hall. By identifying and researching the men who signed the wall, a great deal of historical material has emerged about their personal lives as well as providing information about the era in which they lived.

World War II had special significance for Australia because for the first time war was close to home. Many people, especially the young, are not familiar with the conditions of life during this important period and the enormous effort that was made to keep Australia free. By focusing on these men who signed the wall an image of their world has emerged.

The enormity and complexity of information about World War II makes it difficult to simplify, so only the basic details have been presented here. The timeline concentrates on the main events affecting Australians and includes extra material to show not just when certain events occurred, but also the reason why they occurred.

Throughout the war, the needs and procedures for both the military and civilian sectors changed as circumstances changed. The chapters detailing these changes are included to provide a background for the men on the wall and also as an aid to people researching their family's military history. Nearly all of the topics mentioned are subjects for further research in their own right.

In addition, this book has also provided an avenue for veterans, their relatives and members of the public to voice their recollections and to provide stories from an era that is quickly fading from living memory. During the war, Australia strengthened the relationship with a firm ally from across the Pacific Ocean and many of these stories include them.

Australia's military heritage has been enhanced by the discovery of the Soldiers' Wall, which provides a tangible and human contact to the past.

CONTENTS

CHAPTER 1

INTRODUCTION AND DISCOVERY

Brisbane's history during World War II is rich with the stories of thousands of individual Allied servicemen who enlisted, trained, visited, returned and recuperated in our fair city.

Major (Retd) Patrick O'Keeffe, OAM, Battle for Australia Commemoration National Council, July 2010

Brisbane City Hall in 1949. *(Courtesy of the John Oxley Library, State Library of Queensland 450609)*

In less than a decade since its opening in 1930, Brisbane's City Hall was fulfilling a vital need for the city, for the State and for the nation. From the beginning of World II in Europe in September 1939, it became a major enlistment venue for servicemen and servicewomen. Conveniently located in the centre of the city, it also catered to the needs of military personnel by providing much needed rest and recreation in the form of dances, concerts and other social events. The citizens of Brisbane were glad to help.

> *In the early stages of the war, State schools from the south side of Brisbane came to City Hall to perform concerts, and by request, gave repeat performances. I was 11 years old when I came with the Cannon Hill State School to sing on stage in the auditorium. Some of the songs we sang were "Onward Christian Soldiers", "There Will Always be an England" and "Land of Hope and Glory". There were many proud parents packing the auditorium. My brother, Cecil Linning, was a Rat of Tobruk at the time, driving ambulances. We all felt very patriotic and that we were helping the war effort.*
>
> Olga Townend, sister of Cecil Linning, AIF 1939-1944, October 2011

City Hall became a very popular dropping-off spot and meeting place for service personnel from military centres and camps in and around Brisbane.

> *I came into Brisbane on leave, including "night leave", and often passed through City Hall. It was the normal thing for many soldiers who were stationed in and around Brisbane to walk through City Hall as recreation.*
>
> Veteran Bertram Watson, AIF 1943-1946, October 2009

Many other soldiers had the same idea.

> *I had enlisted there so I went for a night out on the town.*
>
> Wall Signatory, Walter Huggonson, AIF 1941-1944, April 2012

After the attack on Pearl Harbor in December 1941, the fall of Singapore, the bombing of Darwin and the arrival of the American General Douglas MacArthur in Brisbane, the city was to have a new and more important role in the course of the war. The expansion of the Japanese into the South West Pacific Area had been so rapid that it created a general feeling of panic that mainland Australia would be invaded. Against this backdrop of fear and uncertainty, masses of military personnel came to Brisbane and the number of enlistments rapidly increased.

As the Supreme Commander of the South West Pacific Area, General Douglas MacArthur based his headquarters in Brisbane because it was the closest major city to the warzone. Brisbane became an important training centre as well as the major staging post for military personnel heading to Northern Queensland for jungle training or for deployment overseas. Many had already faced the enemy in the Mediterranean region and the Middle East, and were now preparing to face a new type of enemy in the islands of the South West Pacific Area in totally different conditions.

As the war intensified, the numbers of visitors to City Hall increased as it played host to thousands of Commonwealth and United States servicemen who found themselves at leisure in our city. Some were returning on leave after seeing action, others were convalescing and some were just passing through. Brisbane welcomed them all.

> *The Australian Comforts Fund made a lot of handcrafted items for the troops, e.g., socks, mittens and sweaters. They gave special attention to military people who had no family in Brisbane. Many of them were away from home for the first time. It was the women from the Australian Comforts Fund who handed out welcome kits, which included pencils, in the Red Cross rooms at City Hall.*
>
> Bob Arkell, July 2011

A major part of City Hall's attraction had been the Red Cross Cafe located in the basement on the Adelaide Street side of the building. These tea rooms had been opened during World War II specifically to cater to the needs of military personnel. After the war, they remained open for use by the public and played an integral part in the lives of many Brisbane residents. For nearly 70 years, they held a secret.

DISCOVERY

In October 2008, workmen from Hawley Constructions were renovating the basement area of Brisbane City Hall where the Red Cross rooms were situated. They were asked to put shelves on what had been once a wall in the former men's room, but now formed part of a hallway. The plaster needed to be removed in order that the wall could be examined to see what it was made from and how much support would be needed for the shelving.

While removing some of the old plaster, one of the men, the general foreman, Brian Gough, discovered some writing in pencil. Upon further investigation, this writing was found to be a series of names and numbers that began with QX. QX identified the soldiers as Queensland enlistees in the Second Australian Imperial Forces (AIF). Mr Gough, a former naval Leading Seaman, immediately recognised the significance of his discovery. It was graffiti from soldiers who had visited the Red Cross rooms during World War II. In his own words, he described how he felt at the time.

> *It was a very exciting find, and a weird sensation. I had a good feeling that I had accomplished something very meaningful and historical.*
>
> Brian Gough, August 2010

For two days he scraped the plaster off before he told anyone as he simply enjoyed what he had found. He eventually telephoned his employer, Kevin Hawley. The Brisbane City Council's City Design Section was then notified as well as the Heritage Unit and the Lord Mayor's Office. Mr Gough continued to remove old plaster to reveal the full extent of the writing. Once the plaster removal had been completed, the entire area (2.32 x 1.02 metres) was covered with a secure perspex panel to preserve the graffiti. The wall was immediately Heritage listed and was pronounced to be *highly significant.*

Archaeology – The Use of Pencils

The signing of the wall with pencils is the main reason that the signatures have survived. The soldiers were able to obtain their pencils from City Hall as part of the community's welcome to them. Pencils were more convenient to carry as fountain pens needed constant refilling and were notorious for leaking, while biros were not invented until the 1950s. In any case, if ink from any source had been used to write the signatures they would not have survived for nearly 70 years, because moisture from the plaster used to coat the wall would have affected the ink. As pencils survive moisture well, they are often used by museums and other places for the labelling of specimens, especially if they are being stored in ice.

The use of pencils had another beneficial effect. When pencil is written on to plaster it is extremely difficult to remove. There is evidence that the custodian who tried to clean the wall manually with soap and water was unsuccessful, so the wall had been plastered over instead. Being wartime, when both manpower and materials were in short supply, it is not surprising that cheap, high lime content plaster was used. This was much easier for Mr Gough to remove than the better-quality, more enduring plaster used to cover a small area on the far left-hand side of the wall. Being very difficult to remove, he left this section untouched because its removal was thought to be too damaging to the writing underneath.

Since the end of the war, additional layers of plaster had been applied to the wall and it had also been painted over several times. This gave further protection to the signatures until they were discovered in 2008.

Dating the Wall

By using the material that the soldiers actually wrote themselves, the earliest date is "2/6/41" and the latest date is "October 42". Other sources, including the soldiers' personal Service Records, reveal that this timeframe could be extended from the middle of 1941 until the end of 1942. There is no evidence of any signatures being made from 1943 onwards. This means that the signatures were being made during 18 months of one of the most turbulent periods in Australia's history.

From nearly a million military personnel in World War II, this select group of graffiti writers have provided a sample that is small enough to study in detail and who all have something in common, that is, they were all in Brisbane at some time within the same 18 month period and they all wrote on the wall.

By examining their records it has been possible to obtain a picture of their lives during not only this period, but also throughout the entire war. The wall therefore provides an opportunity to glimpse the soldiers' world during these years by investigating these men who came to Brisbane's City Hall. It has provided a microcosm of a time that is so different to the world of today.

CHAPTER 2

IDENTIFICATION AND CASE STUDIES

Determination of the correct identification of the men was the first primary task. This required extensive research using a number of sources. Although every care had been made to providing the correct identification for each of the signatures, there have been a number of problems that have made this difficult and, occasionally, completely impossible.

Problems with Identifications

All of these features hindered interpretation of the writing.

- Some of the plaster has been intentionally left on the wall since its removal may have destroyed the signatures. This also includes fine traces of the weaker plaster, which has impeded investigations. In some cases, identification has been made using only partial signatures.
- Parts of the wall have been damaged over the years, and several cracks have appeared. There are also a few minor holes that unfortunately occur in the middle of signatures.
- There have also been attempts to clean the graffiti off the wall by past custodians of the basement. Some of the signatures have survived in a partial form, but many were destroyed completely.
- Some of the writing is extremely faint.
- In some cases, soldiers have written over the top of another soldier's signature.
- Much of the handwriting is very difficult to read. The older, more decorative style of cursive writing was often used, which is unfamiliar to modern researchers

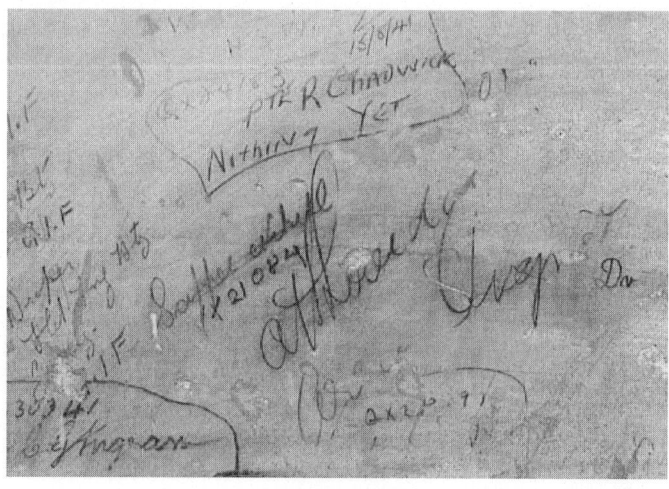

Old cursive writing: "A. H. Loveday, QX 34..., Sigs". *(Image Copyright Brisbane City Council)*

- Some of the handwriting is illegible.
- There are five examples of true graffiti-style signatures which, by their very nature, are convoluted and difficult to decipher.

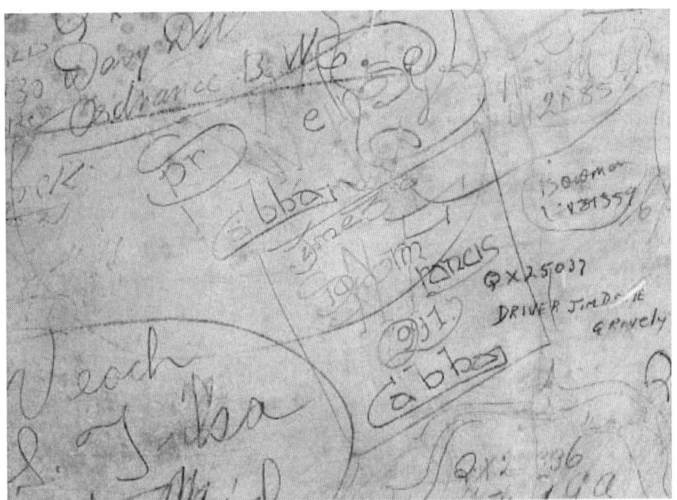

True graffiti-style signatures of Sapper Melrose and Signaller Francis. *(Image Copyright Brisbane City Council)*

Once the writing had been deciphered, there were further obstacles to identification. These were related to the soldiers themselves making errors or to problems with the military records of the period.

- Many of the soldiers were issued with two Service Numbers. In several instances these numbers were confused or completely incorrect.
- The soldiers did not provide enough information to obtain a specific identification.
- As yet, only a small percentage of the soldiers' personal Defence Service Records have been uploaded on to the Internet by the National Archives of Australia. Digitising World War II records is an enormous task that relies on special funding, mainly provided by the families of the individual soldiers. These records can often help in confirmation of identity, for example, by comparing signatures and handwriting. Sergeant Loveday's signature in his service records is the same as his signature on the wall. He therefore was able to confirm his own identity.

However, despite the problems, more than 150 soldiers have been accurately identified. Some of the signatures have been given the most logical identification, but they are not confirmed. These are designated Best Guess. If there is insufficient information or the handwriting is illegible, the soldiers are included in the Unidentified File. The identifications of the soldiers are listed in Appendix 1.

The criteria used to determine identities are surnames, Christian names, initials, service numbers, rank, units, occupation and place names, which are usually where these men were living at the time of enlistment. All of this information is obtainable from the Nominal Roll. The fact that many of the soldiers' details changed throughout the war when they transferred from one unit to another also had to be taken into consideration. Camps in Brisbane were often mentioned and some units were specific to certain camps, which provided additional assistance in determining who the men were.

Case Studies

Once the identification of the individual soldier had been established, it was sometimes possible to obtain his Service Records from the National Archives of Australia. At this point in time, there have been 26 records uploaded on to the Internet. These records include the soldier's personal details, his units, his postings, any disciplinary incidents as well as medical information. Approximately 50 per cent of these files also contain photographs. From these records, it is possible to trace the soldier's military career from the time of his enlistment until his discharge and, in some instances, beyond this. From all of this information, case studies have been written.

List of Case Studies

1. CROSS, J.E.
2. McGILL, J.E.
3. STREETER, M.
4. FAULKNER, R.
5. SCOTT, G.E.
6. HANLEY, S.W.
7. JONES, E.A.
8. HENSON, H.G.
9. WERNER, A.E.
10. RICE, R.F.S.
11. REID, J.
12. DAVIE, M.T.J.
13. LOVEDAY, A.H.
14. DIXON, A.J.S.
15. DAVY, C.
16. MYERS, G.T.
17. FRIEND, R.E.M.
18. HARRINGTON, E.F.
19. JACOBSON, H.I.
20. MILLER, K.D.
21. SAXBY, H.H.
22. GREENHALGH, G.R.
23. BEUTEL, L.R.
24. WESTON, G.H.
25. NEWMAN, T.N.O.
26. JORGENSEN, C.E.

Information has also been obtained directly from relatives of the wall signatories and from several veterans who were in the army in Brisbane during that particular time in history. Additional material has been supplied by the relatives of other veterans, and by members of the public who were very young during the war, but remember it vividly and were happy to share their memories.

Staff from the Australian War Memorial, the National Archives of Australia, the Department of Veterans' Affairs and the Department of Defence have assisted with information and advice. Officers from the Brisbane City Council have provided resources for obtaining information, photography and also for disseminating information to the public about the wall. The John Oxley Library, in conjunction with regional libraries, has provided valuable photographic material.

When combined, all of these sources provide a unique insight into the soldiers' world from this crucial time in our history.

DISCLAIMER

Every care has been made to ensure that all identifications and other material are accurate. However, individual skill and judgement should be exercised when using the information. If necessary, further professional advice relevant to the circumstances should be obtained.

CHAPTER 3

TIMELINE

World War II was the largest conflict in history. It is very well documented and there are many sources for obtaining information. There is a wealth of times, dates and events, all of which are subject to differing interpretation by historians. This overabundance of information makes it difficult to streamline the war. Therefore this timeline concentrates mainly on the major events that affected, directly or indirectly, the Australian soldiers who signed the wall, many of whom served in both the Mediterranean theatre as well as in the South West Pacific Area.

1939

1 SEPT	The beginning of World War II. Germany invades Poland, resulting in Britain and France declaring war on Germany.
3 SEPT	As a British Commonwealth country, Australia also declares war on Germany.
15 SEPT	Prime Minister Robert Menzies announces the formation of the Second Australian Imperial Forces. This was an expeditionary force of volunteers that was initially comprised of the 6th Infantry Division, but was later expanded to include the 7th, 8th and 9th Infantry Divisions as well as the 1st Armoured Division.

1940

JANUARY	Conscription is reintroduced for home defence. Australia starts to send troops to support Britain, mainly in North Africa, Greece, Crete, Cyprus and the Middle East.
27 MAY to 4 JUNE	**Evacuation of Dunkirk**. More than 338,000 British and French troops are ferried to England by ships, including civilian vessels. The Germans gain control in Europe.
10 JUNE	Italy declares war on the Allies. Mussolini's forces in North Africa aim to capture Egypt from the British, take control of the Suez Canal and the international supply routes, as well as the Arabian oilfields, and link up with the Italian-controlled areas of East Africa.
10 JUNE	**The Fall of France**. With this setback, enlistments into the AIF in Australia increase. Militia members are prevented from joining the AIF in order to protect the numbers for home defence.
JULY	The Vichy French Government is formed. After the defeat of France, this government collaborates with the Germans. The Vichy Government consequently takes control of the French Mandated Territories of Syria and Lebanon. It is challenged by the Free French forces based in London under Charles De Gaulle.

	Censorship is introduced in Australia under the National Securities Act.
10 JULY to 15 SEPT	**The Battle of Britain**. This is the first major campaign to be fought using only air power. Many Australians participate in the fighting as part of the Royal Air Force. Britain's victory prevents Germany from gaining air superiority and causes Hitler to abandon his plans to invade Britain. The Allies therefore retain their base from which they can launch attacks on the Germans in mainland Europe.
DECEMBER	**Operation Compass**. In the first major military operation of the war, the British and other Commonwealth Forces enter Libya from Egypt to stop the Italian invasion.

1941

3 JAN	The Italians defending the township of Bardia in Libya near the Egyptian border are attacked by the Australian 6th Division. This was the first major battle for the Australians in World War II. The township falls after three days and 36,000 prisoners, as well as a lot of useable war equipment, are captured.
21 JAN	The Australian 6th Division attacks the coastal town of Tobruk. The Italians had built a 30-kilometre wall, including an anti-tank ditch, around the town. With support from the Royal Air Force, who bombed these defences, the Italians are defeated and surrender to the Allies after one day's fighting; 25,000 prisoners are captured.
2 FEB	Due to concerns about the Japanese expansion in South-East Asia, the 22nd Brigade from Australia's 8th Division is sent to Malaya to reinforce the British.
6 FEB	Libya's second-biggest city, Benghazi, is captured by the Australian 6th Division. Operation Compass has been very successful for the Allies.
7 FEB	Italian Tenth Army surrenders. German Lieutenant-General Erwin Rommel is appointed by Hitler as commander of the Afrika Korps.
14 FEB	Lieutenant-General Erwin Rommel with his Panzer army arrives in Tripoli and takes command of the German Afrika Korps and the remaining Italian Army.

Like the Italians, Rommel's goal was to enter Egypt. In order to do this, he needed a harbour for unloading his supplies. Similar to Benghazi, Tobruk had a deep-water harbour that was strategically significant for supply lines. Without the use of this harbour, Rommel's supplies had to be brought in over 1500 kilometres of desert from Tripoli. It was therefore crucial that Tobruk, which was much closer to Egypt than Benghazi, remained under Allied control. The Australian General Leslie Morshead was asked to hold Tobruk for four weeks, but in the end, he held it for eight months.

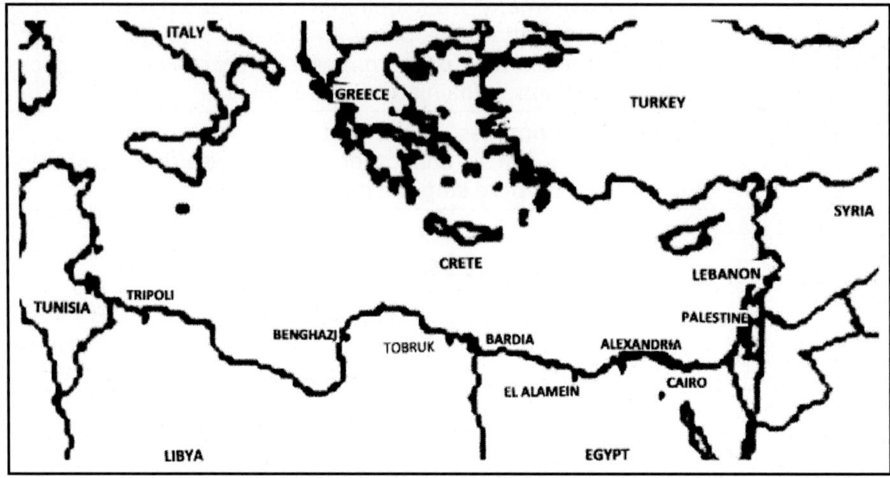

Map of North Africa and the Middle East *(Lyris Mitchell 2012)*

2 MARCH	**Operation Lustre** begins. This is the transportation of Allied troops and equipment to Greece to fight the German invasion.
11 MARCH	The Lend Lease Act is passed by the US Congress. This program refers to the supply of materials to Allied nations. Most of the deliveries are by North Atlantic convoys using the Merchant Navy. This is Britain's lifeline.
24 MARCH	Rommel starts his advance towards Egypt.
APRIL	The Australian 6th Division is sent to Greece in early April as part of Operation Lustre and was replaced by the 9th Division in Tobruk. Greece falls to the Germans about one month later.
3 APRIL	Benghazi is captured by Rommel's forces.
10 APRIL	**Siege of Tobruk** begins.

The German troops were well equipped, outnumbered the defenders by two to one and were led by a military general who at this point had never been defeated in battle. They fought very hard to take Tobruk, but the defenders were able to hold their ground, including the important harbour area.

13 APRIL	Corporal John Edmondson of the 2/17th Infantry Battalion earns **Australia's first Victoria Cross of World War II** at Tobruk.
26 APRIL	2/22nd Infantry Battalion, 23rd Brigade, 8th Division, arrives in Rabaul, New Britain (Lark Force).
30 APRIL to 4 MAY	**The Battle of the Salient**. Rommel is able to gain a wedge into Tobruk's perimeter called the Salient. Germans retain approximately a sixth of Tobruk. They remain a threat, but like other enemy-held areas, are constantly subjected to the Australians' aggressive action.

The Australians became a thorn in Rommel's side at Tobruk. They held up his invasion of Egypt, robbed him of the services of many of his most experienced men and denied him the port facilities. This gives the Allies time to amass forces and equipment at El Alamein in anticipation of Rommel's advance into Egypt. The Royal Navy and the Royal Australian Navy provide a link to the outside world for the Allies throughout the siege, bringing in supplies and shipping out the wounded. The Australians were given the name "Rats of Tobruk" by the Germans because they lived in tunnels and pits. However, they wore this name with pride. From August to October, they were gradually withdrawn by sea, with only the 2/13th Infantry Battalion remaining until December. They were replaced with other Allied troops. Like Gallipoli, Tobruk is a very famous episode in Australian history.

20 MAY to 1 JUNE	**The Battle of Crete**. Like Greece, Crete also comes under German occupation. There are approximately 8000 Commonwealth troops captured.
24 MAY	Britain's largest battle cruiser HMS *Hood* is sunk by the German Flagship *Bismarck*.

This had an enormously demoralising effect on the British. The cry went out "Sink the Bismarck", which began a famous naval chase and battle. Hitler had intended to use the *Bismarck* to disrupt the North Atlantic convoys and thereby isolate Britain from its supply lines. If successful, Britain would have been forced to surrender and the Allies would not have a base in western Europe.

27 MAY	The German battleship *Bismarck* is sunk in the North Atlantic. This is a profound morale booster for the Allies. After several attacks, an ageing biplane launches from the Royal Naval ship the *Ark Royal* and fires a torpedo, which badly damages *Bismarck's* steering gear. This prevents the ship from manoeuvring and renders it vulnerable to attack from Royal Naval ships, which ultimately sink it. The world sees the damage that can be inflicted on such a large vessel by one plane from an aircraft carrier. The use of naval aviation greatly influences later sea battles.
8 JUNE	**Operation Exporter** is the invasion of Vichy French-controlled Syria and Lebanon led by the Australian 7th Division with other Allied units, including the Free French. This is to prevent the Germans using the airfields and harbour facilities within these territories in order to launch an invasion of Egypt from the north-east.
22 JUNE	**Operation Barbarossa**. Germany invades Russia.
14 JULY	An armistice is signed when the Allies are victorious in Syria and Lebanon.
15 AUG	Soldiers from the 27th Brigade of the 8th Division arrive in Singapore to join the 22nd Brigade.
20 NOV	HMAS *Sydney* is sunk off the West Australian coast by the German cruiser *Kormoran* with the loss of all 645 on board. This is the **Royal Australian Navy's biggest single loss in World War II**. The wreck is not found until 2008.
7 DEC	**Attack on Pearl Harbor**. The Americans enter the war. Aircraft from Japanese carriers attack Pearl Harbor in Hawaii, as well as Guam, Wake Island and Midway. Japan declares war on US and United Kingdom.
8 DEC	(Asian time zone) Japanese troops land in Malaya and Thailand. Due to the positioning of the International Date Line, this actually occurs two hours earlier than the attack on Pearl Harbor.
8 DEC	US airfields in the Philippines are bombed, destroying many planes on the ground. The United States and Great Britain declare war on Japan.
9 DEC	Australia declares war on Japan.
10 DEC	The Japanese Air Force sinks HMS *Prince of Wales* and HMS *Repulse* off the coast of Malaya, which ends Allied sea power in the area. Japanese troops invade the Philippines.
12 DEC	A detachment from the 8th Division stationed in Darwin is sent to Timor (Sparrow Force).
17 DEC	Another detachment from the 8th Division is sent to Ambon in the Dutch East Indies (Gull Force).

16 DEC	The Japanese invade Borneo.
17 DEC	2/2nd Independent Company arrives on Timor to assist Sparrow Force.
22 DEC	First US troops arrive in Brisbane. Their ships were diverted from their mission to the Philippines.
23 DEC	General Douglas MacArthur begins a withdrawal from Manila to Bataan.

The Government puts plans in motion to start bringing home the AIF from the Middle East to defend Australia. The 6th and 7th Divisions returned in early 1942, but the 9th Division remained in Egypt with the British Eighth Army. Sections of the 6th Division went to Ceylon (Sri Lanka). RAAF personnel stay in Europe with the Royal Air Force in order to continue the war against Germany.

1942

JANUARY	The Manpower Directorate is established to monitor and control Australia's workforce.
11 JAN	Japanese capture Kuala Lumpur in Malaya and invade Dutch East Indies.
23 JAN	Japanese capture Rabaul on New Britain and invade Bougainville.
30 JAN	**The Siege of Singapore**. The British withdraw to Singapore, which is deemed impenetrable.
31 JAN	The last of the organised forces leave Malaya.
3 FEB	Port Moresby is bombed, which increases the threat to Australia.
15 FEB	**The British surrender in Singapore**. More than 15,000 Australians are captured and sent to Changi POW prison. This was an enormous military defeat for the British. It was to have a profound effect on the relationship between Australians and the British during the war as the Australians now look to the Americans to be their major ally.
19 FEB	**Darwin is bombed**; 252 military personnel are killed and 11 ships are lost.

This is the first time that the Australian mainland was ever attacked by a foreign power. The attack was larger in scale than the one on Pearl Harbor. The same Japanese naval force had been used for both bombing attacks. By November 1943, Darwin had been bombed 64 times.

20 FEB	The Japanese invade Timor. Like New Guinea, Timor was strategic to Australia's defence.
22 FEB	US President Roosevelt, fearing that General MacArthur could fall into Japanese hands, orders him to relocate to Australia.

By the end of February, Australia had suffered a crucial blow. Almost all of Australia's 8th Division, including the Bird Forces, had been killed or captured. However, the 2/2nd Independent Company remained free in Timor and mounted a successful guerilla war for over a year, which prevented many Japanese forces from being deployed to New Guinea. Although AIF units had started returning from the Middle East, there was still a desperate need for more fighting men. Regulations were changed to allow militia members to join the AIF.

3 MARCH	Broome and Wyndham in Western Australia are bombed.
8 MARCH	The Japanese make their first landing in New Guinea when they invade Lae and Salamaua.
12 MARCH	General MacArthur leaves Corregidor in the Philippines and arrives in Darwin on 17th.
14 MARCH	Horn Island is bombed. This was the first of nine raids that ended on 18 June 1943.
20 MARCH	After taking the Ghan train, Douglas MacArthur arrives at Terowie in South Australia and makes his famous speech "I shall return".
20 MARCH	Derby in Western Australia is bombed.
5 APRIL	The Japanese Navy attacks Colombo in Ceylon (Sri Lanka).
18 APRIL	The Allied South West Pacific Area Command is formed and General Douglas Macarthur is appointed Supreme Allied Commander from his headquarters in Melbourne. The Pacific Ocean Theatre is commanded by Admiral Chester Nimitz.
18 APRIL	**Doolittle Raid**. United States B-25 bombers attack the Japanese mainland. This is a very positive morale booster for the US and a very negative one for the Japanese.
2 MAY	Japanese conquer Burma.
3 MAY	Japanese occupy Tulagi in the Solomon Islands. They move on to **Guadalcanal** where they begin to construct a large airfield for long-range bombers. From here their aim is to threaten Allied sea lanes as well as launch attacks on other islands.
4-8 MAY	**Battle of the Coral Sea**. The Japanese goal of extending their perimeter from Rabaul is denied by combined American and Australian forces in this famous sea battle.

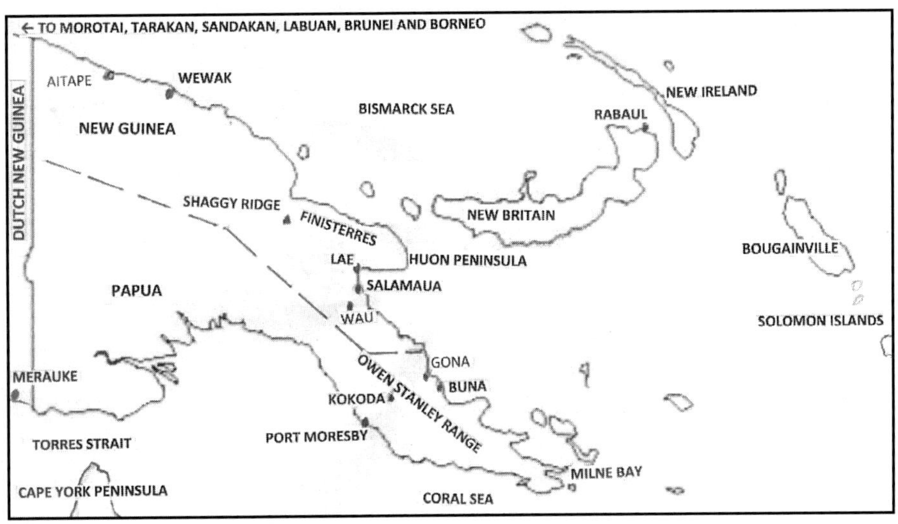

Map of Papua New Guinea *(Lyris Mitchell 2012)*

The capture of Port Moresby was essential to the Japanese plans. Control of the airfields would put Australia within range of land-based bomber aircraft, protect the Japanese supply lines in the Torres Strait and deter the Allies from using Australia as a staging area to launch attacks against them. The decision was made to invade Port Moresby **by sea** using a combined fleet. With the use of intelligence data from coastwatchers and the US naval codebreakers, the Americans were aware of this plan. American and Australian forces succeed in repelling the invasion, damaging the Japanese fleet and reducing the number of enemy ships. The Battle of the Coral Sea is the first battle in history where aircraft carriers and their aircraft were used by both adversaries and none of the opposing ships were within gunfire range of each other.

14 MAY	Rationing is introduced in Australia as a means of controlling civilian consumption of certain basic foods and clothing. The public are issued with ration coupons.
15 MAY	Australian POWs in Changi are now being sent in large groups, e.g., A Force, B Force, *etc.*, to other camps in South-East Asia and Japan to be used as forced labour.
31 MAY	Japanese midget submarines enter Sydney Harbour and sink HMAS *Kuttabul*.
JUNE	Work begins on the **Burma-Thailand Railway** using the forced labour of Allied POWs; 2815 Australians die over a 12 month period.

4-7 JUNE	**Battle of Midway**. This battle is regarded by many as the most significant sea battle of World War II. During a five-minute period, three of the four major Japanese aircraft carriers were fatally damaged and the fourth one sank a few hours later. This is the first conclusive defeat of the Japanese Navy and effectively reduces their carrier fleet. It is a major turning point in the war.
21 JUNE	Rommel's forces capture Tobruk. This forms a staging area for his invasion of Egypt.
21 JUNE	'Maroubra Force' is formed to defend Port Moresby from the Japanese. It consists initially of the Papuan Infantry Battalion and the Australian militia's 39th and 58th Infantry Battalions.
26 JUNE	First Australian troops arrive at **Milne Bay** with a Company of American engineers to build airstrips and wharves.
1 JULY	The Japanese ship *Montevideo Maru* carrying many Australian prisoners of war to Tokyo is sunk by an American submarine. All of the 1053 prisoners and civilian detainees on board perish. **This is Australia's worst maritime disaster**.
15 JULY	39th Infantry Battalion arrives at the village of Kokoda. The village with its airfield lies halfway along the narrow track over the Owen Stanley Range, which connects Buna to Port Moresby.
1-27 JULY	**First Battle of El Alamein**. Rommel's troops try to advance on Alexandria but are prevented by Allied action, including members of the Australian 9th Division.
21 JULY	Douglas MacArthur moves his General Headquarters to Brisbane.
21 JULY to 16 NOV	**The Kokoda Campaign**. After their losses in the Battle of the Coral Sea and the Battle of Midway, the Japanese know that they cannot capture Port Moresby by a sea invasion. They land troops at Gona on Papua's north coast and move towards Buna, which is located at the northern end of the Kokoda Trail. They make a base at Buna in preparation for an overland advance southwards over the Owen Stanley Range.
23 JULY	The fighting between Australian forces and the Japanese at Kokoda begins. The Australians are outnumbered and the 39th Infantry Battalion sustains heavy losses.
25 JULY	Townsville is bombed, followed by raids on 27 and 28 July.

29 JULY	The Japanese capture Kokoda and mount a heavy assault towards Port Moresby. Against overwhelming odds, the Australians are able to delay the enemy until reinforcements can arrive. Then, aided by Indigenous people, they begin the slow and arduous withdrawal back to Port Moresby with the Japanese close behind. The gallantry of the **39th Infantry Battalion** at Kokoda has since become part of Australia's military legend.
30 JULY	Mossman near Cairns is bombed.
7 AUG to FEB 1943	**Guadalcanal Campaign**. With naval support, Allied forces, which are mostly American, land at Guadalcanal and other nearby islands. The main airfield, later called **Henderson Field**, is captured. Codenamed **Operation Watchtower**, this is the first major Allied offensive against the Japanese. The Japanese obtain reinforcements in an attempt to retake the airfield. The fighting is intense and continues for many months, but the airfield remains in Allied hands.
8 AUG	During the first naval battle of the Guadalcanal campaign, the Royal Australian Navy vessel HMAS *Canberra* is sunk in Ironbottom Sound during the Battle of Savo Island.
13 AUG	General Bernard Montgomery takes command of Allied forces in North Africa. He starts to stockpile weapons and supplies at El Alamein in Egypt, thereby creating a massive supply of firepower.
23 AUG to 2 FEB 1943	**Battle of Stalingrad**. This is the largest battle on the Eastern Front, resulting in up to two million combined casualties, including civilians. The German losses severely weaken the Axis cause. It is a major turning point in the war in Europe.
25 AUG to 7 SEPT	**Battle of Milne Bay**. The Japanese send a force of naval marines to Milne Bay in order to capture the airfields. These would be used to launch an attack on Port Moresby. They seriously underestimate the number of defenders and the level of Allied air cover. After very heavy fighting they sustain severe losses and eventually withdraw. It is the **first defeat of the Japanese land forces in the Pacific War** and as such, proves that the Japanese can be beaten. **Queenslander Corporal John French of the 2/9th Infantry Battalion received a Victoria Cross posthumously** for his gallantry during the battle. Milne Bay has also become a famous part of Australia's proud military heritage.
28 SEPT	Along the Kokoda Trail, without supplies, Japanese forces abandon their position just 48 kilometres north of Port Moresby. The Japanese High Command decides that these troops should be used to reinforce Guadalcanal forces. The Australians mount a counter-offensive, forcing the Japanese back to the Buna area.

23 OCT to 4 NOV	**Second Battle of El Alamein**. This is the first large-scale victory for the Allies and the first defeat for the Germans. The Australian 9th Division takes a leading role in the fighting. The victory is a major turning point of the war and begins the German retreat back to Tunisia. Like Tobruk, this is a very famous event in Australia's history.
23-26 OCT	**Battle for Henderson Field**. The Japanese try unsuccessfully to take the airfield from the Americans. This defeat leads to the Japanese Navy preparing to bring an extremely large force of men and supplies to Guadalcanal. The Americans are aware of this plan and mount a naval task force to stop them.
2 NOV	Kokoda village is retaken by the Australians.
10 NOV	Montgomery begins a major offensive against the Germans on the Egypt/Libyan border.
12-15 NOV	**Naval Battle of Guadalcanal**. After a long series of naval battles, this major victory for the Allies deprives the Japanese forces on Guadalcanal from obtaining their reinforcements and supplies. They are unable to take Henderson Field. Without supplies their survival is in doubt. Unknown to the Allies, enemy evacuations begin in December.
13 NOV	Montgomery's Eighth Army recaptures Tobruk.

After their withdrawal from the Kokoda Trail, the Japanese made a heavily defended beachhead on the north Papuan coast. Allied forces attacked the three enclaves and achieved victory, but with an excessive amount of casualties due to both fighting and disease.

16 NOV to 2 JAN 1943	**Battle of Buna**. The Australians join the Americans launching an attack on the airfields on 18th December.
19 NOV to 18 DEC	**Battle of Gona**. Australians capture Gona on the north coast of Papua. "Gona's Gone" is a famous signal.
20 NOV to 22 JAN 1943	**Battle of Sananända**. This coastal town is situated halfway between Gona and Buna. Fighting here was halted until Buna could be captured.
31 DEC	'Merauke Force' is formed to defend the airstrip in Merauke in the south-east corner of Dutch New Guinea.

1943

JANUARY	The 9th Division starts to return to Australia.
23 JAN	Tripoli is captured by Montgomery's Eighth Army.
29-31 JAN	**Battle for Wau**. Wau was an Australian base with an airstrip on the Huon Peninsula defended by a mainly guerilla 'Kanga Force'. This was the last Japanese offensive in New Guinea and they were unsuccessful in capturing this strategic town from the Australians.
2 FEB	The Allies enter Tunisia to confront the Afrika Korps.
9 FEB	The last of the Japanese forces leave Guadalcanal and head for New Georgia.

The Japanese invasion of the Solomon Islands has been the most easterly point of their expansion into the South West Pacific Area. Their defeat at Guadalcanal marks the beginning of their slow withdrawal back to Japan. It is another major turning point of the war.

19 FEB	The Australian Defence Act is amended to allow militia members to serve in the South West Pacific Area.
9 MARCH	General Rommel leaves North Africa for health reasons.
13 MAY	Axis powers officially surrender to the Allies in Tunisia.
14 MAY	The clearly marked hospital ship *Centaur* is sunk by a Japanese submarine off Moreton Island with the loss of 268 men and women. The actual site of the wreck is not discovered until December 2009.
16 MAY	The Royal Air Force launches the famous 'Dambusters' raid on dams in the Ruhr Valley in Germany. Australians form part of the air crews.
4 SEPT to 16 SEPT	**Battle for Lae**. The Australians and Americans launch an assault to recapture Lae and Salamaua. Lae is the major base in New Guinea for the Japanese.
5 SEPT	US paratroops capture Nadzab Airstrip near Lae.
7 SEPT	**Accident at Jackson's Airfield in Port Moresby**. A fully loaded American Liberator bomber crashes on take-off. Australian soldiers from the 2/33rd Infantry Battalion waiting in a truck convoy are hit by the debris and engulfed by the ensuing fire. Sixty-two men are killed and more than 90 are injured. The rest of the soldiers are flown to Nadzab.
11 SEPT	Salamaua is occupied unopposed by the Australian 2/42nd Infantry Battalion.

16 SEPT	Australian forces recapture Lae from the Japanese. It is later to become a major base for the Allies.
19 SEPT to 24 APRIL 1944	**Ramu Valley-Finisterre Range Campaign**. This is a series of actions carried out by the Australian 7th Division in the Huon Peninsula in New Guinea. The Japanese were defeated in the Markham Valley at Kaiapit and also at Kankiryo Saddle north of the Ramu River. The Battle of Shaggy Ridge is a series of battles along the highest part of the Finisterre Mountains where the Japanese held strong defensive positions. The "Pimple" on the summit of the ridge is captured on 27 December. The Japanese no longer posed a threat to Lae and Nadzab. The campaign ended with the capture of Madang.
22 SEPT to 15 JAN 1944	**Huon Peninsula Campaign**. The Australian 9th Division was ordered to remove the Japanese from the coastal parts of the Huon Peninsula. Finschhafen, Sattelburg and Fortification Point are all captured. For his actions at Sattelburg, Sergeant Tom Derrick earns his 2/48th Infantry Battalion's fourth Victoria Cross, making it **the most decorated Australian Army unit in World War II.**
1 NOV	**Battle of Bougainville**. The first Allies land on the island of Bougainville. Fighting occurs over a long period until the Japanese surrender in August 1945. Torokina becomes the main Australian base of operations.

1944

APRIL	The successful New Guinea Offensive victories provide General MacArthur with a solid base for his forces to move point-to-point along the northern New Guinea coast, to Morotai Island and finally to the Philippines. The Australians move on to campaigns in other areas. Allied naval and air support provide assistance whenever possible.
22 APRIL	Aitape, located west of Wewak on the north coast of New Guinea, is captured by the Americans, who develop it as a base area as part of their drive to the Philippines.
6 JUNE	**Operation Overlord-D Day**. The Allies land in Normandy from their base in England. This is the largest amphibious assault in history. It is a major turning point in the war.
19-20 JUNE	**Battle of the Philippine Sea**. This battle is also referred to as the Great Marianas Turkey Shoot because of the enormous losses inflicted on the Japanese planes by the American Navy. Three Japanese carriers are sunk and there is a major loss of naval aircraft and flight crews. This shortfall leads to the introduction of the Kamikaze suicide attack force which was judged by the Japanese to be a more effective use of air power.

25 AUG	Paris is liberated. Free French forces are given control of the French Government.
15 SEPT	US troops land on Morotai Island in the Dutch East Indies. It is used as staging area for American operations in the Philippines and for Australian operations in Borneo. Some Japanese remain on the island, but there is very little interaction with the Allies.
OCTOBER	Australian 6th Division starts to relieve Americans at Aitape.
20 OCT to 31 DEC	**Battle of Leyte**. The Americans invade the Philippines by landing forces at Leyte under the command of General MacArthur. This is supported by the US Navy and the Royal Australian Navy. The Japanese need to maintain control of the Philippines because Allied control of the sea lanes would cut off supplies from Japan to their forces in the south, thereby isolating them from support. In addition, vital fuel and other supplies from their territories in South East-Asia would be prevented from getting to Japan.
20 OCT	General MacArthur wades ashore at Leyte, fulfilling his promise of "I shall return".
21 OCT	HMAS *Australia* is damaged by a suicide Kamikaze plane. This is the first such incident for an Allied ship, but there were many others to come later that were organised as the 'Special Attack Force'. These were mainly land-based aircraft.
23-26 OCT	**Battle of Leyte Gulf**. This is the largest sea battle during the war and is actually a series of four separate battles. The Allied victory here means that the Japanese are no longer a significant naval force, the Philippines are ultimately lost to them and their territories in the south are cut off. General MacArthur has achieved his major objective.
NOV	**Aitape-Wewak Campaign**. Operations begin to clear the Japanese from this part of Australia's territory. They lasted until the war ended in August 1945.
16 DEC to 25 JAN 1945	**Battle of the Bulge**. Hitler's last major offensive fails to halt the Allied advance. The Allies are now able to invade Germany.

1945

JANUARY	Japanese territories in the south that are cut off from the mainland include Bougainville, New Guinea and Borneo. A plan, called **Operation OBOE 6**, is made to invade Borneo. Initially, several nearby islands are occupied by Australian troops. This is Australia's last major campaign of the war. **Sandakan Death Marches**. In January, May and June, Australian and British prisoners of war are marched from the coastal port of Sandakan to Ranau in the interior of Borneo. More than 2000 men die from starvation or disease or are killed by the Japanese. This is the **worst single atrocity against Australians** in World War II.
1 MAY	**Operation OBOE 1**. The Australian 9th Division invades Tarakan Island in the Dutch East Indies to secure airfields for the invasion of Brunei, Labuan Island and Balikpapan in Borneo.
7 MAY	**VE DAY** (Victory in Europe). Germany officially surrenders to the Allies.
10 MAY	Wewak is captured by Australians.
10 JUNE	Australian 9th Division captures Labuan Island in Brunei Bay eight kilometres from the Borneo mainland. After intensive fighting, Japanese opposition ceases soon after 21 June. The Japanese stay on the island until the war ends.
13 JUNE	Brunei is liberated from the Japanese.
16 JUNE	The Australians invade the North Borneo mainland.
1 JULY	**Operation OBOE 2**. With Allied air and naval support, the Australian 7th Division lands at Balikpapan on the east coast of Borneo.
12 JULY	With the capture of Papar on North Borneo's west coast, the Australian offensives end.
6 AUGUST	An atomic bomb is dropped on Hiroshima on the Japanese mainland.
9 AUGUST	Another atomic bomb is dropped on Nagasaki.
15 AUGUST	**VP Day** (Victory in the Pacific). Emperor Hirohito announces Japan's surrender on a radio broadcast. The war has ended. All hostilities were due to cease. This is also referred to as VJ Day (Victory over Japan).
2 SEPT	**VJ Day** (Victory over Japan). General MacArthur, as Supreme Allied Commander, accepts the formal surrender of the Japanese on board the USS *Missouri* in Tokyo Bay. President Truman declares 2 September to be the official VJ Day in the United States.

This timeline includes the more famous battles and events that had impact for the men on the wall. By providing a background where so many historic events are shown to have occurred concurrently, the true war effort by the Australians is put into its proper perspective. They played a major role on two fronts and lost more than 27,000 men and women in doing so. More than 22,000 became prisoners of war of the Japanese and 8600 were held by the Germans. These six years were also filled with individual wartime stories about the men on the wall, which began from the time of their enlistment and continued until their discharge.

CHAPTER 4

ENLISTMENT AND CONSCRIPTION

During World War II, the Australian land forces were comprised of several groups. The largest of these were the militia, also known as the Citizens' Military Forces (CMF), the Second Australian Imperial Forces (AIF) and the Voluntary Defence Corps (VDC). The processes and conditions of enlistment and conscription for these groups changed as the war progressed.

The Militia

The Commonwealth Military Forces section was formed in 1901 after Federation when the militia from the six States were amalgamated into a united force under the responsibility of the Commonwealth Government. The name of this section was later changed to the Australian Military Forces (AMF) but was more commonly called the militia. This was a part-time force of citizen soldiers that operated under the command of a small regular component known as the Permanent Military Forces (PMF). It was only intended for home defence in Australia.

First Australian Imperial Forces

With the advent of World War I, as part of its commitment to the Empire, the Commonwealth Government raised a new force made up of volunteers who were prepared to fight overseas. These new recruits were known as the Australian Imperial Forces (AIF) and they were specifically raised for expeditionary use outside of Australia. It was intended that they would fight the enemy in Europe and the Mediterranean region. The Defence Act of 1903 did not allow members of the militia to serve overseas. It was regarded as a home-based support for the AIF.

After the war, with the AIF disbanded, the militia (now called the Citizen Military Forces) was under the administration of a small permanent group of regular Army officers. The CMF still maintained responsibility for the defence of the Australian mainland. This concept lasted up until World War II. At this point Australia did not have a large permanent standing army with a ready fighting capability. The focus of defence of the nation remained with the part-time citizens' forces.

Brisbane, circa 1940: Militia volunteers at a training camp at Enoggera.
(Courtesy of John Oxley Library, State Library of Queensland 74838)

Second Australian Imperial Forces

Similar to World War I, at the outbreak of World War II, a new force had to be obtained of men who were prepared to confront the enemy outside of Australia. As a result of the ban on overseas service for members of the militia, an expeditionary force known as the 2nd AIF was introduced into the Australian Military Forces in September 1939. Similar to the 1st AIF, this was a voluntary, full-time army and its recruits were destined to be sent overseas. The initial intake was 20,000 men. By February 1940, the first convoy of AIF troops had arrived in the Middle East.

The Volunteer Defence Corps

The third branch of the army, the Volunteer Defence Corps, was established in 1940 by the Returned Services League of Australia (RSL). It was modelled on the British Home Guard and consisted of units of mainly World War I veterans who trained for the defence of the local area. Men employed in essential industries also joined as they were not permitted to enlist in the army. At this stage, they had to use improvised weapons. By 1941 the Military Board had assumed control, issued uniforms and better equipment and trained the men in guerilla warfare, which included intelligence gathering.

In February 1942, the VDC became part of the Australian Military Forces and was formerly raised as a corps in the militia. They were grouped into 25 battalions. The VDC role had been expanded to include volunteers from 18 to 60 years old, which brought their numbers up to nearly 100,000 men. Their activities included the use of anti-aircraft artillery, coastal artillery and searchlights. With training such as this, by March 1942 the VDC units in places such as Broome and Wyndham in Western Australia were able to help defend their towns against enemy attacks. This helped to release regular troops for other duties at a time when manpower was in short supply. Across Australia, the Voluntary Defence Corps had performed an important role in local defence. It was disbanded in August 1945 immediately after the war had ended.

CONSCRIPTION

After Federation, legislation had allowed for conscription of young men into the part-time militia, but this law was rarely implemented because it was so unpopular. From 1911 until 1929, under the Universal Service Scheme, all males 12 to 26 years were directed to undertake various periods of military training in either a cadet or a militia unit. In 1916 and 1917, during World War I, two referenda had been conducted on whether or not to compel conscripted citizens to serve overseas. On both occasions, the public voted against it. The scheme for conscription was abolished in 1929.

Queensland, 1940: Newly enlisted trainee soldiers waiting to embark on a train for Caloundra Camp. *(Courtesy of the John Oxley Library, State Library of Queensland 102308)*

In January 1940, not long after the outbreak of World War II, the rules of conscription were enforced for the second time. The definition of Australia now included its territories such as Papua and New Guinea and the adjacent islands. All males over 21 were required to complete at least three months military training, which boosted the numbers of the militia greatly.

The Relationship Between the Militia and the Second AIF

The 2nd AIF had different conditions of service and unit and command structures to the existing militia. In fact, it was generally regarded that Australia had two separate armies. There was animosity between the two groups of servicemen. The AIF was better trained, better equipped and had higher pay. They regarded the militia as a secondary fighting force due to their part-time attendance, lesser discipline, poor equipment and less training for its members. They were often referred to as "Koalas" who were not to be shot at or exported. They were also referred to as "chocolate soldiers" or "Chocos" who would *melt* in real combat conditions. Their uniforms were compared to the elaborate ones worn by soldiers pictured on the front of chocolate boxes that were sold in Australia in the 1930s.

As the war intensified, part-time militia members were called up for full-time service. Many of them decided to enlist in the AIF. In response, in June 1940, militia men were prevented from joining the AIF as the Government did not want the numbers of men available for home defence to decrease. Unlike England, which had merged its part-time soldiers into the British Army at the beginning of the war, Australia still maintained its two separate and divisive groups. The term Australian Military Forces (AMF) was unofficially corrupted by its detractors to Australian Militia Forces. It took an external enemy threat to help resolve the situation.

December 1941

The events in December 1941 and in the following months produced a major change in the focus of defence in Australia. The attack on Pearl Harbor, the invasion of the Malay Peninsula, as well as numerous successful Japanese attacks and invasions of many other United States and Asian territories in rapid succession, caused a great amount of concern. Australia's homeland was no longer considered as being secure. The Government now had powerful controls. One of the first changes made was the conscription of women for either military or civilian occupational service.

1942

On the 15th February, 1942, Singapore, which was once considered an impenetrable fortress, surrendered to the enemy. Prime Minister Curtain announced that the Battle for Australia was just beginning. Eventually, on the 19th of February, Darwin was bombed.

The prevailing threat of an Australian invasion by the Japanese was regarded by the population as being very real. Many people thought that it was imminent. Civilians in the northern parts of Western Australia, Queensland and the Northern Territory were evacuated to the south. With most of the AIF away fighting the Germans, Italians and Vichy French in the Mediterranean region, the responsibility for the defence of the Australian mainland lay with the militia. There was an urgent need to bolster the numbers of the military on the home front. The Government acted quickly and summoned the AIF home.

Other changes were made in order that the numbers of fighting men increased. The militia units, which were previously separate to the AIF, were now allowed to vote to join the AIF, providing that at least 65% of the established members or 75% of the actual members agreed. The men remained in their original units, but now they were not limited to the Australian Territories and could go anywhere overseas with the AIF.

Enlistments in Australia increased significantly throughout 1942. Legislation was passed that extended the scope of the conscription rules. This now meant that all men aged between 18 and 35, and all older single men aged between 35 and 45, were required to enlist for military service.

In addition, many experienced AIF officers and non-commissioned officers had been transferred to militia units to enhance their members' training and to prepare them for front-line duties. Members of the militia who had been sent overseas to the Australian Territories during 1941 now found themselves on the front-line as the situation worsened. For one militia unit, what was meant to be a simple garrison duty in New Guinea turned into something much more historic. The heroism of the 39th Infantry Battalion is well remembered for its courage when it faced the enemy on the Kokoda Trail. Other militia units fought at such places as Milne Bay. Events such as these showed the enormous capability of even poorly equipped militia units of very young men, although 18-year-old boys were supposedly not allowed to serve outside the Australian mainland.

However, in 1942, the militia with its conscripts was still limited to the Australian Territories. This fact hampered military planning. American conscripts were serving in all areas of the South West Pacific Zone assisting in the defence of Australia, whereas Australian conscripts were not. It was factors such as these that led to changes to the Defence Act in February 1943. These changes meant all militia units were able to join the AIF anywhere in the South West Pacific Zone south of the equator. In January 1943, the 62nd Militia

Battalion pre-empted these changes and went into non-Australian territory at Merauke in Dutch New Guinea. This meant that, for the first time, Australian conscripts were sent to areas outside Australian Territories.

ENLISTMENTS

In Queensland the militia service numbers had started with a Q. If they remained in their unit and elected not to become part of the AIF, they retained their Q number. If they joined the AIF as individuals or when 75% of their militia unit volunteered to become part of the AIF, they were issued with new service numbers, which began with QX. The other States followed suit using the appropriate initials, e.g. Victoria was V and VX. This helps to explain why there are so many variations of service numbers on the wall and also why so many soldiers confused their AIF and militia numbers. Normally, both of these numbers would be stated on the Nominal Roll. The Nominal Roll also displays the enlistment dates for full-time service, but it does not specify whether or not it is militia or AIF. The following list shows the enlistment dates for the men on the wall.

YEAR	1939	1940	1941	1942	1943	1944
January	0	3	3	21	1	0
February	0	0	0	13	1	1
March	0	1	5	12	1	1
April	0	0	3	5	2	0
May	0	1	3	5	1	0
June	0	4	1	4	2	0
July	0	5	6	4	1	0
August	0	1	4	3	1	0
September	0	1	1	4	1	0
October	2	1	3	0	1	0
November	1	0	5	2	0	0
December	1	1	10	1	0	0
Totals	4	18	44	74	12	2
Unknown	1					
TOTAL NUMBER OF SOLDIER						155
ENLISTMENT PRIOR TO PEARL HARBOR (September 1939-November 1941)						55
	35.48%					
ENLISTMENT IN THE 4 MONTHS AFTER PEARL HARBOR (December 1941-March 1942)						57
	37.5%					
ENLISTMENT AFTER MARCH 1942						42
	27.1%					

Table 1 Full-Time Enlistment

This data shows that enlistments increased greatly in the first four months after the attack on Pearl Harbor; 37.5% of all of the enlistments of the men on the wall occurred during this short period when a Japanese invasion appeared imminent. In the earlier part of the war there was an increase in enlistments (5.8%) in June/July 1940 when France fell to the Germans. The actual increase of enrolments was much larger than is shown, but the wall was not available for signatures at that time.

Age at Enlistment

The age limits on enlistment for the 2nd AIF were 20-35 in 1939 and 18-40 in 1943. For the militia it was 18-60. Both the upper and lower age limits were often flouted, especially for men enlisting into the AIF. Many of the front-line troops were found to be veterans of World War I, most of whom would have been over 40 when Australia went into action in 1940. The oldest signatory on the wall was 44 at the time he enlisted into the militia. The youngest was 18 when he enlisted, also into the militia. The figures in Table 2 are for full-time enlistment.

Age	Number	Age	Number	Age	Number
17	0	25	7	33	4
18	7	26	7	34	3
19	22	27	8	36	4
20	20	28	5	37	2
21	18	29	1	41	1
22	14	30	4	42	1
23	9	31	2	43	1
24	11	32	2	44	1
Unknown	1				
TOTAL NUMBER OF SOLDIERS		155			

Table 2 Age At Enlistment

60.64% of the wall signatories were aged 19 to 24 years of age at the time of their enlistment. 85.1% were under 30 years of age. The average age for the enlistment of the soldiers on the wall was 24.09 years.

Dad was so young when he enlisted. He celebrated his 21st birthday at Beirut after the Lebanon/Syrian Campaign.

David Huggonson, son of Wall Signatory Walter Huggonson, AIF 1941-1944. April 2012

In the later part of the war the average age for enlistment dropped as many more young males voluntarily enlisted as soon as they turned 18. The ideas of adventure, duty and becoming a part of Australia's military heritage prevailed with these volunteers. There was also a certain stigma attached to being conscripted. Parental consent was needed for recruits under 21 years.

Neither the RAAF not the RAN had conscription. These services had strong public appeal and attracted many young volunteers. Nineteen-year old Alexander Vallis enlisted into the AIF in March 1942 and then enlisted into the RAAF two months later. He wrote his name on the wall as LAC Vallis (Leading Aircraftman). He stayed in the RAAF until July 1942 when he returned to the AIF.

Both the Air Force and the Navy accepted enlistments from males under 18 years of age. One young man had the misfortune of being born a few months too late.

> *My older brother had been a lieutenant in the navy for several years during the war. My mother worried about him all the way through. When I applied to become a midshipman towards the end of the war when I was nearly 18, I was told that they were not taking any new enlistments as the war was almost over. I was very disappointed at missing out as we had been brought up to be very patriotic. I wanted to do my bit for my country like my older brother. Mum, of course, was delighted.*
>
> Anonymous, August 2011

Upon enlistment, all service personnel were required to fill out attestation papers, which listed their details. These included place and date of birth, occupation, religion, any former military service and next of kin. The next of kin was important as it provided a point of civilian contact if the serviceman or woman should be injured or killed during the war. It was also important for making payments from the soldier's wages. There was a defined order in the NOK relationships with the spouse being the closest next of kin to the soldier, then his children, then his parents, and finally his siblings. Many soldiers like Alfred Loveday and Harold Saxby were married during their war service and so their NOK was changed accordingly. Soldiers were also allowed to nominate people as their NOK from outside the regular list. Ronald Rice nominated his fiancée and Cyril Jorgensen nominated his guardian. The soldiers were also encouraged to make their wills upon enlistment.

The Final Outcome

In total, the army had recruited or conscripted 726,800 personnel during the entire conflict. This represented 73.35% of the total armed forces of 993,900, or 10.38% of the Australian population of 7,000,000. This number was in far greater proportion per head of population than the figures for either Britain or the United States *(Courtesy of the Australian War Memorial).*

During the course of World War II, more than 200,000 militia men had transferred to the AIF. Many others remained in their militia units, which from 1943 onwards, were referred to as the CMF. After demobilisation, the Australian Military Forces were reorganised. In September 1947, a permanent full-time standing army, the Australian Regular Army, was established. In 1980, the CMF was reformed into the Army Reserve. The training became more intensive, better disciplinary techniques were used, and as a consequence pay was increased. The part-time Army Reserve is now seen as an important part of the Australian Defence Force.

CHAPTER 5

RANK AND OCCUPATION

Within the army, the men were defined by their rank and occupation. These determined their pay levels, their responsibilities, their activities, their locations and their overall contribution to the war effort. On occasion, the men moved up the ranks, and in some instances down, and frequently changed their occupations.

RANK

The term *rank* implies a lawful authority to command others. As a soldier moved up the ranks, there was usually an increase in the numbers of men under his control. The following information was supplied by the Australian War Memorial and the Department of Veterans' Affairs. Any rank that is no longer used is in italics.

Commissioned Officers

Commissioned officers obtain their rank and authority to command by being given commissions from the head of state. Depending on their seniority, they can command any number from 30 to several thousand men. The most junior officer rank in the army is Second Lieutenant, then Lieutenant, Captain, Major, Lieutenant Colonel, Colonel, Brigadier, Major General, Lieutenant General, General and Field Marshal. Once an officer has received his rank, it can only be withdrawn in extreme circumstances.

Rank can have its failing. Although the men from World War II reputedly had more respect for their officers than their World War I counterparts, not all of the high command decisions were considered to be correct or worthy of respect by the men. An example of this is the decision to surrender Singapore, which is still open to debate.

> *My brother was in the 8th Division and was present in Singapore when the British surrendered to the Japanese in February 1942. The men were ordered to wear their dress uniforms if they still had them and to line up along the main avenues. Many of the Japanese came into the city riding bicycles. The Australians felt betrayed because they had not been given the chance to fight. With hindsight, the surrender was a horrible mistake, especially when we learnt about the treatment of the prisoners of war.*
>
> Myra O'Shea *née* Harris, sister of Private Geoffrey Robert Harris, AIF 1940-1946, August 2011

There was only one officer who signed the wall, but he is unidentified.

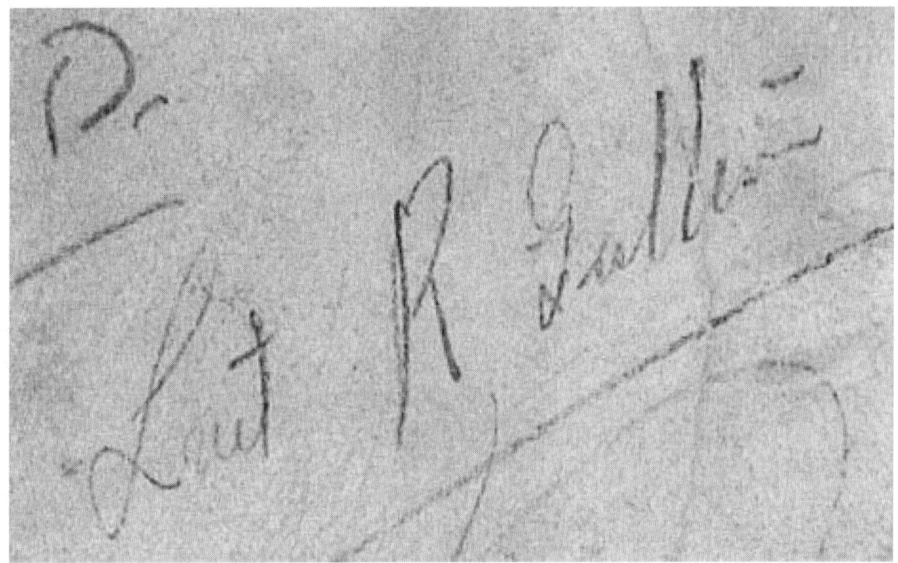

Unidentified Officer, Lieut R. Gallon? *(Image Copyright Brisbane City Council)*

Other Ranks

The signatories on the wall are comprised almost exclusively of men from the army whose ranks ranged from Private to Warrant Officer. They are generally called Other Ranks as opposed to the Commissioned Officer category. These ranks can be given or withdrawn by commanding officers. Although many of the soldiers were given several ranks throughout their war service, the ranks listed below refer to those listed on the Nominal Roll at the time of their discharge. The lowest category of rank is the Rank and File, whose members technically have no rank because they are not in command of anyone. Depending on their particular unit, these men were referred to as Private (74), Bandsman (0), Craftsman (7), *Driver* (4), Gunner (10), *Pioneer* (0), Sapper (14), Signaller (6) or Trooper (0). A total of 115 or 74.2% of the 155 identified men on the wall were Rank and File.

Ravenshoe, North Queensland 1943: Non-commissioned officers from C company of the 2/31st Battalion at training area. *(Courtesy John Oxley Library, State Library of Queensland 283747)*

Non-commissioned officers, referred to as NCOs, are the next most senior in rank. Depending on their level, they are responsible for the maintenance of discipline and good order. These ranks include Lance Corporal (1), Lance Bombardier (0), Corporal (22), Bombardier (2), *Lance Sergeant* (1), Sergeant (10) and Staff Sergeant (2).

Warrant Officers are the most senior NCOs and are issued with warrants under the Defence Act of 1903 in order to facilitate their task of maintaining discipline. There are two levels of seniority, which are both represented on the wall. John Ham is a Warrant Officer Class 2 and the most senior soldier so far identified is Warrant Officer Class 1 James Cross.

CASE STUDY NUMBER 1

CROSS, JAMES EDWARD, QX27537, WARRANT OFFICER CLASS 1

James Cross, a 19-year-old assistant sugar boiler from Sarina in North Queensland, enlisted into the AIF at Brisbane on 11/2/42. He was initially attached to the 101st Convalescent Depot, then sent to the 7th Training Battalion at Redbank, and finally to the 7th Pioneer Company in Brisbane. After some minor disciplinary problems including being Absent Without Leave, he was transferred to the 2/4th Docks Operating Company in December

1942. Docks Operating Companies were responsible for the loading and unloading of ships. They were later referred to as Port Operating Companies. Private Cross was very well suited to work within this unit and rapidly gained promotions.

In January 1943 he was appointed Lance Corporal and a few days later was graded as Group III Hatchman. Hatchmen direct the winchman or crane operator with the loading or unloading of goods into the hatch of a ship. The next month he was promoted to Acting Corporal and this was confirmed in July, just one day before he was promoted to Acting Sergeant. He was just a few days short of his 21st birthday. In September, his unit went to Milne Bay in New Guinea, where his rank of Sergeant was confirmed. After returning to Queensland for several months, he was sent to Lae in March 1945. Six days later he was promoted to Acting Warrant Officer 2, and this rank was confirmed in July. His promotions continued after the war had ended on 15/8/45. In October, he was promoted to Acting Warrant Officer 1 and this was confirmed in February 1946. He was 23 years old. He was transferred to the 33rd Port Operating Company in March before embarking from Lae for Australia in May. On the 4/6/46, Warrant Officer Cross was discharged at Redbank as part of the general demobilisation process.

The former Private James Cross was stationed at Redbank in early 1942 when he signed the wall. He wrote "—Cross, -------- , QX27537, Lost Legion, Redbank". His AWL record at Redbank and his comment "Lost Legion" indicate that he was not satisfied being there and wished to do more for the war effort. His service with the 2/4th Docks Operating Company provided ample opportunity for this.

Similar to Warrant Officer Class 1 Cross, promotions sometimes came very quickly to other soldiers according to the needs of the army and the qualities of the men involved.

Stuart Hanley was promoted to sergeant at the age of 21. He had earned his rank through training, study and by becoming a Signals Operator with the Indigenous unit, the Papuan Infantry Battalion, which involved a high degree of responsibility. He later became a Staff Sergeant and after the war was able to assist with the release of Japanese prisoners of war.

It was not unusual for men to relinquish rank voluntarily in order to obtain a preferred position. James McGill obtained his rank of Lance Sergeant at the age of 21 and reverted to Bombardier once he had completed his training.

CASE STUDY NUMBER 2

MCGILL, JAMES EDWARD, QX18836, BOMBARDIER

James Edward McGill, a 19-year old shop assistant from Mackay, enlisted into the AIF in October 1941. He commenced his gunnery training with the 41st Field Training Battery at Grovely. In March 1942 he was transferred to the 5th Field Regiment with the Royal Australian Artillery (RAA). He was promoted to Lance Bombardier in March and 10 days later, while in Townsville, was made Acting Bombardier. Between August and September he was on duty with the 2/3rd Field Regiment, and in October he attended the Gun Drill Instructions Course. Upon his return he was promoted to Lance Sergeant at the age of 21. In February 1943 he attended a course at the Yorkforce Jungle Training School at the top of the Cape York Peninsula. From there he went with his regiment to the Northern Territory where he attended a Course Field Workshop with the Northern Territory Force Training School. He passed the course and his rank of Bombardier was confirmed. He was detached for duty with the 2/11th Field Regiment in December and returned to his unit, the 5th Field Regiment, in January 1944.

Now in New South Wales, he voluntarily reverted to being a Bombardier from Lance Sergeant with the 5th Field Regiment. Due to the Army decreasing the strength of his unit, he was transferred in December to the Australian Training Centre for Jungle Warfare at Canungra in Queensland. He left for overseas duty from Brisbane in May, arriving at Morotai Island in the Dutch East Indies 12 days later. He was sent to the 1st Base Sub Area Details Depot and remained there until after the war had ended. In October he was sent to 2/12th Field Regiment in British North Borneo, and in December he was transferred to the 2/3rd Tank Regiment. He returned to Brisbane in February 1946 and was discharged from Redbank on 1/4/46 as part of the general demobilisation process. Although he had served with several units during his service, the unit deemed as his most effective was the 2/12th Field Regiment, and this has been included in his discharge papers.

James Edward McGill was with the 41st Field Training Battery at Grovely from 27/10/41 until 3/3/42. He wrote on the wall "QX18836, Gnr. McGill, J.E., 41st Tank Unit AIF Grovely".

Some soldiers lost their rank. This was usually caused by breaches in military discipline. As a result of being Absent Without Leave, Corporal John Reid was reduced to the rank of private. However, he was promoted back to corporal a few months later.

Several of the men were given promotions after hostilities had ceased. They were able to play a prominent role in the aftermath of the war assisting with the clean-up and with the demobilisation process. George Weston was promoted to

Acting Sergeant in October 1945 while he was on Morotai Island working on the docks.

The qualities that had earned the men promotions were still present long after the war had ended.

> *My uncle, George Edwards, exhibited leadership qualities so it was not surprising that he became a corporal during the war. I remember him as being a neat, well-presented man who was also very sociable. He was strong and capable and after the war he became a top tradesman as a solid plasterer.*
>
> Robyn Stephensen *née* Edwards, niece of Wall Signatory Corporal George Edwards, AIF 1942-1945, April, 2011

OCCUPATION

During the war, an individual's occupation took on a whole new meaning. It was no longer simply a means to support oneself, but was also assessed as a means to support the nation at this time of need. It was judged on its ability to contribute to the war effort. Australia's population was too small to maintain a fully operational military workforce as well as maintaining an efficient civilian workforce. Changes had to be made.

Civilian Manpower

At the outset of the war, there were very few government controls over the Australian workforce. Occupations had been divided into categories.

- War industry – these were the *reserved occupations*, which were deemed essential for the war effort and included areas such as engineering and munitions manufacturing. The workers in these industries were not allowed to enlist in the militia or the AIF, although they could join the Volunteer Defence Force.
- Civilian industry – these were listed as being either *essential* or *non-essential*. Essential occupations included, for example, those necessary for food production or metal production. Non-essential included domestic service and furniture making.

As more men and women enlisted or were conscripted into the armed forces, it soon became apparent that there would be a labour shortage. There would not be enough manpower to fill both wartime and civilian occupations. A number of measures were taken to combat the problem. Luxury items were phased out and rationing on petrol was introduced, but there was still a labour shortage. There was no difficulty finding work even for the inexperienced.

Early in the war I was a newly arrived, inexperienced 17 year-old from the country looking for work in Sydney. I applied to work in a factory that made walkie talkies, bullets and other ammunition. I was in the electronic section working with coils and wires. The factory was very advanced for its time and there were a lot of clever people who worked there. Teams of bigwigs were always visiting to check us out.

Anonymous lady, January 2012

After the Japanese entered the war in December 1941, the number of enlistments and conscriptions increased dramatically and the demand for manpower became acute. The Government set up the Directorate of Manpower in January 1942. This agency had wide-sweeping powers in the provision of labour in both military and civilian areas. It created a *Schedule of reserved occupations and industrial priorities* which described the essential and non-essential industries. It also included a list of *protected industries* that required a permit for any change of employment. The highest priority was given to weapons production and then to other military requirements such as the making of military clothing.

I worked in a protected industry at the tannery at Kedron making leather for military boots. All of the staff wished to be "over there" fighting the enemy, but we had to stay at our jobs.

Anonymous, April 2012

Employers in *unprotected industries* had to apply for labour through the National Service offices. The Directorate had the power to determine the hiring of staff and the type of work performed. People from non-essential occupations were placed into essential areas. Everyone had to have identity cards that showed where they were employed, and there were constant checks to ensure that everyone was making a contribution to the war effort.

I was a Junior Draftsman working for the Ford Company at Eagle Farm. We made barges for the army's Water Transport Unit, so we were considered a protected industry. This meant that we could not join the army, but had to continue working. Not many young adults worked here. There were mainly males, like myself, who were too young to enlist, and the much older men who supervised us. I worked for Bill Atkinson who was in the same architectural firm as G. G. Prentice who designed City Hall. We had some young women working as welders, which was really unusual.

Roy Woolley, March 2011

Women filled many of the positions formerly occupied by men, such as farm workers, which were now organised by the Land Army. However, their numbers were too small to provide all of the necessary manpower within the occupations traditionally performed by males. They often met with opposition from unions and male co-workers. Nevertheless, their contribution to the war effort was extremely valuable.

> *I had been working as a machinist for the Australian Knitting Mills for eight years making underwear. In 1943 Manpower shifted me to Pelaco Shirts where I made men's shirts for the army. The heavy khaki material was very hard on my hands and it was difficult to work with.*
>
> Florence Hughes *née* Keir, wife of Wall Signatory Ronald Hughes, January 2012

Brisbane: Uniform production at a clothing company during World War II.
(Courtesy of the John Oxley Library, State Library of Queensland 184431)

Many women wanted to assist the war effort as volunteers with organisations such as the Salvation Army, the Red Cross and the Australian Comforts Fund.

The women from the Australian Comforts Fund sent parcels of small luxuries to the Australian soldiers and food parcels to England, and provided meals for sailors when the ships pulled into port.

Bob Arkell, July 2011

Ramu Valley, Papua New Guinea, 1943: Australian Comforts Fund Christmas hampers arrive for the soldiers from the 2/31st Battalion.
(Courtesy of the John Oxley Library, State Library of Queensland 283935)

However, the women's main responsibility was caring for their families. The whole nation was mobilised for war, including the children, who had to wear identity discs and often faced unique situations.

As a 10-year-old child, I remember going with my father to Indooroopilly State School and digging air-raid trenches, getting rubber plugs to hold between my teeth and having a gas mask. We had air-raid drills, but when the trenches filled up with water, no-one would go near them. The girls were really scared of the frogs that were in the water.

Bob Arkell, July 2011

The children also found a way to directly help the war effort.

> *As kids, we used to go around and collect aluminium scrap, e.g., saucepans and lid, etc., and put it into our billycarts and then take it to the collection bin at the Indooroopilly State School. We knew it was going to be melted down to make aircraft.*
>
> Bob Arkell, July 2011

Brisbane City Hall, 1942: Pens used for aluminium donations to the war cause. *(Courtesy of the John Oxley Library, State Library of Queensland 102825)*

The shortage of metal affected many areas of the working population.

> *Both my father, who was a pharmaceutical chemist, and my uncle worked in protected industries. My uncle was employed at the Royal Brisbane Hospital as a surgical appliance maker, e.g., braces and calipers. As steel was in very short supply, he took scalpels home to sharpen on his stone wheel so they could be reused. He made them very sharp.*
>
> Roy Woolley, March 2011

Even the higher echelon of society made contributions. During the war the decorative copper ceilings in some of the City Hall's main reception rooms mysteriously disappeared. They have never been found. It is assumed that they were donated as part of the war effort.

Many sacrifices were made to keep the war effort moving. The majority of the population was still under the impression that the Japanese might invade Australia and the Government was happy to allow this belief to continue until the latter part of 1943. This was an added inducement to keep the population hard at work. Many of the workers had very severe working conditions.

> *We worked from Monday to Friday from 7.30 a.m. until 6.00 p.m. and on Saturdays from 7.30 a.m. until 4.00.pm. We had half an hour for lunch each day. I rode my pushbike from Morningside to Eagle Farm and crossed the river on the old Apollo Ferry at Bulimba. Petrol was heavily rationed so very few people had cars.*
>
> Roy Woolley, March 2011

The production and supply of basic necessities also came under the jurisdiction of the Directorate.

> *My father was the Superintendent of the Apple and Pear Board during the war. He and his team of marketing officers were responsible for the acquisition of all fruit, vegetables and honey on behalf of the Federal Government. This food was then distributed in portions to the military forces and to the public. As well as ensuring that everyone was able to obtain their ration, it also avoided black marketing of these essential supplies.*
>
> Bob Arkell, July 2011

During the war there had been a severe shortage of all essential supplies and the standard of living decreased greatly. It was not until much later in the war, with the threat of a Japanese invasion over, that workers could start returning to peacetime industries and the quality of life improved. The civilian population had endured hardships and infringements on their freedom, but endured it in order to help with the war effort. It was into this world of austerity and hardship that the soldiers returned when on leave and after being discharged.

Military Occupations

The 1942 Manpower Directorate also had the power to dictate the occupation of members of the armed forces. An early initiative was to allow women to serve in positions such as signals and anti-aircraft, where previously they had not been permitted to work. In another move, the Voluntary Defence Corps was admitted into the AIF, which freed soldiers from local defence activities to work in other areas. From February 1942 onwards there were many militia units that became part of the AIF and this boosted the number of men who could be sent overseas. AIF reinforcements now came from a central pool as opposed to the previous system where each State supplied its own reinforcements.

The AIF reached its maximum number in 1942, when it provided more than 11 divisions of fighting men. The logistic support required was enormous and demand for personnel in these areas was greater than for combat troops. Upon enlistment, the men had some influence in which occupations they would prefer. This was based on physical fitness, education, aptitude and previous experience. Lawrence Beutel had been a farrier in his civilian role and therefore was placed in the unit that provided pack animals. Both Private Greenhalgh and Private Saxby had been drivers before enlistment and so initially they were placed in areas where their experience could be utilised. For veteran Peter Lahanas, it was an easy choice.

> *Because my English was poor, I was asked what job I would like to do. Since I had worked in a cafe in Murgon, I chose to be a cook. I was sent to the camp at Ascot Racecourse, and trained as a Group One Cook. I passed the exams with flying colours and even taught the instructors a thing or two. We were also trained in butchery and I learnt how to cut up a bullock and could cut and name each of the different cuts of meat.*
>
> Veteran Peter Lahanas, AIF 1942-1944, October 2010

Many of the men who enlisted were labourers and farmhands with very little training or formal education. The army provided basic training and then allocated the men into areas where their services were needed. More specialised training was provided and a soldier with useful skills would then be available for postings. Henry Jacobson, Keith Miller, Gilbert Myers, Thomas Newman and George Scott were all sent overseas with the Infantry as riflemen. James McGill became a bombardier and Henry Henson, a former railway porter, qualified as a commando and a signaller. George Weston was a former plumber who became initially a Driver Mechanic then a Specialist Winchman at the docks. James Cross, an assistant sugar boiler, became a Hatchman whose job it was to direct winchmen and crane drivers.

Like many of the soldiers, Colin Davy had two occupations within the army. He was an anti-aircraft gunner as well as being a motor-vehicle mechanic, and saw active service with both positions.

Although most of the soldiers had their own individual and uniquely different employment records with the army, two of the case study soldiers had very similar careers. Both Mervyn Streeter and Royal Faulkner were 19-year-olds when they enlisted into the army in late 1941. Both men underwent gunnery training at Redbank for the Infantry. They were then transferred to garrison duty with Coastal Defences on the same day and then to 13th Garrison on Moreton Island. In August 1942 they became artillery gunners and were transferred to the same battery with the Anti-Aircraft Fixed Defences, and in August 1943 to the same battery with the 56 Composite Anti-Aircraft Regiment. They were both upgraded at the same time. Streeter became a Predictor, which he subsequently relinquished, and immediately became a Fire Control Operator. Faulkner became a Gunlayer. They both departed from Cairns for Red Island Port on the York Peninsula in December 1943.

From this point onwards their service records differ. By 1944, Australia was no longer regarded as being in danger from Japanese attacks and the army was discharging many of its soldiers to assist the civilian population. Gunner Streeter was flown in April 1944 to Townsville, and a few days later he was discharged from Redbank. He was given an expedited Release to Industry to work on a dairy farm, which was part of the essential food-production industry. He had worked on a dairy farm prior to his enlistment.

CASE STUDY NUMBER 3

STREETER, MERVYN, QX23167, GUNNER

Mervyn Streeter was a 19-year-old Lad Porter when he joined the AIF on the 20th November 1941 at Rockhampton. He also worked in the dairy industry. He was sent to Redbank for gunnery training with the 11th Infantry Training Battalion. In March 1942, Private Streeter was detached to the unit guarding the coastal defences at Cowan on Moreton Island and was transferred to the 14th Garrison Battalion in April. He had been hospitalised in Brisbane with inflamed eyelids and then spent time at the 101st Convalescent Depot at Coorparoo until May when he rejoined the 11th Infantry Training Battalion. He was transferred to the 13th Garrison Battalion on Moreton Island, but was sent to Enoggera Camp Hospital a few days later with kerotitis (inflammation of the cornea of the eye). On the 17/8/42 he became a Gunner and was transferred to Anti-Aircraft Fixed Defences with the 37th Anti-Aircraft Battery at Mareeba.

In August the following year this unit became the 137th Heavy Anti-Aircraft Battery of the 56th Composite Anti-Aircraft Regiment and he was graded as a Group II Predictor, which he subsequently relinquished. He was then graded as a Group II Fire Control Operator. Predictors are devices that assist gunners in tracking and firing on their target. Fire Control Operators then have the responsibility of hitting the target. In December 1943 he embarked from Cairns for Red Island Point on the Cape York Peninsula. Here he relinquished his Fire Control Operator status at his own request. In April 1944, he flew to Townsville from Horn Island and was transported to Redbank where he was given an early discharge on 12/4/44 to return to the dairy industry.

He had been in Brisbane from 22/11/41 until at least August 1942, during which time he visited City Hall. He wrote on the wall "QX23167, Pte M.N. Streeter, Ubobo, B.V. Line" in a wavy ellipse. He gave his address at the time of his enlistment as Ubobo, which is on the Boyne Valley railway line in the Gladstone area.

South Queensland, World War II: Two members of the Coastal Defences Unit. *(Courtesy of the John Oxley Library, State Library of Queensland 105700)*

Gunner Faulkner had to wait for two more years before he could be discharged. He had been a labourer prior to enlistment but not in an essential industry. He travelled back to Brisbane by ship in September 1944 and was sent to numerous training battalions until the war ended and did garrison duty afterwards. He was finally discharged in April 1946 as part of the general demobilisation process. Both men had similar careers in the army but Streeter's connection to an essential industry had given him priority for discharge.

CASE STUDY NUMBER 4

FAULKNER, ROYAL, QX24982 (Q5982), GUNNER

Royal Faulkner, a labourer from Avondale in Queensland, enlisted into the AIF on New Year's Eve 1941 in Maryborough at the age of 19. Like many new recruits he began his AIF service at the Brisbane Exhibition Grounds and was then sent to the 41st Field Training Battery at Grovely until 26/1/42. He was transferred to the 7th Infantry Training Battalion at Redbank and in March was detached to Coastal Defence duties and then to 14th Garrison Battalion at Cowan on Moreton Island. In May he was transferred to 13th Garrison when the 14th Garrison Battalion moved to Cairns. He stayed with the 13th Garrison Battalion until August when he became a Gunner and transferred to the Anti-Aircraft Fixed Defences with the 37 Anti-Aircraft Battery at Mareeba.

On the 14/8/43 that unit became the 137th Heavy Anti-Aircraft Battery with the 56th Composite Anti-Aircraft Regiment. He was given proficiency pay then upgraded to a Group III Gunlayer on the 19/8/43. Gunlayers are responsible for correctly sighting the gun on to the target. In December, he embarked for Red Island Point, which was located on Cape York. In January 1944 he had treatment for contact dermatitis. He returned to Brisbane in September. He was sent to New South Wales and participated in training battalions until the end of the war. He was then posted to 1st Garrison Battalion. He was discharged from Redbank on 16/4/46 as part of the general demobilisation process. His war service was considered to be non-operational which meant that he had not been in an active war zone.

Mr Faulkner signed the wall "QX24982, Gnr. R. Faulkner, 41st FTD, Grovely" sometime between 2/1/42 and the 26/1/42 when he was stationed at Grovely.

Another gunner, Cyril Jorgensen, was given four months' leave without pay in 1942 to work as a labourer in the sugar industry. Like Streeter, he was also given an early Release to Industry in 1944 to work in an essential food-production area.

Dangerous Work

Many of the non-combat army occupations were extremely hazardous. Members of the service units were often in the firing line.

When my father, Private Harold Saxby, was in the Middle East, he drove oil trucks in convoys. They usually drove at night with no headlights to avoid the Germans, and the only lights they used were small ones connected to the differential at the rear of each truck, which the driver behind would follow. They drove along narrow desert roads that had soft sand on either side. Following that tiny light for hours at a time, in the pitch black, was very mesmerising and it was easy for the driver to fall asleep at the wheel. If for some reason they lost track of the truck in front of them they could easily drive off the road. It was an enormous task to get a heavily laden truck out of the soft sand. If German pilots spotted the convoy and strafed it, the trucks would have exploded in a massive fireball very quickly. It was dangerous work.

Kaye Phillips *née* Saxby, daughter of Wall Signatory Private Harold Saxby, AIF 1940-1944, July 2011

In many situations, being afraid was only natural especially when driving a potential bomb.

In the Middle East, the men would sometimes touch the sides of the petrol trucks and get a charge of static electricity. This had built up due to driving in the extremely dry desert conditions. It made them very nervous.

Kaye Phillips *née* Saxby, daughter of Wall Signatory Private Harold Saxby, AIF 1940-1944, July 2011

For the combatants, being in close proximity to the enemy was always fraught with danger. The men had to learn to expect the unexpected. Veteran Richard Dulley was in Darwin on 19/2/42 when the Japanese attacked for the first time. He told his family about his lucky escape.

When Darwin was bombed, the airport was one of the main targets. The Japanese flew in tight formation and the bombs fell like raindrops. We did not realise that they were bombs at first, and from our army position just outside the airfield we just watched them coming down. The bombs got bigger and bigger as they got closer. A bomber from the outer part of the formation dropped his bomb and we saw it heading right for us. We all just fell to the ground. It landed about 10 metres from where we were. Fortunately it was the wet season and the ground was soft and boggy and so the bomb exploded when it went deep into the ground. If it had hit hard ground, we would have all been wiped out. It was scary stuff!

Veteran Richard Charles Dulley, AIF 1940-1945, February 2012

In extreme cases, a soldier's occupation may help to keep him alive.

> *My brother's time in Changi was horrendous. However, he said that he was fortunate as he had been in training with the medical corps and was therefore able to stay with the doctors. They received better treatment from the Japanese because they wanted the doctors to keep the Australians soldiers alive so they could be used as slave labour.*
>
> Myra O'Shea *née* Harris, sister of Private Geoffrey Robert Harris, AIF 1940-1946, August 2011

Cowra Escape

Australian soldiers did not have to go overseas to meet the enemy. One of the army's responsibilities was to maintain the security of enemy prisoners of war in Australia. Cowra in New South Wales was a major prison camp housing mainly Japanese and Italians. In August 1944, one of the largest mass prisoner escapes of the war occurred. Corporal Richard Dulley was present at the time and described this incident to his son, John.

> *I was at Cowra when the mass outbreak occurred. I had been training new recruits when we were ordered to go looking in the surrounding countryside for Japanese prisoners who had escaped. One of the men was pushing his bayonet into a large haystack when he hit something. The Japanese may have no fear of death, but this guy sure screamed when he was stuck with a bayonet. He was recaptured.*
>
> Veteran Richard Charles Dulley, AIF 1940-1945, February 2012

Conquering Adversity

It was often necessary for the men to change their occupations for medical reasons. At least four of the wall signatories had to transfer to other areas where their skills could still be utilised. Gilbert Myers was a highly experienced infantryman who transferred to a baker's unit due to eye problems. Ronald Rice, a former 'Z' Special Unit member, was limited to sedentary duties after a knee injury. He became a General Details Depot staff member.

After the war ended, Staff Sergeant Stuart Hanley overcame his debility with his feet and performed duty at prisoner of war camps in South Australia assisting with the release and repatriation of the inmates. For another wall signatory, Walter Huggonson, his misfortune turned into a benefit for others long after the fighting had stopped.

In late 1944, Dad was badly burnt in an accident at his workshop in New Guinea. He was sent to Greenslopes Hospital and then to Repatriation. When they found out that he had been a bootmaker and saddler before the war, and because there was a serious lack of skilled workers in this essential area, they immediately gave him the job of making artificial limbs for returned soldiers. The limbs were made of wood and were strapped to the body with leather. He continued working for them for 20 years after the war.

David Huggonson, son of Wall Signatory Walter Huggonson,
AIF 1941-1944, April 2012

Some soldiers had a variety of ranks and occupations as they transferred from one unit to another. Albert Dixon (*CS 14*) had a long list of both. His rank at various times had been private, gunner, craftsman, sapper, driver, lance corporal and acting corporal. His occupation went from being a civilian plumber to being a soldier who worked with artillery, provost companies, artillery workshops, vehicles, general maintenance, water-transport maintenance and hospital maintenance with the Royal Australian Engineers.

The various combinations of occupations, training and postings have contributed to the enormous range of positions that were filled by the men on the wall. Soldiers identified their position in the army with their rank and their occupation and, particularly for the lower ranks, these were closely associated with their units.

CHAPTER 6

UNITS I: THE INFANTRY

The military structure of the army is well demonstrated on the Signature Wall due to the fact that many of the soldiers have included divisions, battalions, companies, platoons or sections along with their names. It was not unusual for soldiers to be part of several different units throughout their service careers, and therefore the unit name on the wall is not necessarily the same unit included in their discharge papers.

When combined, the units associated with the wall collectively represent practically all of the major battles, events and activities that are now part of Australia's World War II historical record. They also reveal the broad cross-section of the type of units that made up Australia's land forces during this war.

Two Separate Armies

The organisation of the units for World War II varied considerably throughout the war as there were many factors involved. There were several theatres of war, including Europe, North Africa and the Pacific, as well as two separate armies. The Australian Military Forces consisted mainly of the militia and the Second Australian Imperial Forces (AIF). The militia units were the pre-war part time units, which were mobilized in December 1941. Originally called the Citizen Military Forces (CMF), the term *militia* was used from 1930 until the end of 1942, when the former part-time army became known once again as the Citizen Military Forces (CMF), although the term *militia* remained in usage. The Second AIF were the units specifically raised in 1939/41 for service overseas.

The Naming of the Battalions – The Militia

After World War I, when the First AIF had been disbanded, militia units were regarded as the mainstay of Australia's defence. These militia units were raised in the same areas, followed the same structure and were given the same numerical designations as the original World War I AIF units, as well as gaining the AIF units' battle honours. The militia battalions were also given the name of the regions from where the recruits were drawn. Hence the 25th Infantry Battalion was known as the Darling Downs Regiment. With the advent of World War II, conscripted men as well as volunteers were placed into militia units and they could only be stationed in Australia or its Territories.

The Naming of the Battalions – The Second AIF

Australia's involvement in World War II meant that more men were required and therefore additional divisions had to be formed. The Second AIF was formed not long after the war began in 1939 and these soldiers were all volunteers and destined to be sent overseas. In contrast to the naming of the militia units, the Second AIF units retained a straight numerical designation. The Government opted to name these new AIF units from the 1st Infantry Battalion onwards, but distinguished them from the militia units by placing the prefix *2/* in front of the AIF number, for example, the 2/25th Infantry Battalion.

In June 1940, militia members were prevented from joining the AIF in order to preserve the strength of the militia for home defence. However, after the war with Japan had commenced the regulations were changed during 1942 to allow militia members to voluntarily join the AIF, but they would still stay within their own unit. Some of the militia units became AIF units, while others maintained their separate status. The militia units that were incorporated into the AIF from 1942 onwards retained their original unit names and numbers. However, each individual man was given a new service number.

Like the militia units, recruits for the AIF were mostly raised from local areas and, wherever possible, given the same number as the earlier World War I units from the same locality. Therefore by World War II, there were many battalions that formed one part of three distinct units with the same number. The naming of the three Brisbane-based 9th Infantry Battalions, for example, was like this:–

1. *World War I*, 9th Infantry Battalion, 1st AIF, August 1914 until 1919
2. 1921 onwards, 9th Infantry Battalion (Moreton Regiment), now a militia unit
3. *World War II*, continues as 9th Battalion militia unit and in 1943, as part of the CMF incorporated into the 2nd AIF, disbanded 12/12/45
4. *World War II*, 2/9th Infantry Battalion, 2nd AIF, formed in Brisbane, November 1939, disbanded 3/1/46

Brisbane, December 1939: AIF Infantry procession in Queen Street with the Treasury Building in the background. *(Courtesy of the John Oxley Library, State Library of Queensland 108476)*

Throughout the war, the composition and numbers within units varied as circumstances changed. Some battalions like the 31/51st Infantry Battalion, by necessity, were combined. This was due mainly to depleted numbers of men in the units caused by a very high number of casualties or by redeployment. It was also not unusual for units to have name changes during the war, for example, the artillery unit 2/13th Field Regiment became the 2/1st Medium Regiment while in the Middle East in 1941.

Military Structure

The units are organised according to a set of criteria based mainly on the numbers of men in each section. In 1941, the basic structure for the infantry was made as follows:

Organisation	Strength	Made up of	Commanded by
Army		2 or more corps	General
Corps	30,000+	2 or more divisions	Lieutenant General
Division	10,000-20,000	3 brigades	Major General
Brigade	2500-5000	3 battalions	Brigadier
Battalion	550-1000	4 companies	Lieutenant Colonel
Company	100-225	3 platoons	Major or Captain
Platoon	30-60	4 (later 3) sections	Major or Lieutenant
Section	9-6		Sergeant or Corporal

Courtesy of the Australian War Memorial

The Regiments

The militia infantry units commonly used the term *regiment* in their name to represent a territorial allegiance. The Cavalry/Armoured Corps used regiment as their equivalent of a battalion as well as squadron instead of company and troop instead of platoon. The Artillery Corps also used regiment but their equivalent of a company was a battery.

Maintaining Numbers

Once a unit had completed its training and had its full complement of men and equipment, it was considered to be operational and ready to be sent to any place where it was needed. Extra men could be acquired by being Taken on Strength (TOS), that is, as needed, in order to keep up the necessary strength in numbers of personnel. During wartime, it is usual for units to be at full strength if possible.

When a soldier was absent for more than seven days, his name was added to the X List, which meant that he could be replaced in his absence. This system was used to maintain the necessary number of active personnel in order for the unit to operate effectively. A soldier was not considered to be on active service if he was in basic training, in medical care, at a course of study, being Absent Without Leave (AWL), in detention or for any other reason. After a prolonged absence, a soldier may find himself assigned to another unit.

Theatre and Battle Honours

Unit Honours take two forms. Theatre Honours are awarded to all units who have participated creditably in a theatre of war, e.g. the South West Pacific 1942. A Battle Honour refers to a specific battle or event in which the unit performed very well, e.g. Buna-Gona, 16 November 1942-22 January 1943. The units listed below earned many Battle Honours, including better-known ones such as Tobruk and El Alamein in North Africa and Kokoda and Milne Bay in Papua New Guinea.

Only certain units are eligible to be considered for honours and there are rules governing the granting of the honour. The records of individual soldiers do not state whether or not the soldier was present at a particular battle or event, but in some cases, it can be reasonably assumed that he was with the unit at a particular time and place. This can be said of Sergeant Scott, a Rat of Tobruk, who was shot during the fighting.

CASE STUDY NUMBER 5

SCOTT, GEORGE EARNSHAW, SX1150, SERGEANT

George Scott was a salesman from South Australia who enlisted into the AIF on 27/11/39 at the age of 22. His unit was the 2/10th Infantry Battalion. In March 1940 he embarked from Sydney for Scotland. After training in England, the battalion embarked from Glasgow in November and went to Egypt. In March 1941, like many of the soldiers from the 2/10th Battalion, he was detached for special duty with Lustre Force, which was due to be sent to Greece. However, there is no evidence that any embarkation took place and he returned to his unit on the 28/3/41. In April, his battalion was sent to help in the defence of Tobruk in Libya. On 1/5/41, the enemy under Rommel's orders had penetrated Tobruk's defences, and during the night of 3/5/41 and the morning of the next day the Allies launched a counter-assault, which was successful in defending the town, but claimed a lot of casualties. On 4/5/41, Private Scott was shot in the fourth toe of his left foot and evacuated to hospital. He embarked for Australia in March 1942. The next time that he faced the enemy was against the Japanese with the 2/10th Battalion at the Battle of Milne Bay in August 1942.

The second half of Sergeant Scott's service record is missing, but his other papers provide information. His proceedings for discharge provided advice about malaria, so it can be assumed that he caught this disease while in New Guinea. The 2/10th Infantry Battalion is listed on both his Discharge Proceedings and the Nominal Roll as being his major posting at his discharge on 31/7/45. The battalion's last action was conducted in Borneo after which many of the longer-serving soldiers like Sergeant Scott were given an early discharge. He had attained the rank of sergeant.

The 2/10th Infantry Battalion was camped at Kilcoy in Queensland in 1942 before proceeding north by convoy to Milne Bay in Papua New Guinea. This would have provided George Scott with the opportunity to come to Brisbane and sign the wall. He wrote "SX1150, G.E.S.".

Army matters were conducted through various Headquarters. If these were located in Active Service areas, Headquarters senior staff, like all formation and unit commanders in the field, were required to keep War Diaries, which detailed daily activities. Headquarters staff also maintained the soldiers' personal records.

Headquarters and Administration (Miscellaneous)

Headquarters 2nd Australian Corps	Dobbin
Australian-New Guinea Administration Unit	Taylor, W
Land Headquarters	Sankey
2/1st Headquarters Guard Battalion	O'Brien
1st Personnel Staging Camp	Bowman, Grace
2nd Advanced 2nd Echelon and Records	Davie
Qld Echelon and Records	Davie

AUSTRALIAN INFANTRY CORPS

During World War II, the majority of soldiers were placed into Infantry Battalions. Each soldier's main weapon was a rifle and each man was responsible for his own gun

There is a very broad range of these fighting units represented on the wall. Some of the men had returned from fighting the Germans, the Italians or the Vichy French in the Mediterranean region and were preparing to defend Australia from the Japanese. Others were newly recruited and were being trained to join the more experienced soldiers in combat.

Divisions 1 to 5 were the pre-war militia divisions, while Divisions 6 to 9 were formed for the 2nd AIF. The 3rd and 5th Infantry Divisions as well as elements from other militia divisions participated in active service in combat areas. Many of the militia brigades served in more than one division. The units and the men associated with them are listed below.

Brisbane, 1940: Soldiers at the Enoggera Army Camp displaying their rifles
(Courtesy of the John Oxley Library, State Library of Queensland 124166)

Militia

1st Infantry Division

This militia division was responsible for the defence of Sydney and remained in Sydney throughout the war.

2nd Infantry Division

34th Infantry Battalion	Veigel

In 1941, the 34th Infantry Battalion was located in Wollongong NSW. It was under the overall control of Eastern Command, with its headquarters in Sydney. It later became an AIF unit with the 28th Infantry Brigade.

3rd Infantry Division

22nd Infantry Battalion	Bancks, Cooper

(South Gippsland Regiment), 4th Infantry Brigade. This unit was located from March 1942 in Warwick, Caloundra, Maroochydore and then did extensive service in New Guinea.

29/46th Infantry Battalion	Floyd, Glasson, Harrison, Hughes, McNaughton

(East Melbourne Brighton Rifles), 4th Infantry Brigade. This unit was located at Warwick, Caloundra, Mt. Gravatt and Maroochydore from March 1942 until March 1943. The 29th and 46th Battalions merged in August 1942.

As part of the 4th Infantry Brigade, the 22nd and the 29/46th Infantry Battalions both served with the 5th Infantry Division in New Guinea in the latter part of the war.

58/59th Infantry Battalion	Connell

(Essendon, Coburg, Brunswick/Hume Regiment). The 58/59th Infantry Battalion fought with the 3rd Infantry Division in the Salamaua Campaign and on Bougainville.

4th Infantry Division

48th Infantry Battalion	Saxby

This was a South Australian battalion that was under the control of Southern Command with its headquarters in Melbourne.

5th Infantry Division (formerly Northern Command, HQ, Brisbane))

25th Infantry Battalion	Anderson, Johnston

The 25th Infantry Battalion (Darling Downs Regiment) was located at Chermside in Brisbane in 1941. The unit participated in the Battle of Milne Bay, 27 August -7 September 1942 as part of 'Milne Force'. The battalion went to Bougainville in late 1944 as part of the 3rd Infantry Division, where a member of the unit, Corporal Rattey, was awarded a Victoria Cross.

11th Infantry Brigade

31/51st Infantry Battalion	Friend

(Kennedy/Far North Queensland Regiment). Initially this battalion was directly under the control of the Militia Northern Command from its headquarters in Brisbane. From early in 1940, the 31st Infantry Battalion, like the 51st Infantry Battalion, was raised in Northern Queensland, and as part of 11th Brigade, was given the task of defending Far North Queensland. In April 1943, as rural workers were released by the Government for essential work, the numbers in the battalions were depleted and the 31st and the 51st Infantry Battalions merged. In June the same year the 11th Infantry Brigade was sent to perform garrison duties in Merauke in the south-east of Dutch New Guinea, becoming part of the 'Merauke Force'.

'Merauke Force'

62nd Battalion (Merauke Regiment)	Spry

The 62nd Infantry Battalion was a militia unit raised from soldiers serving in the 14th Garrison Battalion in Torres Strait in December 1942. In January 1943, the battalion went to Merauke and was redesignated 'Merauke Force'. It was the area's principle infantry unit and its main purpose was to hold the airstrip and the port, which provided an important Torres Strait base. The 11th Infantry Brigade, which included Robert Friend from the 31/51st Infantry Battalion, later arrived to assist. The Japanese never invaded this area, but maintained air attacks. The 62nd Infantry Battalion returned to Australia in February 1944 and was disbanded in May the same year.

Papuan Infantry Battalion	Hanley

This was an Indigenous battalion formed in 1940 by volunteers, many of whom were formerly in the Royal Papuan Constabulary. In 1942, there were 300 Papuans enlisted. On the 23 July of that year, the battalion ambushed enemy troops who were advancing towards Kokoda. Afterwards, the unit formed stretcher teams to help with the Allied sick and wounded. In later campaigns members of the Papuan Infantry Battalion were used as scouts and for reconnaissance behind enemy lines. Sergeant Hanley joined the battalion in June 1943 as a Signals Operator.

CASE STUDY NUMBER 6

HANLEY, STUART WILLIAM SX30974 (S36732) STAFF SERGEANT

Stuart Hanley was a 19-year-old milkman from Laura in South Australia when he enlisted part-time into the militia on 17/9/41. He was allocated to Australian Signals in the 4th Military Division at Largs Bay in South Australia. He became a full-time member on 16/12/41 and transferred to the 8th Military District Training Centre located at Toowoomba in preparation for duty in New Guinea. He went to the 5th/11th Field Training Regiment at Grovely in Brisbane on 10/2/42. The following June, during training in the Goondiwindi area, he transferred to the 13th Field Regiment Signal Section.

In July, he sailed to Port Moresby. He was classified as a Signals Operator Grade II in October and in December he undertook a Signals Training Course. On 7/1/43, he officially enlisted in the AIF in the field. He was appointed Acting Lance Sergeant in June and transferred to the Papuan Infantry Battalion. He was promoted to Sergeant in January 1944 at the age of 21. In September, he contracted malaria for the first time.

After his promotion to Staff Sergeant in January 1945, he left Port Moresby and travelled to South Australia where he was married. By April 1945 he was still on leave when he contracted malaria again. In May, his medical classification was changed to B2, which meant fit for duty but with a debility. This was due to his having flat feet and bunions. He was then reallocated for duty at various prisoner of war camps, including Sandy Creek. He was discharged on 27/11/45 at Hampstead in South Australia.

Sergeant Hanley was stationed at Grovely from 10/2/42 until 20/4 42, when he was able to write on the wall "S36732, Sig. Hanley, S.W., Australian Corps of Signals, attached 11th Field Reg., Grovely. Another South Australian".

The 2nd Australian Imperial Forces (AIF)

6th Infantry Division

Formed in October 1939, it was the first division to be part of the Special Forces for Overseas Service for the 2nd AIF. Its losses were particularly heavy, not just from casualties, but also from losing thousands of men as prisoners of war to the Germans in Greece and Crete.

2/1st Infantry Battalion	Darlington, O'Brien
2/6th Infantry Battalion	Gutteridge

2/7th Infantry Battalion	Dean, McKinnon, McLeod, R., Newman, Snell

7th Infantry Division

In common with the 6th and 9th Divisions, the 7th Infantry Division served in both the Middle East and the South West Pacific Area. The division earned distinction in both areas, which included Tobruk, Syria, Kokoda Trail, Milne Bay and Borneo.

2/9th Infantry Battalion	Jacobson, Marshall
2/10th Infantry Battalion	Scott, Miller, K.
2/12th Infantry Battalion	Dare, Goodwin
2/14th Infantry Battalion	Cranston
2/16th Infantry Battalion	Cook, Rieman, Robinson
2/25th Infantry Battalion	Newman
2/31st Infantry Battalion	Harvatt, McDermid, Tarbuck
2/33rd Infantry Battalion	Davie, Myers

New Guinea, 1943: Members of the 2/31st Infantry Battalion after marching from the Finisterre Range. *(Courtesy of the John Oxley Library, State Library of Queensland 283659)*

8th Infantry Division

When war with Japan became increasingly probable in 1941, the decision was made to send most of the 8th Infantry Division to Malaya to reinforce the British forces and to provide an Australian presence in other South-East Asian areas. The division was poorly equipped and was unable to withstand the Japanese invasion. The result was the tragic loss of almost an entire division due to death or capture by the enemy.

2/26th Infantry Battalion	Martin

After the fall of Singapore on 15/2/42, the majority of the 2/26th Infantry Battalion spent three and a half years as prisoners of war in camps mainly at Changi, Burma, Thailand, Borneo and Japan.

9th Infantry Division

This division has the distinction of spending more time in combat than any other division. It was the last Australian division to leave North Africa and was therefore present at the Battle of El Alamein.

2/15th Infantry Battalion	Casey, Chalmers, Davis, Meehan, Ritchie, Rowe
2/32nd Infantry Battalion	Howard
2/43rd Infantry Battalion	Saxby

The Army had three other Infantry Divisions.

10th Infantry Division

This was a militia division that was formed briefly at Newcastle from April 1942 until August 1942. It was disbanded early due to manpower shortages.

11th Infantry Division

Once the Japanese had been defeated at Milne Bay, the 'Milne Force' was redesignated as the 11th Infantry Division in October 1942. It remained active in New Guinea and New Britain until the end of the war in August 1945.

12th Infantry Division

Based near Darwin, the Northern Territory Force consisted of army units that were rotated at different times for duty in order to protect the Northern

Territory. For 15 days from 31 December 1942 until 14 January 1943 it was redesignated briefly as the 12th Infantry Division. The Northern Territory Force was disbanded at the end of the war.

Infantry Training Battalions (ITB)

These soldiers were either trainees or instructors.

1st Infantry Training Battalion	Hancock
2nd Infantry Training Battalion	Faulkner
7th Infantry Training Battalion, Redbank	Cross, Darlington, Faulkner, Newman
11th Infantry Training Battalion, Redbank	Miller, K., Streeter
18th Infantry Training Battalion, Palestine	Scott
23rd Infantry Training Battalion	Hunter
25th Infantry Training Battalion	Osborne, Saxby
29th Infantry Training Battalion, Goondiwindi	Miller, K.
32nd Infantry Training Battalion	Faulkner
2nd Australian Infantry Special Group (attached to 2nd Infantry Training Brigade)	Faulkner

Machine Gun Battalions

During World War II, one Machine Gun Battalion was raised for each AIF Division in order to provide support for the Infantry. Each machine gun company was allocated to a different infantry battalion and in each campaign they remained attached to these units throughout the fighting. In common with other infantry battalions, the Machine Gun Battalions had their own signalmen, like Signalman Abrahams.

As part of the 6th Infantry Division and later, the 7th Infantry Division (February 1944)

2/1st Machine Gun Battalion	Abrahams

The 2/1st Machine Gun Battalion had participated in the Greece and Crete campaigns. It was in Queensland from June 1942 for a few months. The battalion later participated in Operation OBOE.

As part of the 7th Infantry Division and later, the 9th Infantry Division (from January 1942)

2/2nd Machine Gun Battalion	McDermid

The 2/2nd Machine Gun Battalion is particularly famous for its role at El Alamein.

Pioneer Battalions

Pioneers were infantry soldiers who performed light engineering tasks as well as being assault troops. They were therefore multi-skilled men who were recruited to help the Royal Australian Engineers build roads, camps, fortifications etc. As World War II progressed and more infantry were needed on the front lines, many of the pioneers transferred to the fighting.

Special Pioneer Companies

The Special Pioneer Companies also used multi-skilled men. These companies were not part of the Pioneer Battalions, but were special units set up from March 1942 until October 1942 at Redbank for construction projects. After they were disbanded in October they formed the 31st Employment Company. They never officially had the *2/* prefix, although some of the men included it when they signed the wall. This signified they were part of the 2nd AIF.

7th Pioneer Company, Redbank	Cross, Dean, Doolan, Newman
8th Pioneer Company, Redbank, No. 1 Platoon	Chaplin, Jacobson, Snell
31st Employment Company	Hill

Parachute Battalion

(Also referred to as Paratroop Battalion)

This specialised infantry unit was formed in late 1942 with 40 volunteers and by March 1943 had sufficient numbers to form a battalion. Most of the men were riflemen or artillery gunners who had previously been in active service. Prior to joining the battalion, the men trained with the 1st Parachute Training Battalion at Richmond Air Force Base. This qualified them to wear the maroon berets that symbolised elite airborne forces. They are commonly referred to as 'Red Berets'. Additional training specifically for jungle warfare was conducted at Canungra in Queensland. The unit never saw action outside of Australia. It was prevented from going to Borneo by the lack of available aircraft.

1st Parachute Battalion	Jones
1st Parachute Training Battalion (RAAF Base, Richmond, NSW)	Jones

CASE STUDY NUMBER 7

JONES, EARLE ALBERT, NX38209, PRIVATE

Earle Albert Jones, a farmer from Ulmarra in New South Wales, had enlisted in the Citizen Military Forces in 1936 and joined the AIF in July 1941. He was initially sent to the 1st Field Training Regiment in Cowra for gunnery training, and then to the 2/13th Army Field Artillery Regiment at Ingleburn. This unit was later reformed into the 2/1st Medium Artillery Regiment. In September 1941 he embarked with the regiment for the Middle East. His unit formed part of the 1st Australian Corps. He left the Middle East in March 1942.

In the following February he was sent to the 1st Parachute Training Battalion at Richmond in NSW. He was assessed as medically fit for all duties and qualified as a parachutist on 29/4/43. From June until August he was detached to the 1st Australian Signals Training Battalion, and on 26/8/43 he was appointed Special Grade 2 Signalman to complete his training. He was officially transferred to the 1st Parachute Battalion on 21/9/43. In October 1945, not long after the war had ended, he ceased to be entitled to parachutist pay. He was discharged on 16/11/45 as part of the demobilisation process.

He wrote on the middle of the far right side of the wall "NX 38209, GNR Jones, E.A., 2/1 Med Regt., RAA" while he was a member of the 2/1st Medium Artillery Regiment sometime prior to September 1941 when he left Australia for the Middle East.

Infantry units could not function on their own as independent entities and therefore required that men from other areas with specialised skills be incorporated into the Infantry as required by circumstances. Therefore, an infantry brigade group may be composed of three infantry battalions, men and equipment from the Cavalry/Armoured Corps, Artillery, Engineers, Ordnance, a machine gun battery, plus men from the Signals Corps, the Medical Corps and numerous areas of the Australian Army Service Corps.

CHAPTER 7

UNITS II: COMBAT (ARMS)

In addition to the Infantry, the Army was organised into specific functioning corps which were directly involved in the fighting. These Combat (or Arms) Corps included Cavalry/Armoured, Artillery, Signals, Engineering, Survey and Intelligence, which all had their own traditions and structures. Most of these corps are represented by wall signatories.

CAVALRY/ARMOURED CORPS

From very early times, the cavalry has been associated with horses and mounted soldiers known as troopers. As technology advanced the horses were gradually replaced with mechanised armoured transport of various kinds, but the men were still referred to as troopers. The organisation for this corps was comprised of division, brigade, regiment, squadron, troop and section. In 1941, three cavalry divisional regiments were Australia's only armoured units.

Divisional Cavalry Regiments

Initially, each of the 2nd AIF 6th, 7th and 9th Divisions was allowed a cavalry reconnaissance regiment equipped with armoured vehicles. Armoured support for the infantry consisted of mainly light tanks and scout carriers, which were very well suited to the desert terrain of North Africa and the Middle East. The 8th Division was not provided with support because it was thought incorrectly that they would not need it in Malaya. In December 1941, four militia Light Horse regiments were added to the cavalry regiments as reconnaissance battalions.

8th Divisional Cavalry Regiment (later 9th Division Cavalry Regiment)	Lennane

By early 1943 the Australians were fighting the Japanese in South East-Asia in mainly impenetrable jungle conditions. Most vehicles were unsuited to the dense jungle terrain. The decision was made to convert these cavalry regiments to light infantry and by late 1943 the cavalry units were amalgamated with former Independent Companies under the command of Cavalry Regimental Headquarters.

Independent Companies

In 1940, Independent Companies were raised to reinforce the numbers of men in the 2nd AIF. These were small special units that were highly trained in sabotage, raids and guerilla warfare and had the ability to fight independently without assistance from other units. Recruits had to be extremely fit physically. By 1942, there were eight Independent Companies. The men were usually referred to as "commandos". In late 1943, when the Independent Companies were amalgamated with the divisional cavalry regiments, the new units were designated "Commando Squadrons".

2/2nd Commando Squadron (formerly 2/2nd Independent Company)	Hodge

This unit operated independently until the end of the war. It was part of Sparrow Force and is famous for its guerilla war in East Timor against the Japanese in 1942-43. The commando training had provided survival skills that allowed not only the commandos, but also soldiers from other 8th Division units who had evaded capture and joined them, to remain independent. The unit was listed as missing by the army after the other units in Sparrow Force had been captured. Communications with Australia had failed, but Signalman Max Loveless eventually built a wireless that had enough power to contact the mainland. In order to prove their identity, the signaller was asked the name of Jack Sargent's wife. The response was "Kathleen", which was easy because the signaller was Jack Sargent himself. This is a very famous story.

The unit was supported by the Timorese population during this time, but Japanese reprisals led to the tragic loss of 40,000 to 60,000 people. The unit was never captured by the enemy and was withdrawn from Timor in December 1943. It went on to fight in New Guinea and New Britain.

2/3 Commando Squadron (formerly 2/3rd Independent Company) operated as part of 2/7th Cavalry (Commando) Regiment	Henson

This unit received high praise for its excellent service in Noumea, New Guinea and Borneo.

Training Centres

The 7th Infantry Training Centre (a cover name for commando training) was located at Foster on Wilsons Promontory in Victoria before moving to Canungra.

7th Infantry Training Centre	Henson
Commando Training Battalion, Canungra	Henson
1st Cavalry (Commando) Training Battalion	Henson

CASE STUDY NUMBER 8

HENSON, HENRY GEORGE, NX 38826, SIGNALLER

Henry Henson was a 21-year-old porter with the NSW Railways before enlisting with the AIF on 15/7/41 at Paddington in Sydney. He was sent to the Eastern Command Signals Training Depot at Tamworth and then was officially transferred to the 7th Infantry Training Centre in Victoria where the recruits were being trained to become commandos. In October, he was transferred to 2/3rd Independent Company. Signaller Henson went to Woodside Camp near Adelaide for one month before embarking from Sydney in December for garrison duty in New Caledonia. His unit returned to Sydney in August 1942. In September, he was sent to Queensland, and in May 1943 he transferred to the 1st Commando Training Battalion at Canungra.

In late 1943, the independent companies and the cavalry regiments were amalgamated, and as from the 10/10/43 Signaller Henson became part of the 1st Cavalry (Commando) Training Battalion. In January 1944 he returned to his former unit, the 2/3rd Independent Company. It was now called the 2/3rd Commando Squadron and formed part of the 2/7th Cavalry (Commando) Regiment. The unit was stationed on the Atherton Tableland. In March Signaller Henson attended the First Australian Army School of Signals for a Regimental Signaller Refresher Course, which included Morse Code operations, map reading and cable work. He qualified at the course and was retained in the role of Signaller.

In June 1945 his unit left Townsville for Morotai Island in the Dutch East Indies. From here it left for service at Balikpapan in Borneo. By the end of July the offensive operations ceased and Signaller Henson relinquished his Grade 2 Signal Operator's status at his own request. He was transferred to the 2/1st Composite Anti-Aircraft Regiment Workshops. After the war ended he returned to Brisbane in November and was given an occupational discharge a few days later on 29/11/45. This was in order for him to resume his former civilian position as part of an essential industry with the NSW Railways.

Signalman Henry George Henson was in Brisbane at the end of 1942, which is when he most probably went to City Hall. He wrote on the wall "QX38826, Sig. H.G. Henson, 3rd Aus. Ind. Coy" and included the (blue) double diamond heraldic symbol of his unit.

AUSTRALIAN ARMOURED CORPS (AAC)

This corps was created in 1941 to supply personnel to man the increased numbers of armoured vehicles that had been manufactured.

Armoured Divisions

Australia's 1st Armoured Division was raised early in 1941 in order to be deployed to the Middle East. However, with the outbreak of the Pacific War it was retained in Australia and formed a key defence against a possible Japanese invasion. By September 1943 the threat of the invasion was over and the division was disbanded. Two more armoured divisions and one brigade were raised from the reorganisation of Cavalry Divisions, but these too were disbanded in 1943, although some elements of their units survived independently. Only the 4th Armoured Brigade Group survived until the end of the war as a major supplier of armoured units to other formations.

World War II: Downhill run for an armoured vehicle. *(Courtesy of the John Oxley Library, State Library of Queensland 64775)*

1st Armoured Division Advanced Reinforcement Depot	Davie
1st Armoured Training Regiment	Davie
2/5th Armoured Regiment	Davie

As part of 1st Armoured Division and 1st Armoured Brigade, the 2/5th Armoured Regiment was initially located at Grovely in Brisbane in July 1941, but in October it was relocated to Greta in NSW to join the rest of the 1st Armoured Brigade. In August it was sent to Edgeroi in NSW to conduct exercises. In early 1943 the regiment moved to the Geraldton area in Western Australia with the rest of the 1st Armoured Division. However, the unit was never deployed outside Australia. The 2/5th Regiment moved to Southport in Queensland in March 1944. The unit was equipped with tanks and carriers.

Carrier Platoons and Companies

Carriers are light armoured tracked vehicles with up to four troopers manning them. They were used for transporting equipment such as weapons and occasionally for personnel. The artillery used them as tractors for ordnance. Carriers were equipped with Bren machine guns and the vehicles were therefore also used as gun platforms. In 1941, infantry battalions were issued with 21 carriers and by 1943 they were allowed up to 33. They were organised into platoons and companies. The carrier was the most numerous fighting vehicle in history and was very well suited to desert conditions, but like most of the armoured vehicles, was unsuitable for jungle terrain. It was therefore used mainly for taking supplies to the front line and providing defence for the areas behind the lines.

29th Infantry Battalion "Carriers"	Harrison, McNaughton
5th Carrier Company	McLennan

ROYAL AUSTRALIAN ARTILLERY (RAA)

The Royal Australian Artillery had been in existence since the 19th century. Based heavily on the British system, the organisation was comprised of regiment, battery, troop and detachment. An Infantry Division was normally supplied with three artillery field regiments comprised of three batteries each and an Anti-Tank Regiment. Medium Field Regiments were comprised of only two batteries. A battery, commanded by a major, was comprised of two troops with four guns each. The private soldiers were known as Gunners and corporals with specialist skills as Bombardiers, for example, Bombardier McGill.

Field Regiments

2/2nd Field Regiment	Dixon
2/3rd Field Regiment	McGill
2/5th Field Regiment	Davie, Jordon Jorgensen, McGill, Werner
2/9th Field Regiment	Werner
2/12th Field Regiment	McGill

2/13th Field Regiment	Dobson, Hanley, Jones, Moir, Mudge, Werner
2/15th Field Regiment	Edwards
2/17th Field Regiment	Jorgenson
5/11th Field Training Regiment	Hanley (on attachment), McGill

Medium Regiments

2/1st (formerly 2/13th Field Regiment)	Jones, Stevens

Mountain Battery

1st Mountain Battery (New Guinea)	Werner

CASE STUDY NUMBER 9

WERNER, ALLAN EDWARD, QX24293, CORPORAL

Allen Werner, a clerk from Auchenflower in Brisbane, joined the AIF in October 1941 at the age of 19. He began gunnery training for the Royal Australian Artillery at Grovely with the 41st Field Training Battery and in the following March he was sent to the 5th Field Regiment. In September, Gunner Werner was transferred to the newly formed 1st Mountain Battery. With his unit, he embarked in October from Townsville for Port Moresby. After recovering from an illness in December he re-joined his unit, which was at Buna at this time. In July 1943 he attended a Signals Course and qualified as a signaller. While on duty in August he fractured his finger while attempting to catch a football. The matter was investigated by an officer from 1st Mountain Battery and Gunner Werner was cleared of all blame. He left New Guinea for Cairns in November on leave. Upon his return to duty, he was taken on strength to the 2/9th Field Regiment.

In March 1944 he embarked from Brisbane for Merauke in Dutch New Guinea and was upgraded to a Group 2 Signaller. He left Merauke in October for Thursday Island, and in November returned to Queensland. Private Werner was then sent to several different units for short-term duty. These included the 28th Army Canteen Service Officers' Club, the 73rd Forward Ammunition Depot, the 13th Field Regiment and the 7th Advanced Ammunition Depot on 13/8/45. Private Werner was promoted to Acting Corporal in May and confirmed as Corporal in August. He was finally discharged from Redbank as part of the general demobilisation process on 22/8/46.

Gunner Werner, as he was known then, was stationed at the 41st Field Training Battery at Grovely from 27/10/41 until 3/3/42. It was most probably during this time that he signed the wall. He wrote "Gnr A Werner, Grovely, QX" along with his mate's name "Gnr H Drew". Gunner Drew was later stationed at Paga Point in Port Moresby.

Coastal Fortress near Brisbane, January 1942: Australian soldiers preparing a mortar for firing. *(Courtesy of the John Oxley Library, State Library of Queensland 169995)*

Coastal Defences (attached Infantry)	
1st Garrison Battalion	Faulkner
13th Garrison, Moreton Island	Faulkner, Streeter
14th Garrison Battalion	Faulkner, Streeter

Coastal Defences (New Guinea)	
Paga Coastal Defence Heavy Battery (Paga Point was a gun emplacement on a headland protecting Port Moresby Harbour).	Drew

Anti-Aircraft	
11th Gyro Gun Sight (Militia)	Moran
32nd Heavy Anti-Aircraft Battery	Murphy, Smith, N.

37th Heavy Anti-Aircraft Battery	Faulkner, Streeter
141st Heavy Anti-Aircraft Battery (Mobile)	McEwen
137th Heavy Anti-Aircraft Battery (Part of 56th Composite Anti-Aircraft Regiment)	Faulkner, Streeter
57th Composite Anti-Aircraft Regiment, LE	Baker
2/3rd Composite Anti-Aircraft Battery	Jackson, Reid
2/9th Light Anti-Aircraft Battery	Reid
113th Light Anti-Aircraft Battery	Davy, C., Reid
114th Light Anti-Aircraft Battery	Davy, C., Ingram
158th Light Anti-Aircraft Battery	Davy, C.
235th Light Anti-Aircraft Battery (Milne Bay)	Davy, C., Reid

Anti-Tank Regiments

1st Anti-Tank Regiment	McKenzie
2/3rd Tank Attack Regiment	McGill

Training

41st Field Training Battery, Grovely	Baker, Davie, Draper, Faulkner, Ham, Lawson, McGill, McLeod, E., Werner, Weston, Wallace, Gunner M. (Unidentified)
41st Field Training Battery (Anti-Tank), Grovely	Hunter
101st Anti-Tank Field Training Battery, Grovely	Davy, C., McGill, Wallace
Unspecified Training Units, Grovely	Ingram, Jordon, Jorgenson, McEwen, Parkinson, Stevens
1st Field Training Regiment, Cowra	Jones
RAA Services Training Regiment	Dixon

AUSTRALIAN ARMY CORPS OF SIGNALS

It is impossible to underestimate the importance of signals and communication during wartime. The Signals Corps was, and still is, responsible for installing, maintaining and operating all types of communication equipment and for keeping communication links open between units. Each army division had its own signal allocation. The men were known as signallers although they were often referred to as signalmen.

Militia

Northern Command Signals	Loveday, Rice
Australian Signals, Largs Bay	Hanley
13th Field Regiment Signals Section	Hanley
3rd Signals Squadron, 1st Motor Brigade (attached)	Rice
3rd Signals Company, 5th Motor Regiment, J Troop (attached)	Rice

AIF

1 Composite Signals Section	Street
Brisbane Fortress Signals, Fort Lytton	Gosper, Street
3rd Infantry Division Signals	Plymin
Australian Corps of Signals (attached to 11th Field Regiment, Grovely)	Hanley
1st Multi-channel Wireless Transmitter Section (Radio Communication)	Francis, N.
Signals Fixed Defences	Gosper
35th Wireless Task Section	Loveday
38th Wireless Task Section	Loveday
1st Independent Signals Group	Loveday
18th Lines of Communication Signals, New Guinea	Loveday
19th Lines of Communication Signals, Queensland	Loveday
Torres Strait Signals	Burr

Training

1st Australian Army School of Signals	Henson
Signals Training Battalion, Bonegilla	Jones, Loveday
New Guinea Force Training Centre (Signals)	Hanley

ROYAL AUSTRALIAN ENGINEERS (RAE)

The Royal Australian Engineers were primarily responsible for the provision of movement capability for the Allied troops. Their tasks included the building of roads, bridges, airstrips and landing grounds as well as the clearing of mines and booby traps. They also laid minefields and engaged in demolition work to impede enemy movement. The engineers were also responsible for the provision of purified water. They were called sappers because from the earliest times engineers dug saps (tunnels) into enemy territory. In 1941, the RAE organisation was comprised of company (or squadron), platoon and section. After the war they formed regiments. The men were often required to work very close to the front lines and were therefore trained soldiers.

Field Companies

These were the combat engineers who worked at the front-lines. There were normally three of these companies allocated to each Infantry Division.

Militia	
18th Field Company	Gulliver
21st Field Company	Nihill

AIF	
2/9th Field Company	Clark
2/11th Field Company	Solomon
2/15th Field Company	Edwards

Logan River, World War 2: Sappers practising bridge building. *(Courtesy of the John Oxley Library, State Library of Queensland 187087)*

Field Park Companies/Squadrons

These units held large amounts of supplies and equipment for the field companies. They normally stayed in a stationary position behind the front lines, but could be mobilised when needed. There was one Field Park Company allocated to each division.

2/1st Field Park Squadron	Chaplain
2/25th Field Park Company	Miller, K.
51st Field Park Company	Dendle

Docks Operating Companies

Docks Operating Companies (later referred to as Port Operating Companies) were a vital and essential link in supply lines. As such, they were prime targets for the enemy. These companies were responsible for the loading and unloading of ships and the handling of supplies and military equipment. As part of the Royal Australian Engineers, the men were entitled to be called sappers.

2/1st Docks Operating Company	McLeod, E., Weston
2/2nd Docks Operating Company	Smith, D.
2/4th Docks Operating Company	Cross, Francis, L.
2/8th Docks Operating Company	Okey
2/10th Docks Operating Company	Draper, Weston
2/2nd Port Operating Company	Arnold
2/3rd Port Operating Company	McKinnon
2/4th Port Operating Company	Francis, L.
2/10th Port Operating Company	Davy, C.
33rd Port Operating Company	Cross
Unspecified Operating Company	Taylor, L.

Maintenance	
2/1st Port Maintenance Company	Lawson
7th Hospital Maintenance Platoon	Dixon
115th Hospital Maintenance, Heidelberg	Dixon
13th Maintenance Platoon	Dixon
Cape River Meat Works Maintenance Section	McDonald

Water Transport	
13th Water Transport Company	Dixon
19th Water Transport Company, Mt Martha	Dixon

Other Engineering Units	
12th Army Troop Company	Dull
2/11th Army Transport Company, Deagon and Sandgate	Creffield
2/1st Mechanical Equipment Company	Parkinson

AUSTRALIAN SURVEY CORPS (ASC)

The major task of the surveyors was to produce maps. Initially the survey units were Royal Australian Engineers militia units that were sent to other units to provide assistance with military operations. They separated from the RAE in 1932. In the early 1940s, the corps was expanded to be able to incorporate their own militia units. They served in both the Middle East and the South West Pacific regions. Women were able to join the survey units in Australia and New Guinea. By the end of the war the Survey Corps was 1700 strong, and had produced more than 1400 new maps of the theatres of war. They were commended by many senior staff, including General Macarthur. Their service was formally recognised in 1948 when they were given the title of Royal Australian Survey Corps.

Survey Unit	
1st Field Survey Company	Melrose
2/1st Survey Regiment (RAA)	Viquerat

SPECIAL UNITS

Two commando groups were formed separately as part of the Allied Intelligence Bureau and were attached to Special Operations Australia. They were multinational combined forces units made up of volunteers from all branches of the military. They conducted covert operations in the South West Pacific Zone which were far more clandestine than other commando groups. Their actions were kept secret for many years after the war had ended.

The work of both of these units was regarded as being very dangerous and many of the personnel were killed either in action or executed by the Japanese. 'M' Special Unit members' primary role was to provide intelligence on the enemy's movements via radio from coastal positions. They were known as Coastwatchers and there were approximately 400 in the South West Pacific Zone.

Members of the 'Z' Special Unit had training in espionage, explosives and parachuting. The unit trained in many places in Australia, including Fraser Island. They specialised in raiding operations like Operation Jaywick, where, posing as Asian fishermen on board their famous boat, HMAS *Krait*, members of the unit entered Singapore Harbour and destroyed seven Japanese ships. Many of their training techniques and operational procedures are still in use today. The unit has received considerable publicity in the popular culture with programs like *Heroes*, *Attack Force Z* and *Spyforce* depicting stories from what is often seen as a uniquely Australian commando force.

This elite unit consisted of little more than two thousand men and women over its three years' existence. Two of its representatives are on the signature wall. These are Doolan and Rice

CASE STUDY NUMBER 10

RICE, RONALD FRANCIS STEPHEN, QX48705 (Q100784), SERGEANT

Ronald Rice from Brisbane described himself as a radio mechanic when he enlisted into the militia in December 1941. He was 19 years and 10 months old. In the following January he was called up for full-time duty. He was sent to Northern Command Signals Training Depot at Lytton in Brisbane until May when he was sent to Townsville and transferred to the 3rd Signals Squadron, which was attached to 1st Motor Brigade. In July he was sent to do three courses in Gympie. He completed a Carrier Pigeon Course, a Signal Electrician Refresher Course and an Uplift Serial Course for Telephone Mechanic Trainees. He was now officially classified as an Instrument Mechanic.

In January 1943, Signalman Rice transferred to the AIF and joined the 'Z' Special Unit Land Headquarters in August. He was promoted to Acting Sergeant in the following month and departed for service in New Guinea. In November, the rank of Sergeant was confirmed. He was 21 years old. He was on active service for the 'Z' Special Unit in New Guinea from 24/9/43 until 9/1/44 when he left Port Moresby by plane for Townsville. This was a top-secret unit and no details of his service have been supplied in the Sergeant's records.

From February until October he was admitted to hospital with a succession of BT Malaria relapses. In April he transferred from the 'Z' Special Unit to the Queensland Lines of Communication General Details Depot at Redbank for reallotment and in May he fractured his left kneecap. He was assessed medically as B2 (fit for sedentary duties only) due to his left knee making him unfit for long marching. He became a staff member for the Queensland Lines of Communication. Sergeant Rice was discharged at Redbank as part of the general demobilisation on 27/3/46.

Earlier in his army career, he had been located at Lytton from 7/1/42 until 11/5/42. It was during this period that he most probably came to City Hall and his name was written in true graffiti style on the wall "Sig. R. Rice, Gabba", most probably by his mate, Norman Francis.

Author's Note: Sergeant Rice's identity has not been confirmed, but he is the only R. Rice listed in the Nominal Roll as being a Signaller. In addition, his records show that he was in Brisbane at the right time to be included on the wall and he was located at Lytton, which was attached to the Woolloongabba ("Gabba") Camp.

The army had another corps that completed the structure of the Arms Corps in World War II. This was the Intelligence Corps, whose main role was to provide commanders with information about the enemy.

Like the Infantry, all of these specialised Combat Corps had depended on the Combat Support Corps in order to operate successfully.

CHAPTER 8

UNITS III: COMBAT SUPPORT

After Federation, when the State militia units were amalgamated to form the Australian Military Forces, there were two main service corps supporting the army. The Ordnance Corps was responsible for the supply and storage of ammunition, machinery, vehicles and weapons as well as maintenance. The Service Corps was responsible for the transport and supply of other provisions. At the outbreak of World War II in 1939, these two corps continued to provide support services to the front-line combat units, which enabled them to operate effectively in the field. Several other corps such as the Provost Corps and the Medical Corps also provided essential combat support.

The army needed their support teams wherever fighting units were sent. This meant they were often in close proximity to a war zone. The men in all of these corps formed part of the retinue of assistance to the divisions and were often transferred from one unit to another. It was not unusual for them to have more than one occupation during the course of the war. The Combat Support Corps has many representatives on the wall.

AUSTRALIAN ARMY ORDNANCE CORPS (AAOC)

In 1942 the Ordnance Corps was streamlined so that its main functions were the responsibility for ordnance supplies to army units. This included non-perishable items such as guns, ammunition, uniforms etc. Initially the corps had workshops but these were later transferred to the Australian Electrical and Mechanical Engineers Corps. The AAOC was organised into battalions, companies, platoons and sections, but its members were normally attached as small sub-units to the larger formations as support staff.

2nd Base Ordnance Depot	Phipps
113th Light Anti-Aircraft Ordnance Workshop	Chadwick, Reid
7th Advanced Ammunition Depot	Werner
73rd Forward Ammunition Depot	Werner
2/4th Army Field Workshop, Middle East	Harrington
1st Ordnance Workshop Company, Middle East	Harrington
4th Ordnance Workshop Company, Middle East	Harrington, Huggonson
2nd Tank Ordnance Workshop Company, Rutherford	Harrington, Huggonson
2/3rd Ordnance Workshop Company, Ipswich	Huggonson
Ordnance Base Workshop	Davy, D.

1st Parachute Maintenance Platoon	Hobbs
Headquarters Northern Command Ordnance Workshop (HQNCOW)	Hatfield
Queensland Lines of Communication Ordnance Workshop	Reid
Australian Ordnance Training Regiment (AOTR)	Harrington

AUSTRALIAN ELECTRICAL AND MECHANICAL ENGINEERS CORPS (AEME)

The Electrical and Mechanical Engineer Corps was officially formed in December 1942. It was responsible for the co-ordination and organisation of the workshops for the separate Ordnance, Signals and Royal Australian Engineers Corps. Its main responsibilities were the maintenance, recovery and repair of machinery, vehicles, electronic equipment and weapons. The men were generally referred to as craftsmen. The corps was used in all phases of the war and remained in the rear echelon.

Brisbane, August 1942: Army personnel undergoing workshop training at Central Technical College. *(Courtesy of the John Oxley Library, State Library of Queensland 207333)*

Workshops	
1st Infantry Troops Workshop	Kurkowski
2/1st Advanced Workshop	Harrington, Popp
2/1st Composite Anti-Aircraft Workshop	Henson
2/4th Light Anti-Aircraft Workshop	Reid
2/13th Composite Anti-Aircraft Workshop	McDuff
2/1st Artillery Field Workshop	Dixon
102nd Brigade Workshop	Davy, D., Friend
2/72nd Light Detachment	Ramsden
242nd Light Aid Detachment	Friend
Townsville Area Workshop	Friend
New Guinea Lines of Communication Area Workshop	Harrington
3rd Infantry Division Workshop	Harrington
11th Advanced Workshop	Harrington
2/2 Tank Workshop Company	Huggonson
2/2 Base Workshop Company	Huggonson

Salvage Unit	
34th Lines of Communication Salvage	Gutteridge

AUSTRALIAN ARMY SERVICE CORPS (AASC)

The Army Services Corps was mainly responsible for the supply of perishable items. This included the very important supplies of food and fuel as well as postal functions. The AASC was also responsible for the provision of transport.

Supply	
6th Infantry Division Supply Column	Pascoe, Greenhalgh
2/1st Supply Depot Company	Greenhalgh
2/2nd Supply Depot Company	Saxby
2/5th Supply Depot Company	Greenhalgh, Saxby
2/8th Supply Depot Platoon	Saxby
229th Supply Depot Platoon	Caldow
7th Infantry Division Petrol Company, Palestine	Saxby

Food Supply

2/1st Field Butchering Platoon	Campbell, Greenhalgh
2/3rd Field Butchery Platoon	Vallis
12th Field Baking Company	Myers
26th Field Baking Platoon	Myers
3rd Independent Farm Platoon	Dawson
Divisional Food Supply (Unspecified)	Huggonson

Laundry Services

3rd Stationary Laundry	Freeman
3rd Infantry Division Mobile Laundry and Field Decontamination Unit	Veigel
Mobile Laundry and Field Decontamination Unit, Liverpool	Smith, R. (Unidentified)

Motor Transport

1st Armoured Division Transport Company	Miller, R.
131st General Transport Company	Wyatt
160th General Transport Company	Cardwell
5th Movement Control Group	Betts
10th Movement Control Group	Munro
2/96th Transport Platoon	Harris

Bougainville circa 1945: Truck convoy of Australian Infantry moving through a devastated area. *(Courtesy of the John Oxley Library, State Library of Queensland 124086)*

Equine Transport

Horses, donkeys and mules were used to carry equipment and supplies. In heavy jungle conditions, they were instrumental in getting the wounded to hospital.

1st Auxiliary Horse Transport Company, Enoggera (Militia)	Beutel, Dawson, Lee
2nd Pack Transport Company	Beutel

Training

Northern Command Army Trades Training Depot	Smith, J.
Army Trades Training Depot, Gaythorne	Reid
Army Trades Training Depot, unspecified	Caldow, Edwards, Marshall
Qld Lines of Communication, Army Trades Training Depot, Woolloongabba	Whebell

AUSTRALIAN ARMY CATERING CORPS (AACC)

Raised in March 1943, the AACC was responsible for the provision and transportation of food, the management of canteens in the camps and in the field, and the administration and training of personnel.

Townsville, 1939: Soldiers peeling potatoes in front of a camp kitchen.
(Courtesy of the John Oxley Library, State Library of Queensland 283639)

Canteens	
Northern Territory Force Canteens	Ham
28th Army Canteen Services	Werner

AUSTRALIAN ARMY PROVOST CORPS (AProvC)

The Provost Marshals (i.e. the 'Provos'), also referred to as Military Police, were formed in 1912. They were responsible for traffic control along supply routes, security duties, maintaining personnel discipline, crime investigation, military detentions and the management of enemy prisoners of war. The soldiers in this section were either provost staff or detainees.

1st Armoured Division Provost Company	Miller, R.
1st Provost Company, Palestine	Dixon
2nd Provost Company, Palestine	Dixon
7th Provost Company, Queensland	Greenhalgh

3rd Guard Compound, Brisbane	Saxby
2/1st Detention Barracks, Grovely	Saxby
4th Detention Barracks, Grovely	Greenhalgh
9th Detention Barracks	Beincke
2nd Aust. Corps Field Punishment Centre	Greenhalgh

AUSTRALIAN ARMY MEDICAL CORPS (AAMC)

Raised in 1902, the AAMC was responsible for the provision and the training of staff for all medical, nursing, dental, psychological, veterinary and sanitary services. It became the Royal Australian Army Medical Corps in 1948. The soldiers in this section were either patients or staff.

2/1 Australian General Hospital	Harrington
2/7th Australian General Hospital	Ross
2/9th Australian General Hospital	Harrington
117th Australian General Hospital	Saxby
121st Australian General Hospital	Saxby
106th Casualty Clearing Station	Pemble
111th Casualty Clearing Station	Saxby
101st Convalescent Depot, Coorparoo	Cross, Cooper, Drake, Jacobson, Johnston, Leigh, Miller, K., Warner, Wright
102nd Convalescent Depot	Miller, K., Saxby
2/2nd Convalescent Unit, Coorparoo	Grace
2/3rd Convalescent Depot	Davy, C.
2/10th Convalescent Depot	Beinke
2/1st Field Ambulance	Greenhalgh
2/3rd Field Ambulance	Harrington
2/4th Field Ambulance	Carnaby
2/5th Field Ambulance	Saxby
2/13th Field Ambulance	Freebury, Millgate

Also

63rd British General Hospital, Middle East	Harrington

SPECIALIST UNITS

These were smaller units that had highly specialised roles. They include band, education, legal, pay and chaplains.

Band

Band units of the Australian Army became a corps in 1968. Military bands have consistently provided musical support to the army, enhancing morale and improving public relations.

1st Entertainment Unit	Fletcher
3rd Infantry Division Entertainment Unit	Fletcher
3rd Infantry Division Signals Entertainment Unit	Plymin

Australian Army Education Service (AAES)

The Australian Army Education Scheme was set up in March 1941 and in October 1943 it was renamed as the Australian Army Education Service. The main aim of the Education Scheme was to provide vocational education to the men in order to enhance their skills, build morale and to provide a basis for demobilisation and repatriation. It prepared men for citizenship and also created a diversion from the daily routine. Marcellus Davie qualified to attend the 4th Armoured Brigade Swim School in the summer of 1944 which would have been a very welcome diversion from the heat. All of the soldiers on the wall undertook army training courses at some point during their service.

Each corps had its own training organisation with a centralised system for the initial training of recruits, who are then allocated to a corps where they receive their specialised training before being allocated to units in the field. Centralised training was also provided for skills that were common across the various corps. This was done at Army Trades Training Depots and at Motor Trades Training Depots. The World War II War Diaries *(Courtesy of the Australian War Memorial)* constantly refer to courses that have been provided for both the enlisted men and the officers.

Many of the courses were specialised for particular occupations. Ronald Rice, a Signaller with the militia, attended a Carrier Pigeon Course, a Signal Electrician Course and a Telephone Mechanic Course, which qualified him to be an Instrument Technician. This enabled him to later join the highly specialised 'Z' Special Unit. Henry Henson was sent to the 7th Infantry Training Centre in Victoria, which was a cover name for commando training. Here he learnt the skills of sabotage, raiding and guerilla fighting. He later attended a refresher course that included Morse Code operations, map reading and cable work. He qualified at the course and was retained in the role of Signaller.

Attendance at a course often had extra benefits. Corporal John Reid attended a formal Artillery course which he did not pass. However, his attendance at the course assisted him to regain his rank after being demoted.

CASE STUDY NUMBER 11

REID, JOHN, QX24899, CORPORAL

John Reid was an unemployed labourer when he enlisted into the AIF at Townsville on 30/12/41 at the age of 22. He was sent to the Australian Trades Training Depot at Gaythorne and later transferred to South Brisbane, classified as a Fitter Trade Group 1 and then transferred to the 113th Light Anti-Aircraft Ordnance Workshop, located at Kedron. He was promoted to Acting Corporal in October. He embarked from Brisbane in October 1942 for New Guinea where he was transferred to the 235th Light Anti-Aircraft Battery at Milne Bay. His promotion to Corporal was confirmed in November. For one year from April 1943 until April 1944, he was transferred or attached to several units as needed. This included the Fortress Workshops in Lae, and finally, the 2/4th Light Anti-Aircraft Regimental Workshop with the Australian Electrical and Mechanical Engineers (AEME), which remained as his last and most effective unit.

In April 1944, he left Port Moresby by plane to attend the Land Headquarters Electrical and Mechanical Engineering School in New South Wales. He attended the four-month Artillery Course but failed overall. Lack of experience and education were cited as the reason that he failed, but he was described as a "consistent trier". He returned to his unit in Queensland (Atherton Tableland) in August. In December he was AWL for two days and was reduced to the rank of Private. However, as a result of his course, in January he became a Graded Trade Group I Fitter (Instrument), and in February 1945 he was promoted again to Corporal. He rejoined his unit in April after recovering from an unspecified knee problem. He applied for demobilisation priority in November and was discharged on 6/12/45 as part of the general demobilisation.

John Reid was in Brisbane from 3/1/42 until 13/10/42. During this period, he wrote on the wall "QX24899, J. Reid, Ayr, NQ" in large letters.

Australian Army Legal Department (AALD)

Legal practitioners from AALD were available to supply general legal advice to all ranks. There were several instances of breaches of discipline by the men on the wall for which they may have required legal assistance. This includes numerous cases of being AWL and at least 11 courts martial. There is one documented case of the legal services being used by a soldier who signed the wall.

Legal Section, HQ 6th Infantry Division	Greenhalgh

Australian Army Pay Corps (AAPC)

The AAPC was originally established in 1914 and was granted the title of "Royal" in 1948. The members of this section are responsible for the financial administration and payment of wages to the men. They are attached to other units as clerks but have the standard ranking structure of other soldiers in the infantry. Corporal Davie had been a former member of the Artillery Corps and the Armoured Corps, but had not been sent overseas. His transfer to the Queensland Advanced 2nd Echelon provided the opportunity for him to go to Morotai Island where he became part of the 2/33rd Infantry Battalion.

107th Depot Cash Office	Davie

CASE STUDY NUMBER 12

DAVIE, MARCELLUS THEODORE JAMES, QX25037, CORPORAL

M. T. J. Davie, also known as Jim Davie, enlisted in the AIF in Toowoomba on 10/12/41 at the age of 22. He had previously been a labourer from Jondaryan employed by the Railway Department. He trained with the 41st Field Battery at Grovely and was a Driver for the Royal Australian Artillery. He then transferred to the 5th Field Regiment and in April 1942 to the 2/5th Armoured Regiment. In June, after a stay in hospital with gum infections and teeth problems, he was able to rejoin his regiment which had relocated to Western Australia. It formed part of the 1st Armoured Division, which was a component of the 3rd Australia Corps defending Western Australia. The 2/5th Armoured Regiment entrained for Queensland in April 1944. On 15/3/45 he transferred to 107th Depot Cash Office with Queensland Advanced 2nd Echelon. His former unit had not been deployed overseas at any time and this transfer provided the opportunity to go.

He embarked from Brisbane in May 1945 and disembarked at Morotai Island in the Dutch East Indies (now Northern Indonesia). The war ended on 15/8/45. In September he was medically assessed as B1 "unfit for prolonged marching or standing" due to knee problems and sent for relocation to the 2/33rd Infantry Battalion as a clerk. He was promoted to Corporal in February 1946 and returned to Brisbane. He was discharged in April. Marcellus Davie died on 9/2/87 at the age of 77.

Mr Davie was stationed in Brisbane from 10/12/41 until 3/3/42. It was during this period when he was with the 41st Field Training Battery at Grovely that he signed the wall twice. His first graffiti reads "QX25057, Driver Jim Davie, Grovely" and his second contribution reads "QX25037, Driver M.T.J. Davie, AIF, Grovely". Each was written in a different handwriting, but it is the latter signature that corresponds to his handwriting on his army attestation form.

Australian Army Chaplains

Chaplains are non-combatant officers from various religions who administer pastoral care and advice to the men. All of the men on the wall would have had access to a chaplain.

Two other military formations are represented on the wall.

Royal Australian Air Force (RAAF)

No. 3 Initial Training School	Vallis
RAAF Air Crew, Voluntary	Newman

The British Royal Air Force (RAF)

204 Group, Egypt (detached)	Saxby

Wherever the combat units went, either at home or abroad, numerous combat support corps went with them. The army would have been ineffective without them whatever their location.

CHAPTER 9

LOCATIONS AND TRANSPORT

Australian soldiers during World War II could reasonably expect to be sent to multiple destinations away from home. Many of the men had probably never left their local area prior to their enlistment into the army. The army kept records of these movements as well as the transport used to get the men to their various locations.

The men were sent anywhere that they were needed, including the front line. The main reasons for these movements were transfers, postings, leave, training and occupation. Sergeant Alfred Loveday, as a specialist wireless operator, was posted to many locations in both Australia and the South West Pacific Area.

CASE STUDY NUMBER 13

LOVEDAY, ALFRED HENRY, QX34660 (Q191480), SERGEANT

Alfred Loveday, a labourer from Maryborough, enlisted into the Citizen Military Forces at Lytton in May 1940 at the age of 22. He was classified as a specialist Signals Operator Group II and sent to Cowan on Moreton Island and later to Lytton while staying at the Victoria Barracks in Brisbane. He was promoted to Acting Corporal, then Corporal, and then attached to the Area Signals Mount Isa Mines Force. In August he was promoted to Acting Sergeant and then Sergeant in January 1942 at the age of 24. He was married in February 1942.

In July he enlisted into the AIF, and after six weeks duty at Warwick was transferred to the Australian Signals Training Battalion, which was part of the 2nd AIF Special Signal Section located at Bonegilla in Victoria. In October he was transferred to the Wireless Task Group with the 35th Wireless Section and then to the 1st Independent Signals Group, initially until July 1943. He then joined the 38th Wireless Task Section, and in August was transferred to the Queensland 19th Lines of Communication Signal Section. From here he was transferred overseas. He embarked from Townsville via the Canberra on 26/8/43 and disembarked in Port Moresby three days later, where he became part of the 18th Lines of Communication Signals.

In February 1944 he left Port Moresby to attend a course in Brisbane on the operation and maintenance of the No. 133 Wireless Set. He rejoined the 38th Australian Wireless Task Section in May. In August he embarked from Townsville aboard the Ormiston to Port Moresby, and in October sailed from Lae on the Cape Victory for Munda Point on the island of New Georgia in the Solomon Islands. He stayed there until August 1945, when he sailed for the coastal village of Torokina on Bougainville, where he spent the last few days of the war. In October, Sergeant Loveday left Torokina by plane for Amberley. He was taken on strength by several different units, including his own 38th Wireless Task Section, while awaiting the determination of his demobilisation priority. He was finally discharged at Redbank on 11/3/46.

Sergeant Loveday was in the AIF when he wrote on the wall sometime after July 1942: "A. H. Loveday, QX 34---, Sigs" in an old-style script.

Brisbane, 1941: Alfred Loveday on leave with his fiancée Hedy outside the Brisbane General Hospital. They had been visiting Mr Loveday's 19-year-old brother Len. *(Courtesy of Judith Calvert, daughter of Alfred Loveday)*

LOCATIONS

Collectively, the men on the wall have ties to places in every Australian State and to many overseas locations. For the majority of the men, the Nominal Roll supplies information about where they were born, where they enlisted and where they were living at the time of enlistment. In some cases these locations were unknown and the records were incomplete. For other soldiers, even though their identifications have not been confirmed, they have supplied place names with their signatures. In addition, the individual National Archives records have provided comprehensive location records for the men in the case studies. All of these contributions have been added to the data base, which is located in Appendix 2.

Place of Birth

Upon enlistment, the date and place of birth were clearly marked on the soldier's attestation papers as one of the means of identification for administration purposes. This information was also used to determine if the soldier was a "natural born or a naturalised British Subject", which was important from a loyalty perspective, especially in a time of war. It was assumed that anyone born in a British Commonwealth country would have allegiance to the King and therefore to the Allied cause. However, one soldier on the wall, Wilhelm Kurkowski, was actually born in Germany. He was of Polish descent and worked as a craftsman in infantry workshops. He may have been required to produce the correct naturalisation papers before he was allowed to enlist. Today this would be called proof of Australian citizenship.

STATE	CAPITAL CITY	COUNTRY AREAS	TOTAL	%
QUEENSLAND	11	73	84	54.19%
NEW SOUTH WALES	5	27	32	20.64%
VICTORIA	13	7	20	12.90%
SOUTH AUSTRALIA	1	2	3	1.94%
WESTERN AUSTRALIA	0	1	1	0.64%
TASMANIA	1	1	2	1.29%
TOTAL	31	111	142	91.58%
OVERSEAS	12	(7.74%)		
UNKNOWN	1	(0.64%		
TOTAL	155			

Table 3 Place of Birth

More than 90 per cent of the men who signed the wall were Australian born. The largest single group were men who were born in the country areas of Queensland (47%). Only 7.1% were born in Brisbane. The country areas of New South Wales are well represented with 17.4% of the wall signatories.

Place of Enlistment

Upon entering the army the soldiers signed an Oath of Enlistment which formed part of their attestation papers. The location where they took this oath was regarded as their place of enlistment. Many men came from country areas to major cities to enlist. In some cases it was necessary to enlist outside the normal recruitment centres. This was usually due to the fact that they were training in the field or on operational service. Many militia men enlisted into the AIF while in the field.

STATE	CAPITAL CITY	COUNTRY AREAS	IN THE FIELD	TOTAL	%
QUEENSLAND	62	41	3	106	68.39%
NEW SOUTH WALES	15	3	0	18	11.61%
VICTORIA	9	1	3	13	8.39%
SOUTH AUSTRALIA	5	0	0	5	3.22%
WESTERN AUSTRALIA	0	4	0	4	2.58%
TASMANIA	0	0	0	0	0.0%
TOTAL	91	49	6	146	94.18%
PAPUA/NEW GUINEA					
PORT MORESBY	4	(2.58%)			
IN THE FIELD	2	(1.29%)			
UNKNOWN	3	(1.93%)			
TOTAL	155				

Table 4 Place of Enlistment

The majority of enlistments for the men on the wall were made in Brisbane (40%). City Hall was the major centre for taking recruitments, but there were also many areas in the surrounding suburbs such as Kelvin Grove and Lytton where the army had establishments. In Sydney, Paddington was the main centre for enlistments.

Place of Residence at the Time of Enlistment

The place where the soldier was living at the time of his enlistment was also recorded on his attestation paper. This was regarded as his home address, but it frequently changed throughout the war, especially if the soldier married at some point during his war service.

In Queensland, the number of locations recorded for place of birth, enlistment and residences collectively add up to one major city and more than 80 country centres. As an enlistment venue and as a welcome centre, City Hall had played a major role. Many visitors to the wall are able to find an affinity with the men by identifying with the locations that the soldiers had included with their signatures.

The Camps

There were many camps set up around Australia and overseas to house both militia and AIF soldiers. They provided food and shelter, which was usually in the form of 6-8-man tents, as well as washing amenities. There were administration areas and medical centres. Many soldiers, like Gunner Streeter, were sent to camp hospitals with minor medical problems, which helped to ease the pressure on the larger hospitals. Some of the camps mentioned in the records and on the wall include Chermside, Deagon, Eumundi, Gaythorne, Woolloongabba, Southport, Hughenden and Bonegilla. There were hundreds of camps in Australia and overseas that were set up to cater for the soldiers' needs.

Charleville, 1944: Army camp at hospital grounds. *(Courtesy of John Oxley Library, State Library of Queensland 70699)*

In Brisbane transport into the city by the soldiers on leave was by train, bus, tram and taxi. Five men sharing a taxi from Grovely would pay one shilling

(10 cents) each, which was a lot of money then *(Courtesy of Sidney Calam and Ron Culbert)*. Men coming into the city from camps located outside Brisbane had transport especially organised for them. They were generally trucked into collection points where they were able to access city transport.

> *We came from army leave collection venues such as the Leave and Transit Depot (LTD) at Indooroopilly, and the General Details Depot (GDD) at Greenbank. The soldiers were trucked from their units to these collection points in order to get transport into the city.*
>
> Veteran Bertram Watson, AIF 1943-1946, October 2009

There was not a plentiful supply of city transport at night so the soldiers had to be very careful in finding the means to get back to camp before their nightly curfew came into effect. This was referred to as *tattoo*.

The camps were also major training areas for the troops. One of the camps located at Wilsons Promontory in Victoria was designated No. 7 Infantry Training Centre, but it was really a secret training centre for commandos specialising in demolitions and sabotage. Signaller Henry Henson trained there.

For many of the new Queensland recruits, the first place they encountered was the Northern Command Reception Camp at the Brisbane Exhibition Grounds, and from there they were sent to other camps for training. Enoggera was also one of the main reception camps for Queenslanders joining the AIF and maintained specialised units such as 2nd Pack (Horse) Transport Company. Enoggera's connection with horses goes back to World War I. The camp was also extremely well placed with regard to transport as it was located at a tram terminus and had a railway station close by.

> *Enoggera was a very large camp, but I was never stationed there.*
>
> Veteran Peter Lahanas AIF 1942-1944, October 2010

Redbank was also a very large camp. The first Queensland battalion of the 2nd AIF, the 2/9th Battalion, began its training there in November 1939. Some of Redbank's specialised areas were the preparation of Pioneer Companies as well as providing gunnery training.

The camp that is mentioned most often on the wall is Grovely, where the 41st Field Training Battery was located. This was an Artillery unit. Grovely was also home to many infantry units from the 7th, 8th and 9th Divisions and had provided training before they were deployed to the Middle East and Malaya. The camp also provided courses for military drivers and supplied workshops for the vehicles. The Mess Hall was built on the site, which now houses the Grovely State School (*Courtesy George Londos*).

North Queensland 1943: The Men's Mess at Rollingstone Army Camp.
(Courtesy of the John Oxley Library, State Library of Queensland 247411)

Conditions in the camps were basic. Veteran Peter Lahanas, was a cook, who transferred to many different camps and therefore had a unique perspective of the soldiers' world at that time.

> *At Woolloongabba there were only a few tents in the middle of the grounds, so the majority of the soldiers slept in the grandstands on bags that were filled with hay. Later we were sent to a camp at Yeerongpilly where there were tents to sleep in. There was a dance here every Saturday night, but I never went as I couldn't dance.*
>
> Veteran Peter Lahanas, AIF 1942-1944, October 2010

Army meals had a certain notoriety. With the strict rationing that was in place, the soldiers, in common with the civilian population, were restricted to a limited variety of food.

> *As an army cook at several camps in the South East Queensland region I normally prepared what were called rations, and this was fairly monotonous food. The favourite meal for most of the soldiers was roast beef and mashed potatoes with gravy. We also made boiled cabbage and very rarely boiled beans. Desserts were mainly rice custard and rock cakes. The eggs and milk that we used were*

> *mainly powdered and did not taste all that nice. However, on one or two occasions the cooks were allowed to prepare individual recipes and this went over very well with the men. I made a Greek dish of meat and macaroni with rich tomato gravy and the men lined up for seconds.*
>
> Veteran Peter Lahanas AIF 1942-1944, October 2010

Senior staff were also subjected to a limited food range. Even the officers who dined at the American camp at Ascot were supplied with ration food. However, there were some cases where special allowances were made. The army cooks found a way to directly boost morale when feeding the fighting men.

> *At the Exhibition Grounds there were 12 cooks and we fed 2200 men. Sergeant Kent from Victoria was our superior. All of the supplies were locked up. The men going to P.N.G. were fed at the Exhibition Grounds. We were only allowed to feed these troops fresh food, and definitely no canned goods, as they were going over to fight and they deserved good meals. We also fed the soldiers returning from P.N.G. Again, only fresh food was supplied to them as they had lived on rations for months. The reason we were at the Exhibition Grounds was because that was where the train carried the troops from.*
>
> Veteran Peter Lahanas, AIF 1942-1944, October 2010

The World War II army camps had been a vital component of the soldiers' world in providing a home and preparation of their future roles. After the war, some of the camps, like Enoggera, were retained as military establishments. Today, it is one of the largest army sites in Australia. Other camps were put to different uses. The Commando Training Camp at Wilsons Promontory became a holiday village and Bonegilla, also in Victoria, was transformed into the Migrant Reception and Training Centre, which has since become an Australian icon. However, most of the camps have disappeared and the land has been used for housing estates, industrial estates and other purposes.

Overseas Postings

During the war, according to Australian War Memorial figures, more than 590,000 army personnel served overseas. Many of the men on the wall formed part of this group who were given overseas postings. For Albert Dixon, his posting to the Middle East marked the beginning of new medical problems as well as a change in his army occupation. In later years he was to have several changes in his occupation and these coincided with changes in his locations.

CASE STUDY NUMBER 14

DIXON, ALBERT JOHN STANLEY, VX736, SAPPER

On 26/10/39, Albert Dixon, a 23-year-old plumber from Carnegie, joined the AIF in Melbourne. He was posted to the 2/2nd Field Regiment with the Royal Australian Artillery at Seymour. Here he suffered the first of many problems with his throat and ears that were to affect him throughout his military service. In April 1940 he embarked for Kantara, which is a town along the banks of the Suez Canal. From there he went to the Gaza Strip in Palestine. At Deir Suneid, after further medical problems including two bouts of sandfly fever, he was found to be medically unfit for field service and was transferred to the 2/1st Artillery Field Workshops at Beit Guya. In February 1941 he was transferred to 1st Provost Company and was appointed Lance Corporal on the same day. He was graded to Group II Provost Duties in March and upgraded to Acting Corporal in August. He undertook training at the AIF Services Training Regiment prior to returning to Australia in February 1942.

He embarked from Brisbane in August for Port Moresby and in March 1943 was graded as a Group III Mechanical Transport (M.T.) Driver. In August he was sent to the Headquarters of the New Guinea Forces where he was graded as a Group I Plumber. In February 1944 he returned to Australia in March and was sent to Victoria. Here he joined the 13th Maintenance Platoon, the 13th Water Transport Company and the 19th Water Transport Company at Mt. Martha, and in May, the Royal Australian Engineers at the 115th Australian General Hospital at Heidelberg. He was medically assessed on 20/6/44 as B2 (sedentary duties only) due to his hearing problems. In March 1945 he transferred to the 7th Hospital Maintenance Platoon. He was discharged at Royal Park on 31/8/45 as part of the general demobilisation.

His unit was listed on his discharge papers as the 2/2nd Field Regiment and on the Nominal Roll as a Plumber with the Royal Australian Engineers. Albert Dixon was in Brisbane prior to leaving for New Guinea on 28/8/42. This is when he most probably signed the wall. He wrote "VX736, A. Dixon" in a circle. It is very faint and located next to the frame on the right-hand side of the wall.

Anti-aircraft Gunner Colin Davy was sent to Milne Bay in October 1942. This was just a few weeks after the Japanese had tried unsuccessfully to take this strategic target in a very hard-fought battle. As a base camp, it was famous for its high humidity, insects and tropical diseases. It rained very often and mud was a constant problem.

CASE STUDY NUMBER 15

DAVY, COLIN, QX30922, GUNNER

After his enlistment in March 1942 at age 19, Colin Davy from Proserpine trained with the 101st Anti-Tank Training Battery at Grovely and then transferred to the 113th Light Anti-Aircraft Battery. In October 1942 he left Brisbane for New Guinea where he joined the 235th Light Anti-Aircraft Battery at Milne Bay. It was here that he succumbed to malaria in December. In April the following year he was classified as a Grade II Mechanic and transferred to the Australian Electrical and Mechanical Engineers (AEME) where he worked as a motor-vehicle mechanic attached to the 235th Light Anti-Aircraft Battery. He remained in Milne Bay until April 1944, when he returned to Australia for recreational leave.

In August 1945 he was sent to the Dutch East Indies where as an anti-aircraft gunner he provided protection from Japanese air attacks. He was initially stationed at Morotai Island in what is now Northern Indonesia, and then was transferred to Tarakan Island in Borneo. He returned to Australia in January 1946. During his service period he received many fines for breaches of discipline, but also received numerous proficiency pay increases. He was discharged in July 1946.

From March to October 1942, Colin Davy was stationed in Brisbane. He wrote on the wall

"QX30922, Gnr Davy, 101 A/Tank Fld Trg Bty, Grovely, AIF" and "Proserpine" in a square under Harris's Rangers.

Milne Bay had three airfields and remained a very important staging site for the Allies until September 1943 when other sites in New Guinea became available.

Overseas Locations

From their collective records, research has shown that the men on the wall went to many locations outside of Australia. These include:

- BORNEO – Tarakan Island, Labuan Island
- BRITISH ISLES – England, Scotland
- CEYLON (SRI LANKA) – Colombo
- DUTCH (NETHERLANDS) NEW GUINEA – Merauke
- MALAYA
- MIDDLE EAST – Libya, Egypt, Palestine, Lebanon, Syria, Gaza Strip
- DUTCH (NETHERLANDS) EAST INDIES – Morotai Island

- NEW CALEDONIA – Noumea
- PAPUA/NEW GUINEA – including Port Moresby, Lae, Kokoda Trail, Milne Bay, Bougainville (Bougainville is geographically located in the Solomon Islands)
- SINGAPORE
- SOLOMON ISLANDS – New Georgia Island, Munda Point
- TORRES STRAIT ISLANDS

New Guinea, 1944: Australian soldiers at Dobodura near Lae. *(Courtesy of the John Oxley Library, State Library of Queensland 447400)*

Most of these locations were operational war zones. In Australia, the Northern Territory was also considered a war zone due to the constant Japanese attacks. However, other vulnerable parts of the Australian mainland such as Townsville and the Atherton Tableland were not considered to be operational areas. This made a difference to the status of the soldiers in these locations with regard to army benefits after the war.

TRANSPORT

At the beginning of the war, Australia was divided into military districts based on State boundaries. This was mainly for administrative purposes. These

districts are often referred to in the soldiers' records as they moved from one area to another.

1st MD Queensland	5th MD Western Australia
2nd MD New South Wales	6th MD Tasmania
3rd MD Victoria	7th MD Northern Territory
4th MD South Australia	8th MD Papua/New Guinea and Islands

The 7th and the 8th Military Districts were added after Japan had entered the war.

Army echelon sections were set up at Headquarters and each district had a Records Office that kept track of the soldiers' movements and other details. Lines of Communication had been set up that provided the troops with essential supplies and kept open communications using established transport routes. There were numerous army sections such as the General Details Depots, the Personnel Staging Camps and Leave and Transit Depots set up to deal with postings, troop movements, the housing of soldiers prior to transport, the transport itself and the reception at new postings.

Travel within Australia was not without its difficulties. Although trucks were used extensively, it was the railway network that became the most important method of moving men and supplies. The railway gauges for each State were different and it was necessary to detrain and then entrain at the borders. There had been no central organisation of the railways until 1943. With coastal shipping facing the possibility of Japanese attack, moving men and supplies to the Northern Territory meant using a combination of trains and trucks overland.

Men moving overseas nearly always travelled by ship, but Australia did not have many ships of its own. His Majesty's Transport ships (HMT) were commonly used as troopships. For example, Dixon (*HMT Y5*), Scott (*HMT X4, HMT L13*) and Harrington (*HMT44*) all travelled to the Middle East by these English ships. Harold Saxby had the interesting experience of being transported to Colombo by the glamorous passenger liner *Mauretania* in December 1940. This brand-new Cunard White Star liner had been requisitioned by the British Government in 1939, painted grey, armed with small weapons and turned into a troopship. It conveyed Australian troops to Suez, India and Singapore during the early stages of the war.

Many civilian ships had been converted to be used as troop carriers. Steamships such as the SS *Sea Witch*, SS *Strathallan* and SS *Thedans* carried soldiers to New Guinea and other parts of the South West Pacific. The *Katoomba*, a civilian coastal vessel that was used as a troopship in both World War I and World War II, conveyed Stuart Hanley from Lae to Bowen in February 1944.

Queensland, March 1940: Off to war for these soldiers being farewelled at the railway station. *(Courtesy of the John Oxley Library, State Library of Queensland 107684)*

The Katoomba. *(Courtesy of the John Oxley Library, State Library of Queensland 65355)*

The ships usually travelled in large convoys with the Royal Australian Navy providing escort.

> *During the war my parents lived in the lighthouse on Lady Elliot Island at the southernmost tip of the Great Barrier Reef. The shipping convoys taking men and supplies north to the battle zone stayed inside the reef, which protected them from Japanese submarines. In December we heard the horn of a destroyer escort as it approached the island. From on board we were signalled in Morse code "Merry Christmas" as the ship passed by. It was from my brother who was an officer on board the destroyer. My mother was overjoyed to hear from him, but worried about where he was going.*
>
> Anonymous, August 2011

The Americans also assisted with transport for the Australians to this part of the war zone. The USS *Tulsa*, a US naval gunboat that is mentioned on the wall, spent many months in 1943 escorting troopships and supply vessels in the New Guinea-Australian region.

Queensland, circa 1940: Qantas flying boat used as a troopship. *(Courtesy John Oxley Library, State library of Queensland 197407)*

Although ships carried the bulk of thousands of soldiers, there was air travel available in special circumstances. Thomas Newman was transported from Port Moresby to Townsville by air ambulance after being shot near Salamaua, and Robert Friend was taken by air ambulance from Merauke to Cairns after his accident with a shotgun. Mervyn Streeter was provided with air travel from

Horn Island to Townsville when he was given an expedited early discharge to industry. Like the ships, many aircraft were provided by civilian companies.

In New Guinea, because of the mountainous jungle terrain, troops were transported by massive airlifts. There is one airlift that was very well documented because of the tragedy that occurred just before the troops were due to fly to the Lae region from Port Moresby. On 7/9/43 a fully loaded American Liberator bomber crashed on take-off, killing 60 Australian soldiers waiting in truck convoys to emplane. The *Official History of World War 2* has this description for the accident:

> *Ammunition continued to explode and the fires to blaze for an hour while the remainder of the battalion emplaned, according to schedule. Time could not be wasted, for weather over the Owen Stanleys usually made flying unsafe in the afternoon. Saddened by the freak tragedy, 540 members of the 2/33 and brigade headquarters were flown to Tsili Tsili. By 12.30 p.m. the weather had closed in over the mountains. During the day 59 transport planes arrived at Nadzab.*
>
> (Second World War Official Histories, Australia in the War of 1939-1945, Volume VI, The New Guinea Offensives, Chapter 13, The Fall of Lae , pp 358-359. Courtesy of the Australian War Memorial)

The well-travelled Private Gilbert Myers had been present at Jackson's Airfield on that day. He was an experienced infantryman who had witnessed death in the Middle East and on the Kokoda Trail. However, this incident at the airfield had occurred away from the enemy and would have been unexpected. It illustrates just how dangerous travel could be during wartime.

CASE STUDY NUMBER 16

MYERS, GILBERT THOMAS, NX20608, PRIVATE

Gilbert Thomas Myers was a 24-year-old labourer from Mallangaree in New South Wales when he enlisted into the AIF at Lismore in June 1940. He left Sydney in August to sail to Palestine. He joined the 2/33rd Battalion, which, as part of the 7th Australian Division, fought in Egypt and later took part in the invasion of Syria and Lebanon. Having spent more than 16 months in the Middle East, he embarked with his battalion in February 1942 for Adelaide. The 2/33rd Battalion stayed in Australia on leave and for training and eventually moved to Strathpine, north of Brisbane. Private Myers was encamped there until August 1942 when his unit embarked for Port Moresby. In September, the battalion was sent to the Kokoda Trail to reinforce the Australian units. They participated

in the fighting on the trail as the Japanese retreated northwards. Losses were very heavy and the unit left New Guinea In December for Brisbane.

In February 1943 Private Myers experienced eye problems and in May he developed malaria symptoms. In July, the battalion embarked from Townsville for New Guinea. On 7th September, a severe tragedy occurred at Jackson's Airfield in Port Moresby. Sixty soldiers were killed and more than 90 were injured. The surviving members of the unit went on to fight the enemy at Lae. Information about this accident was suppressed in the records, so it is unclear whether Private Myers was injured or not. In December he had malaria again.

He left Port Moresby for Townsville with his unit in February 1944. Due to his medical condition, which included eye problems and malaria, he could no longer stay with the 2/33rd Battalion. In October, he was sent to the 12th Field Baking Company. He was discharged in Sydney on 8/9/45 as part of the general demobilisation.

Private Myers was in the Brisbane area several months prior to 31/8/42. It was during this period that he most probably signed the wall "NX 20608 Pte G.T. Myers".

Like so many soldiers, Private Myers had travelled to a multitude of places that he could never have imagined as a young man from the country. His world had been vastly expanded. While performing his duty, he had witnessed numerous events that have become part of the historical record. The price he paid was the detrimental effect to his health.

CHAPTER 10

MEDICAL

The medical system had changed very little between the wars and was still largely similar to World War I. The sick and the wounded were progressively moved away from the fighting to first aid by stretcher bearers and then to casualty clearing stations, field ambulances, ambulance trains, dressing stations, camp hospitals and general hospitals, referred to as AGH's (Australian General Hospital). Hospital ships, like the AHS *Centaur*, carried patients home from overseas locations.

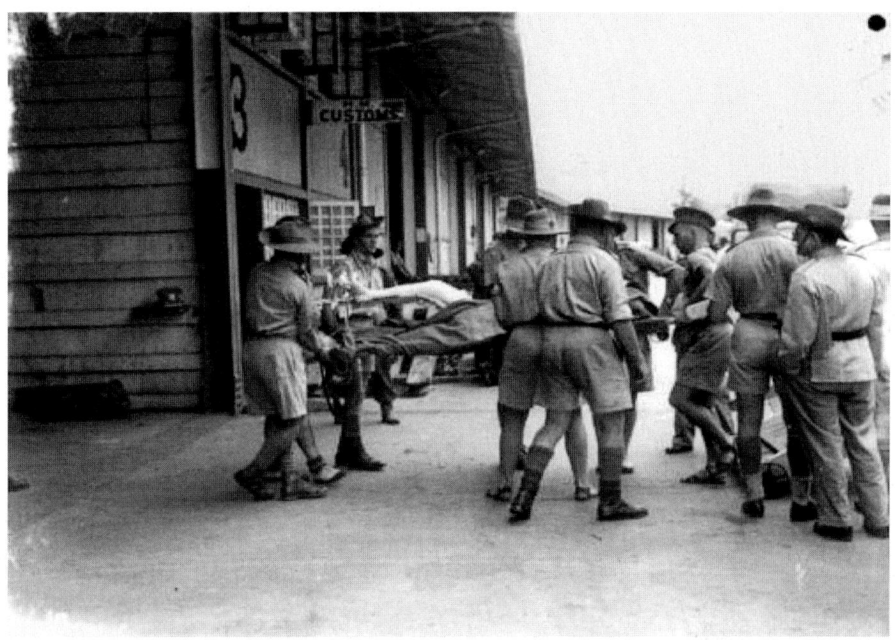

Brisbane, 1942: Patients being taken from a hospital ship. *(Courtesy of the John Oxley Library, State Library of Queensland 104056)*

New additions to the medical evacuation system were the use of Papuan stretcher-bearers (the 'Fuzzy-Wuzzy Angels') and pack animals to carry patients to hospital in the jungle regions of South-East Asia as well as the first use of air ambulances. There were many specialist military hospitals such as the Infectious Diseases Hospital in Port Moresby. New specialist clinics were established like the Malaria Clinic at the 102 Convalescent Depot in Brisbane that was attended by Private Keith Miller.

With regard to the treatment of patients, medical staff had many advantages over their earlier counterparts. Field medical experiences gained during World War I, better knowledge of illnesses, diseases and the treatment of injuries as well as improved medical techniques all contributed to a better system of patient care. One of the largest assets was the introduction of the

use of antibiotics, especially penicillin. Although it was only beginning to be introduced, antibiotic treatment made a vast impact on the survival rate of patients with bacterial infections. In addition, immunisations were available for some diseases such as typhoid. Tropical medicine provided a new range of diseases for the medical staff to learn to diagnose and treat.

After being discharged from hospital, the patients could be sent to a convalescent unit or a recreational camp, followed by light duties in a depot or training camp. Veteran Private Bertram Watson, having returned from New Guinea due to malaria, had recovered at Burleigh Heads Convalescent Depot. He described it as a "real holiday" compared to what he had been through in Papua and New Guinea.

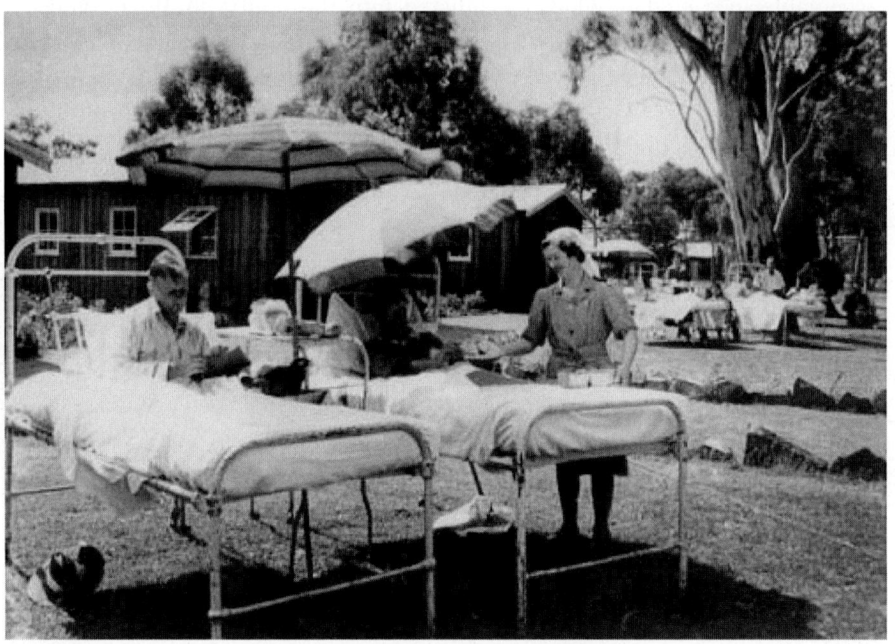

Queensland, circa 1943: Tea and sandwiches for patients recovering in the sunshine. *(Courtesy of the John Oxley Library, State Library of Queensland 129891)*

The Environment

Extreme environmental conditions could easily affect the health of the men. In the desert regions of North Africa the days were very hot and dry. Water was rationed and dehydration was a constant problem. The desert nights were extremely cold and most of the men had to sleep on the ground. Sandstorms were a common occurrence. In South-East Asia the days were very hot and humid. The nights could be cold if at high altitudes. Soldiers complained of the

constant rain and the mud that made all activity difficult. Heavy jungle growth and steep hillsides hampered movement for both men and vehicles. Soldiers' limited rations, poor hygiene and washing facilities, insects and parasites as well as the constant threat of disease and an enemy presence all increased the stress on the soldiers and added to the problems for the medical staff.

Initial assessment

A medical assessment was part of the enlistment process. It was from these results that a determination was made on whether or not the candidate was suitable for enlistment, and, in conjunction with other test criteria, where they were to be placed in the army. Stuart Hanley had flat feet, but this was medically acceptable in a soldier when he enlisted into the militia in 1941. When he joined the 2nd AIF in 1943 it was also allowable because he could still perform his duties as a signaller. However, this condition combined with bunions that appeared in 1945, caused severe pain when walking, which caused him to be reclassified to sedentary duties only.

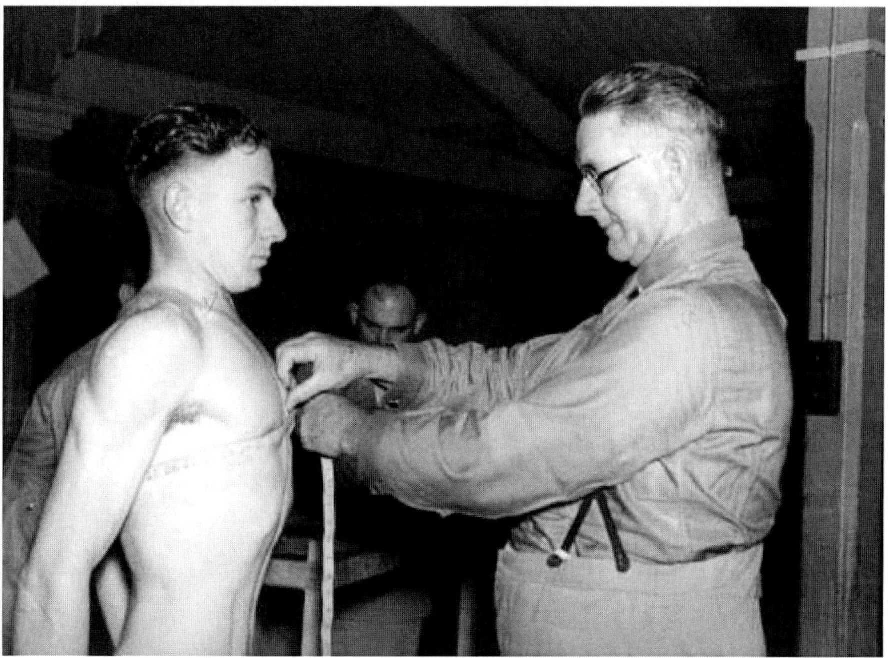

Brisbane, circa 1940: Medical inspection for a new military recruit. *(Courtesy John Oxley Library, State Library of Queensland 164955)*

Sapper Herbert Dull had lost the index finger on his right hand in a childhood accident that limited his options in the army. However, due to his

experience servicing farm engines and water supplies, he was regarded as a water-tap expert and placed with the Royal Engineers.

For their assessments, the medical staff used a list of classifications that changed very little as the war progressed (see Appendix 3). A soldier's medical classification made a large impact on his/her army service.

> *I was initially rejected by the AIF in October 1942, being classified as B1 due to being blind in my left eye. I was limited to desk duty in the CMF, which I did not like very much. In July 1943, I was called up by the AIF and reclassified as A2. After training in navigation and seamanship, I was able spend the rest of the war manning supplies and personnel in small watercraft in the Lae region of New Guinea. I felt that I was doing much more for the war effort than just sitting at a desk.*
>
> Veteran Bertram Watson, AIF 1943-1946, October 2009

Some positions in the army required additional assessment as the soldiers in these units needed a high level of physical fitness. Men in the Pioneer units had to be especially fit and strong as they were expected to assist the engineers with the heavy labour. Parachutists like Earle Jones, 'Z' Special Unit members Sergeant Rice and Corporal Doolan, and Independent Company/Commando members like Allan Henson, had to pass additional physical examinations before they could join these units.

> *My father was physically fit for all of his life. He jogged and played golf until just a few years before he died.*
>
> Jenny Middleton *née* Coop, daughter of Captain Donald Coop, 'Z' Special Unit, AIF 1939-1946, October 2011

A soldier's medical classification was often changed throughout his service as the need arose. Some of the reclassifications made a soldier unfit to remain in the Army. One soldier suffered from epilepsy, but this was not discovered on his initial medical assessment. Once it was realised that he had this condition his medical classification went from A1 to D and he was given a medical discharge.

Medical Conditions

Of the 155 men identified on the wall, there exists detailed medical information about the conditions of 26 of them based on the National Archives of Australia records and relatives' information. The Nominal Roll has revealed that all of the men identified on the wall returned from the war alive, but the records of the

26 case studies show that many of these men had developed chronic medical problems.

Practically every soldier was absent from his unit at some point for medical reasons. If this was likely to be more than five to seven days he was placed on the X list, which meant he could be replaced in his absence. When it was time for him to return to duty, he did not necessarily return to his former unit, but had to wait to be *taken on strength*, that is, as the need arose, to be either taken back into his own unit or transferred to another unit. This is the case with George Weston, who was in the 2/1 Docks Operating Company prior to going into hospital with an eye problem and was subsequently transferred to the 2/10 Docks Operating Company upon his discharge.

Some problems were apparent from the very first day of being in the army.

> *I was called up as an 18-year-old in Murgon where I was working in the Busy Bee Cafe with my uncle. At this stage I was in the Infantry. We were taken to the Brisbane Cricket Ground in Woolloongabba and fitted out with uniforms. The pants, called jungle pants, were 2-3 sizes too big. This was deliberate so they could air and help fight tinea.*
>
> Veteran Peter Lahanas, AIF 1942-1944, October 2010

Skin problems were extremely common throughout the war. The uniform material was also known to cause contact dermatitis, which explains the skin irritation suffered by Royal Faulkner that was made worse by the hot and humid climate of the tropics.

It was not surprising that the men wore very little clothing, especially in hot climates. Sapper Dixon was admonished in the Middle East for neglecting to wear a shirt while on duty as it was thought to provide some protection from insect bites and thus lower the malarial attack rate. Although the men were unaware of it at that time, the risk of skin cancer from being shirtless would manifest itself in later life.

> *After his time in the Middle East, my husband, Corporal Stephen Chuck, developed melanoma. The cancer eventually spread to his salivary glands and he died.*
>
> Gladys Chuck, wife of Corporal Stephen Chuck, AIF 1940-1945, June 2011

The records show a wide variety of problems that various men experienced, including an infected finger; cellulitis of the left elbow; fibrositis of the right deltoid muscle (chronic pain, stiffness and tenderness of the chest muscle); an

ingrown toenail; fibroma of the foot; fibroma of the tendon sheath of the left ankle; and an ulcer on the right ankle.

Mouth problems include tooth and gum infections, cavities and gumboils. One soldier suffered from parotitis (infection of the parotid salivary gland).

Smoke emitted when a gun was discharged was known to cause irritation to both the eyes and the skin. Men in the artillery were therefore especially susceptible to eye problems. These included inflamed eyelids and keratitis (infection of the cornea), both of which were suffered by anti-aircraft Gunner Streeter.

George Weston was diagnosed with pterygium of the right eye, which is a membrane growing over the cornea. It is often caused by prolonged exposure to harsh-climate conditions, especially wind. He was a winchman at the docks. Infantryman Private Myer's worsening eye problem was unspecified, but it eventually limited him to sedentary duties only.

Ear problems experienced by the men included middle-ear infections which can be very severe.

> *We were sent to Toorbul Point and practised on the landing barges from Toorbul to Bribie Island in preparation for P.N.G. Unfortunately I picked up an ear infection, probably from the bore water, and was sent to Greenslopes Hospital where I stayed for one month and I missed going to New Guinea with my unit. I lost the hearing in my left ear.*
>
> Veteran Peter Lahanas, AIF 1942-1944, October 2010

The Risk of Infection

Many illnesses were spread by close contact with other soldiers. Even fit men were liable to catch childhood diseases if they had not already experienced them. Six of the men on the wall caught either measles, German measles (*rubella*) or mumps (three cases). These patients were all hospitalised. There were no vaccines available at this time and these diseases in adults could be quite serious, unlike their usual course in children.

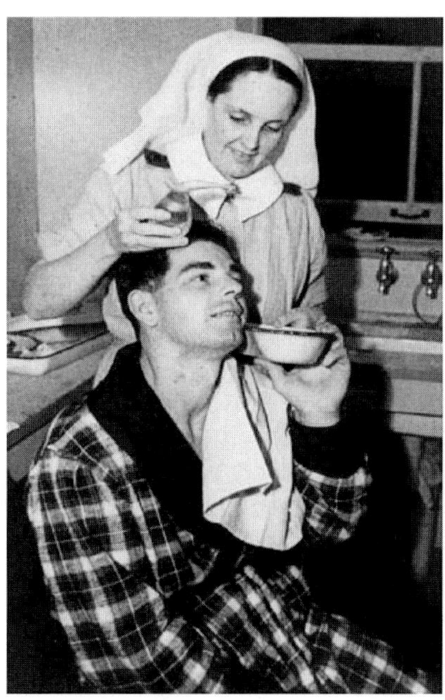

Brisbane, 1943: Nursing sister and her patient. *(Courtesy of the John Oxley Library, State Library of Queensland, 171975)*

Often the living conditions, both in Australia and overseas, were, by necessity, fairly primitive. Experience from World War I had shown the devastating effect that poor sanitary conditions and hygiene had on the health of the men, such as at Gallipoli where gastrointestinal diseases were prevalent. In World War II the necessity of clean drinking water and proper sanitation was more appreciated and there was better prevention of these illnesses. Some soldiers even devised their own method of maintaining hygiene, using whatever was at hand.

> *My father told me that the petrol-tanker drivers in the Middle East drove by night and camped by day under camouflage nets. There was a severe shortage of water and the little that they had was used only for drinking and was heavily rationed. The men used petrol to wash their clothes and even their bodies. The petrol dried very quickly in the hot climate. This form of washing had not only a drycleaning effect, but also helped to repel insects such as lice and fleas.*
>
> Kaye Phillips *née*, Saxby, daughter of Wall Signatory Harold Saxby, AIF 1940-1944, July 2011

Nevertheless, dysentery and gastroenteritis were constantly being reported and the affected men often ended up in hospital. Such infections could result in being given antibiotics and placed in isolation. The Australian soldiers in World War II may have been better prepared than their World War I counterparts, but gastro-intestinal problems were still experienced by many of the men who signed the wall.

Influenza

Another potentially severe infectious disease that caused concern was influenza. During 1918 and 1919, millions of people worldwide died from an influenza pandemic. By World War II, antibiotics were being used, but these were only helpful against the secondary bacterial infections, particularly pneumonia. Antibiotics could not control the viral disease of influenza itself. Anyone diagnosed with influenza was usually placed into hospital and then sent to a convalescent unit until they were completely recovered. New recruits coming into the camps from rural areas, such as Stuart Hanley and Cyril Jorgensen, often quickly developed respiratory infections. This was due to a lack of previous exposure to such infections, which resulted in the patient having very little immunity. There was no influenza immunisation available at this time.

All upper respiratory tract infections (URTI) were treated as potentially serious. The specific symptoms were generally not stated in patient records, but simply referred to as URTI. Severe colds that may have had the additional symptoms of tonsillitis, laryngitis and sinusitis were reported frequently, as were bronchitis and pneumonia. The patients were usually sent to hospital for treatment. Just a few days after enlisting in the 2nd AIF, Private Jones spent five days in Casualty in Cowra with URTI during the winter of 1941. This happened just a few days after arriving from his farm. The following year Private Beutel was training in Toowoomba during winter when he was sent to the 117th Australian General Hospital with URTI. Keith Miller's chronic catarrhal maxillary sinusitis was severe enough for him to be given an early medical discharge.

Difficult to Diagnose

South-East Asia had provided new situations and a multitude of possibilities for medical diagnoses. URTI was not the only non-specific illness. Some problems such as cystitis were easy to diagnose. The medical staff would also have found the diagnosis of Alfred Loveday's acute appendicitis very straightforward. Other problems such as the enlargement of axillary lymph glands and an alveolar (lung) abscess affecting Edward Harrington while he was in New Guinea were more difficult to treat. Many conditions such as seizures were at first referred

to as *NTD* (not yet determined) until they were finally diagnosed. Fevers in the tropics were often referred to as *PUO* (*pyrexia* or fever of unknown origin).

Gunshot Wounds

Unfortunately, there was one area where the army medical staff had no difficulty making a diagnosis. Of the 26 case studies of the men on the wall there were three who were wounded in action.

George Scott was wounded by Rommel's troops on the 4 May 1941 during the Battle of the Salient at Tobruk. He was serving with the 2/10th Infantry Battalion when he was shot in the left foot. His recuperation was fairly extensive due to the fact that he would not have been considered fit for duty until he could wear boots again. At this point he was sent to a training unit. He eventually rejoined the 2/10th Infantry Battalion before the unit went to Papua New Guinea in August 1942, where it participated in the Battle of Milne Bay.

Keith Miller, who was also a member of the 2/10th Infantry Battalion, was wounded at Buna in Papua on 24/12/42 when he was shot in the left thigh. His recuperation was hampered by the fact that he also had severe malaria. He was unable to return to his unit until one year later.

During the push towards Salamaua in New Guinea on 29/3/43, Thomas Newman, a member of the 2/7th Infantry Battalion, sustained a gunshot wound to his right-shoulder joint. After recuperating for six months, his medical classification was classed as B, which meant *restricted medical fitness.* He was unable to join his unit and took an early discharge to work in an essential industry.

Accidents

Being injured by gunfire was not restricted to enemy action. Robert Friend, an armourer, was repairing a shotgun in Merauke in the Dutch East Indies on 17/12/43. While being test fired, the chamber of the gun burst, perforating his left eardrum. Fortunately, there were no long-term effects and he fully recovered his hearing.

The RAAF to the Rescue

Sergeant Friend had another accident just a few weeks before his discharge. While on leave near Richmond in Queensland he fell from his motorcycle and broke his left clavicle. He was sent to the RAAF Sick Station Quarters at Garbutt in Townsville and was then airlifted to Cairns for further treatment.

CASE STUDY NUMBER 17

FRIEND, ROBERT EMMET MARQUESS, QX44563 (Q109255), SERGEANT

In September 1941, 21-year-old Robert Friend was called up for full-time duty with the militia and joined the 26th Infantry Battalion at Sellheim. He underwent technical training and was classified as an armourer. He was transferred to the ordnance workshops at Kedron in Brisbane and then to the 31st Infantry Battalion. His unit officially transferred to the AIF in December 1942 and he began training in the field in Northern Queensland. It was early in 1943 that he contracted Dengue Fever and was hospitalised for a month in Cairns. A few days later he was readmitted to hospital with an infected finger. He was promoted to Acting Corporal in February. His unit had now merged with the 51st Infantry Battalion to become the 11th Infantry Brigade's 31st/51st Infantry Battalion (Kennedy/Far North Queensland Regiment).

In June he embarked from Cairns for Merauke in Dutch New Guinea via Thursday Island. His rank of Corporal was confirmed in August and he was appointed Acting Sergeant on the same day. In December he was flown by air ambulance to hospital in Cairns after a shotgun accident. He returned to Merauke in March. In August, while in Townsville, he transferred to the 242nd Light Aid Detachment, and in December 1944 he was sent to Bougainville in the Solomon Islands as part of the 31/51st Infantry Battalion. His rank of Sergeant Armourer was confirmed on 25/4/45 while he was in Bougainville. He was 24 years old.

In July 1945 he was admitted to hospital for 12 days with a severe upper respiratory tract infection (URTI) and a middle-ear infection. In September he left the Solomon Islands from Torokina and went to Rabaul on the island of New Britain. He returned to Brisbane in January 1946. He was eventually discharged at Redbank on 2/4/1946 as part of the general demobilisation process.

Robert Emmet Marquess Friend died in Mt Isa on 22nd September 1966 at the age of 46. His signature on the wall was most probably made during his time at Kedron in March 1942. He wrote "Friend R.E.M., The gift to the fair sex of Brisbane, 109255, E. Company, Sellheim".

Another soldier, Edward Harrington, had not been so lucky. He had been a radio mechanic with the 2/4th Army Field Workshop in the Middle East when he broke his left clavicle on 21/12/41. He was sent to a British hospital for 10 days over the Christmas period. Twelve days after his release he broke his clavicle again and was sent to an Australian hospital for four days. He did not join his unit again until March.

CASE STUDY NUMBER 18

HARRINGTON, EDWARD FREDERICK, VX56551, CRAFTSMAN

Edward Harrington enlisted into the AIF on 5/8/41 at Royal Park in Victoria at the age of 20. He was graded as an Acting Radio Mechanic and transferred to the 2/4th Army Field Workshop. He embarked from Sydney for the Middle East in September and was able to begin working on radios, including tank radios, in such places as Tobruk and Egypt, where the 2/4th Army Field Workshop was stationed.

In December he accidentally fractured his left clavicle and stayed in medical care until the end of January, and in April, he was admitted to hospital with acute enteritis. He left the Middle East with his unit in July 1942. Once back in Australia he was transferred in October to the New Guinea Lines of Communication Workshop in Port Moresby.

He spent several weeks in hospital in July and September with a NYD (not yet determined) condition. His later documentation also reveals that he suffered malaria during his time in New Guinea. He returned to Victoria by hospital ship and then ambulance train. In March he was assessed as being D, "medically unfit for military service" due to being diagnosed with epilepsy. He was given a medical discharge from the army at Royal Park on 21/3/44, but was considered a suitable case for repatriation. He was 23 years old.

He most probably visited Brisbane on his way north to Townsville in October 1942. Since he was a tall man (6'1" or 185 cms), he was able to write his name high up on the wall. He wrote "Pte Harrington, VX56551".

The list of accidents incurred by the 26 men in the case studies also includes a fractured nasal bone, a fractured left wrist, a damaged left knee with possible bone chips embedded in the tissue, a sprained left ankle, and a fractured fifth finger of the right hand, which occurred while playing football when on duty. An enquiry cleared Corporal Werner on this occasion of any wrong doing.

When Corporal George Weston fell down the stairs from the canteen late one Saturday night he broke the glass that he carried in his back pocket. The men had been required to bring their own drinking glasses. This accident resulted in a lacerated buttock, requiring stitching, and leaving a scar which, after the war, Mr Weston humorously described as his "war wound".

A fracture of the left kneecap was enough to make the very fit Ronald Rice from the 'Z' Special Unit unfit for long marching. He went from A1 to B2 which meant that he was *fit for sedentary duties only*. His injury, coupled with his malaria, had prevented his return to New Guinea.

Tropical Diseases

Tropical diseases in the Mediterranean Region and South East-Asia were a major challenge for the medical staff. These diseases are caused by infectious agents found primarily in tropical and subtropical regions and are often transmitted by insects. The constant heat and humidity provided the optimum conditions necessary for mosquitoes and other insects to breed throughout most of the year. For many tropical diseases there was no cure, and emphasis was placed on treating the symptoms and prevention.

Many of the fighting units were badly affected, such as the 2/9th Battalion, which claimed that "extremely large casualties were caused by the fighting and by tropical diseases" *(Courtesy of the Australian War Memorial)*. Henry Jacobson had to face both of these conditions.

CASE STUDY NUMBER 19

JACOBSON, HENRY IVAN, QX28868, PRIVATE

Henry Jacobson, a 19-year-old dairy-farm labourer from Gunalda in Queensland, enlisted into the AIF on 20/1/42 in Brisbane. After initial training he was transferred to the 8th Pioneer Company at Redbank, which was later sent to Goondiwindi. He embarked for New Guinea in November and was transferred to the 2/9th Infantry Battalion. After Private Jacobson joined the Battalion it went on to fight at the Battle for Buna between the 18th and 24th of December 1942, and the Battle of Sananda between the 12th and 24th January 1943. By now the 2/9th Infantry Battalion was seriously depleted of men due to the fighting and disease.

In March the unit embarked from Port Moresby for Cairns. In April Private Jacobson was sent to hospital with malaria and rejoined his unit in June. In July he was again admitted to hospital with malaria. By August he was able to return with the 2/9th Infantry Battalion to Port Moresby, where the unit trained until being deployed to the Finisterre Mountains in New Guinea in December. Between 2/1/44 and 1/2/44, the Battalion was involved in the operations at Shaggy Ridge, which resulted in its capture from the Japanese. The 2/9th Infantry Battalion was responsible for capturing the vital strategic target of Green Snipers' Pimple on 21/1/44.

In May the unit left from Lae for Townsville. While on leave in July, Private Jacobson was sent to Gympie General Hospital again with malaria. He was transferred to the Brisbane Military Hospital with BT (Benign Tertian) malaria, Relapse A, and sent to recover at the 101st Convalescent Depot before rejoining his unit in September. He was given an early discharge from Redbank on 2/11/44 as part of the release of manpower to an essential industry, which in this case was dairy farming.

Henry Jacobson died at Mt Olivet Hospital on 15th September 2004 at the age of 81. He had served with the 8th Pioneer Company from 31/3/42 until 27/9/42. Although some of this time was spent in Goondiwindi, this is the period during which he most likely signed the wall. He wrote "QX28868, Pt. H.I. Jacobson, 2/8 Pioneers, No. 1 Platoon, AIF".

If confronting the enemy was not enough, there was the wildlife. It was not just spiders and snakes.

In New Guinea, large hairy caterpillars caused huge problems if they came into contact with the skin. Even their trail of mucous, which was left as they crawled over clothing and blankets, would cause a horrible rash.

Kaye Phillips *née* Saxby, daughter of Wall Signatory Harold Saxby, AIF 1940-1944, July 2011.

Some of the very small wildlife were the most dangerous due to the fact that they carried tropical diseases such as amoebic dysentery, scrub typhus and tick typhus. Several of the better-known tropical diseases were reported in the case studies.

Hookworm (Anchylostomiasis)

The hookworm nematode parasite is found in the intestines of infected humans. It is a common disease in tropical and subtropical areas. The larvae enter the body by direct penetration of the skin, for instance, by the soldier walking barefoot through contaminated soil. The symptoms include gastrointestinal pain, diarrhoea, colic, nausea and anaemia from low iron and progressive debilitation, which can be treated by drugs. Private Myers developed hookworm while in the tropics.

Sandfly Fever (also known as Pappataci Fever)

This debilitating disease occurs in the moist subtropical regions around the Mediterranean and the Middle East. It is a virus carried in the salivary glands of the blood-sucking female *Phlebotomus* sandfly. *Pappataci* is Italian for sandfly. There is very little protection from these insects as they are so small that they can fit through mosquito nets. Two to five days after being bitten the patient experiences lassitude, abdominal distress and dizziness. The next day there is a rapid increase in temperature (39 -40 C), headaches, joint pains, a flushed face and a rapid pulse due to an increase in the heart rate. After two days the temperature drops to normal, but fatigue, weakness, a slow pulse and low blood

pressure are still present. Recuperation may take a few days or up to a few weeks. Albert Dixon developed sandfly fever twice while he was in the Middle East.

Dengue Fever

Dengue fever is the second most important tropical disease after malaria. The dengue virus is carried by several species of the *Aedes* mosquito, which is found in many tropical and subtropical areas, including South-East Asia and the north-east of Australia.

The main symptoms of the disease are a sudden high fever (39 -40 C), and within two days there may be a rash over most of the body. A second rash, resembling measles, appears soon after that makes the patient very uncomfortable. Other symptoms may include headaches, fatigue, joint and muscle aches, nausea, swollen lymph nodes and vomiting. Treatment includes the provision of fluids for dehydration. Normally simple dengue fever is not fatal, but in less than 5% of the cases some severely infected soldiers develop the much more serious dengue hemorrhagic fever. Symptoms of dengue hemorrhagic fever include bleeding from the nose and mouth and a leakage of fluid from the circulation, which leads to decreased blood supply to the vital organs.

As yet no vaccine has been developed to counter dengue fever, although several are in advanced clinical testing. Robert Friend became infected while in training in Queensland.

Malaria

Malaria was the most prevalent tropical disease to affect the Australian troops. Fifteen of the case study soldiers went to New Guinea. Of these, seven, or nearly 50 per cent, became infected with malaria and all of the other soldiers were most likely exposed to the disease. Malaria could cause frequent relapses that kept the men away from duty for additional periods.

The term *malaria* comes from the Latin *mal*=sick and *aria* =air or miasma. The ancient Romans believed people caught this illness by breathing the sick air of the swampy regions in Italy. It is actually caused by the bite of infected female *Anopheles* mosquitoes that breed in swamps, brackish marshes and other areas. Mosquitoes carry the protozoan parasite *Plasmodium* in their salivary glands, which is transmitted to humans when they are bitten. The Australian soldiers in New Guinea had little protection from mosquitoes so they largely depended on medication to prevent and treat malaria.

In New Guinea, they wore khaki shorts and not much else.

Margaret Woolley, March 2011

Malaria was so devastating in the Milne Bay area that General Blamey, in December 1942, made the wearing of protective clothing compulsory. Men in all the tropical regions were instructed in the use of personal protection in the form of protective gear and repellents such as pyrethrums. Mosquito netting was also used, but was in short supply due to a shortage of cotton. The areas around the camps were drained to prevent mosquitoes from breeding in any pools of water.

North Queensland, circa 1944: Soldiers digging an anti-malarial drain at a Cairns army camp. *(Courtesy of the John Oxley Library, State Library of Queensland 247399)*

There are four *Plasmodium* species that cause malaria. *P. ovale* and *P. malariae* were mild diseases that were uncommon, but *P. vivax* and *P. falciparum* were particularly prevalent during World War II. The species of parasite usually determined the severity of the illness.

P. vivax was the most common infection in Australian soldiers and was referred to as BT (Benign Tertian) malaria. The symptoms include chills, fever, sweats, muscle aches, headaches, vomiting, diarrhoea, coughing and yellowing (jaundice) of the skin and eyes. In rare instances vivax malaria leads to death, but it is mostly known for the debilitating fevers it causes.

P. falciparum was the more severe form of the disease. It was referred to as MT (Malignant Tertian) *malaria*. It included the same symptoms as *P vivax*, but left untreated also produced the extreme symptoms of liver and kidney failure, coma and death. It is one of the few infectious diseases that could be fatal within hours to days if not treated.

Treatment

Malaria was treated during World War II with quinine extracted from cinchona bark and with synthetic drugs such as Atebrin and Plasmoquine. Supply of antimalarial drugs was often a problem. Malaria in the bloodstream can usually be effectively treated if the drugs are taken in sufficient quantity for several days. However, the residual parasites remain in the liver, where they are not affected by drugs. They can reactivate or relapse months or years later. The malarial pattern of remission and relapse is a result of the parasite adapting to both the mosquito and the human host. Although a patient may develop a degree of immunity from one infection, it does not automatically follow that he will be immune to a second infection or to any others that may follow. Keith Miller had a many relapses during the war.

CASE STUDY NUMBER 20

MILLER, KEITH DOUGLAS, QX28788, PRIVATE

Keith Miller was a farm labourer (grazier) from Mt Alford when he enlisted in the AIF at Boonah on 3/1/42 at the age of 20. He was sent to the 1st Infantry Training Battalion at Redbank and to the 29th Infantry Training Battalion at Goondiwindi. He joined the 2/10th Infantry Battalion as a reinforcement in August and embarked for New Guinea. He was taken on strength into the unit after its numbers had been depleted by fighting at the Battle for Milne Bay. On Christmas Eve in 1942 he was wounded in the left thigh in action in the heavy fighting at Buna where the 2/10th Infantry Battalion again had a very high number of casualties. He was evacuated to Port Moresby and then to Brisbane by hospital ship.

He spent the next year in either hospital or convalescent depots. He was being treated for both his gunshot wound and for many recurring serious bouts of malaria. He spent time at the Malaria Clinic and the Orthopaedic Hospital as well as the Mackay Hospital shortly before his return to New Guinea in December 1943. He was then sent to the 2/10th Infantry Battalion to strengthen their numbers. In January 1944, due to an unknown fever, he was suspected of having MT (Malignant Tertian) malaria. However, he was diagnosed with the less-serious BT malaria. He joined his unit in February and returned to Australia three months later.

In July he had another malaria relapse, but was able to return to his unit. In October he was transferred to the 2/25th Field Park Company with the Royal Australian Engineers and was therefore given the rank of Sapper. In April 1944 he was given a new medical classification of D citing chronic Catarrhal Maxillary Sinusitis, and was discharged on medical grounds on 26/5/45.

Mr Miller's entry in the World War II Nominal Roll states his unit as being the 2/25th Field Park Company, but his service records demonstrate that he had also served very effectively in the 2/10th Infantry Battalion. His signature on the wall is partially covered by a good-quality plaster, which would have damaged his signature if removed. However, the writing, which is visible, is clear enough to provide the correct identification. He wrote "Miller, K.D., QX28788, Dalby". He was in Brisbane from 20/1/42 until 28/8/42 with the exception of some time spent in training at Goondiwindi. It was during his stay in Brisbane that he most probably visited City Hall and signed the wall.

The soldiers were regarded as being convalescent due to their original malaria infections or subsequent relapses. It was so common for this to happen that in many cases the men were often not sent to major hospitals, but stayed in Australian camp hospitals until they were able to return to duty. Upon discharge, soldiers like Sergeant Scott were issued with instructions on how to deal with relapses of the disease. Mrs Gladys Jacobson has revealed how her husband Henry suffered severe relapses later in his life.

He suffered a relapse when we were on holiday in Singapore and other places in Asia. It was a very bad attack and caused a lot of stress.

Gladys Jacobson, wife of Wall Signatory Henry Jacobson,
AIF 1942-1944, April 2010

Stress Problems

Malaria was not the only problem to have lingering effects after the war had ended. Many soldiers experienced severe mental stress due to the horrors, deprivations and devastation of the war. During World War II, this condition was generally referred to as Battle Fatigue, whereas today it is often known as Post Traumatic Stress Syndrome. Two of the wall signatories shared the same extremely traumatic event.

On 7/9/43, Private Myers was waiting in a convoy with his unit, the 2/33rd Infantry Battalion, at Jackson's Airfield in Port Moresby. Like the other members of his unit he witnessed the death of 60 of his comrades, and the injuring of 92

more, when a fully laden Liberator bomber crashed into the truck convoy. The mental and physical trauma created by this horrific accident were enormous, yet the survivors had to go on doing their duty and join the fighting to capture Lae.

Camped alongside the airfield with his unit was Private Harold Saxby. He was injured from the fallout of aluminium pieces as the plane exploded. The medical staff had to remove multiple pieces of shrapnel from his legs and feet. Private Saxby had repeated operations on his legs in the following months. The aircraft accident at Jackson's Airfield in New Guinea remained under the Official Secrets Act for many years after the war had ended and this was very demoralising for the family members, who had to wait for a long time to get details. Private Saxby's daughter, Kaye Phillips, stated that the shock and stress that resulted from the accident and the many operations that followed contributed to the onset of her father's diabetes and heart problems and this eventually led to his death in 1980 at the age of 63.

CASE STUDY NUMBER 21

SAXBY, HAROLD HENRY, SX5334, PRIVATE

On 14/6/40, Harold Saxby, a 23-year-old boot repairer from Eastwood in South Australia, reported for duty at Wayville. He was allotted to the 2/43rd Infantry Battalion. On 29/12/40 he embarked for the Middle East, where he was assigned as a driver to the 7th Infantry Division Petrol Company in Palestine. He was detached to the Royal Air Force 204 Group in Egypt for one month. This was part of the Desert Air Force under RAF Middle East Command, which supplied close support to the British Eighth Army. It included Australian squadrons. Before returning to Australia in March 1943 he was transferred to the 2/5th Company AASC.

In May his unit was sent to Brisbane where he was transferred to the 2/2nd Supply Depot Company and embarked for Port Moresby in August 1943. Early in the morning of the 7th September 1943, Private Saxby and his unit were camped alongside the Americans outside the perimeter of Jackson's Airfield in Port Moresby. A fully loaded American Liberator bomber crashed on take-off and exploded. Parts of the plane and burning fuel were spread over a wide area, including the place where Private Saxby was camped. The small tents could not offer protection against the masses of falling aluminium shrapnel. He was struck by multiple pieces of sharp metal and it was his legs that were most severely injured. He was taken to hospital and had many operations to remove the shrapnel and repair his legs. This accident was classified as an official secret and is not mentioned in his records. The records also fail to mention his time spent in hospital afterwards. However, they do mention that he contracted BT Malaria in March 1944

and in May he left New Guinea for Brisbane. He was now medically classified as B2. He was discharged on Manpower Release (MPR) from Wayville, SA on 18/11/44.

Even after his discharge there were more operations to try and remove all of the shrapnel, but they never quite succeeded. Harold Saxby said that the shrapnel "moved around". He often wore a long leather boot, which was designed to protect his ankle, but he had a limp for the rest of his life.

Private Saxby was in Brisbane from May 1942 until August 1943, during which time he wrote on the wall "SX5334, H. Saxby" near the lower right corner.

The problems due to stress were not limited to the army. RAF/RAAF Flight Lieutenant William Dulley's wartime experiences in Europe had left him with far-reaching difficulties. His daughter explains:

Years after leaving the Air Force, Dad developed a 'fear' of flying as a passenger. The horror of flying on bombing raids, claustrophobia and the loud, droning engines of the Lancasters left him quite a mess if he had to take a commercial flight. I remember flying to New Zealand with him in 1975. He was quite anxious on the flight and had to rest up the next day. This was so unlike him. He said he would have been much better if he could be at the controls. It was amazing how the experience of flying off the coast of wartorn England had affected him in that way. With what his nerves had been subjected to, it was a wonder he wasn't a lot worse.

Ros Newlands *née* Dulley, daughter of Flight Lieutenant William Dulley, RAAF 1941-1945, September 2010

For many, the horror of war had been a daily ordeal. Prisoners of war suffered dreadfully under the control of their captors. George Edwards, a wall signatory, had the added anguish of knowing that his brother was a captive of the Japanese.

My father's brother, Stanley, had been a prisoner of war of the Japanese for four years. Like my father he suffered traumatic stress from his wartime experiences. They both had extreme nightmares about the war for the rest of their lives.

Thomas Edwards, son of Wall Signatory Corporal George Edwards, AIF 1942-1945, June 2011

The details of their captivity were generally not disclosed to the families, although the effects were very evident.

My grandfather, John Arthur Bacon, was a prisoner of war in Changi Prison in Singapore during World War II. He had suffered from severe malnutrition. He was very reluctant to talk about it. From his time there he had acquired ulcerated sores on both shins that never completely healed throughout his life.

Kimberleigh Campbell *née* Bacon, granddaughter of Driver John Bacon, AIF 1940-1945, September 2011

Not Talking About the War

For many of the relatives, there was very little that the veterans would tell them about their wartime experiences. George Weston had admitted to his family that he felt very nervous when his ship approached Labuan Island because of the Japanese presence there. He did not comment any further.

My brother George never talked about the more serious side of the war, only the funny stuff.

Ronald Weston, brother of Wall Signatory Corporal George Weston, AIF 1940-1946, November 2010

The family of Flight Lieutenant William Dulley knew that he had crashed in the Bay of Biscay after a bombing raid and had been badly injured, but that was all he had been willing to tell them.

Dad didn't ever speak much about the horrors he encountered during his six years in the Air Force and wasn't even interested in participating in Anzac Day marches. He wanted to put it all behind him and enjoy life to the fullest. When he was in Greenslopes Repatriation Hospital, just before he died, he met a German officer who had served with the Luftwaffe. Dad and this man shook hands and became friends, but neither wanted to recall or compare war stories.

Ros Newlands *née* Dulley, daughter of Flight Lieutenant William Dulley, RAAF 1941-1945, September 2010

Today it is accepted that many of the veterans are extremely reluctant to talk about their war experiences. This reticence is understandable.

To talk about it is to remember it. To remember it is to relive it. No-one should have to experience that more than once in a lifetime.

Anonymous, April 2012

It was not only the soldiers who suffered. Many of the medical staff would have been severely affected by the conditions and incidents that had to be faced throughout the war. There are several ambulance and convalescent staff who have signed the wall. Their efforts and that of all other medical staff are especially appreciated when considering that every one of the 155 identified men had survived to return to Australia despite their many illnesses, accidents, diseases and gunshot wounds.

CHAPTER 11

THE HUMAN ELEMENT

From all the information gleaned from the wall, it is the human element that is the most endearing. From these small entries into the literary world, the men have revealed much about themselves. As well as military data, they have included comments that give some indication about how they felt about certain issues. The wall is a kaleidoscope of feelings, personalities and friendships.

Why Did They Do It?

Many visitors to City Hall, drilled in the modern idea that graffiti is environmental vandalism, have wondered why they wrote on the wall. A number of theories have emerged that try to answer this question. The average age of the men who signed the wall, calculated from New Year's Day in 1942, is 23.83 years. Throughout the centuries, young men, and the not so young, from all over the world have left their names in public places. It made the statement "I was here!" Someone with this in mind most probably jumpstarted the graffiti at City Hall with his own mark of identity.

It was customary for military men in particular to sign things, for example, flags, handkerchiefs, planes and, of course, walls. Pencils had been provided and the wall was conveniently close by. A young man might reason that if the other guys had signed and left their mark, so would he. It would have been seen as an act of bravado, something daring and dashing to do before going off to an unknown future. It would have had the added thrill of doing something slightly naughty, because graffiti then, as now, was regarded as something *one should not do*. The widow of Henry Jacobson has found it hard to comprehend why her husband had signed his name as he had been an extremely law-abiding man.

> *He never got even a traffic ticket throughout his life.*
>
> Gladys Jacobson, wife of Wall Signatory Henry Jacobson, AIF 1942-1944, October, 2009

Henry Ivan Jacobson AIF 1942-1944. *(Courtesy of Gladys Jacobson)*

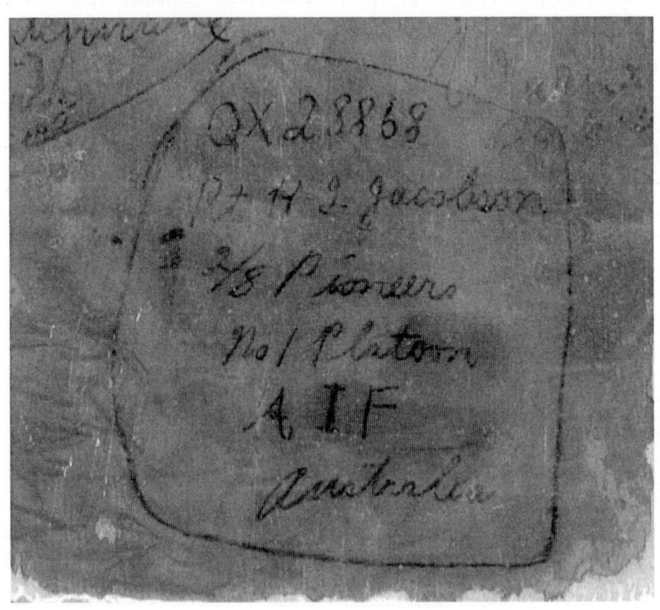

QX 28868, Private H.I. Jacobson, 2/8 Pioneers, No. 1 Platoon, AIF, Australia.

(Image Copyright Brisbane City Council)

Perhaps by signing the wall he had felt unity with the other men and a sense of belonging to a very large team with a common purpose, in this case the army. Henry Jacobson came from a family of team players. He was second cousin to a great Australian cricketing icon, Wally Grout.

The fact that there was an attempt to clean the writing of the wall shows that at least one custodian of the Red Cross tea rooms was not too happy about the graffiti being there. Nevertheless, more than 180 men managed to write their names before the wall was covered over with plaster in late 1942.

A Sense of Pride

They appear to have exhibited a great deal of pride as they freely and openly wrote their names, service numbers, places of origin and the names of their units on this public wall. It told people who and what they were. Some of the men wrote the name of the places where they had lived before enlisting, such as Thomas Newman's "Tara" and Roy Dendle's "Late of Springsure". When they wrote the name of their unit, it also carried with it the unit's previous history. For instance, Corporal William Davis included the 2/15th Battalion with his signature. This unit had fought with great heroism and endurance in the North African campaign in 1941, most notably at Tobruk and El Alamein, before he had joined the battalion. His pride was obvious. Similarly, Signalman Arthur Abrahams included his unit, the 2/1st Australian Machine Gun Battalion, which had fought bravely in North Africa as well as Greece and Crete in 1941.

Some men went one step further by proudly showing their unit's heraldry. Signalman Henson included the double diamond (blue) of his unit, the 2/3 Australian Independent Company. This colour patch is still easily recognised by many visitors to City Hall.

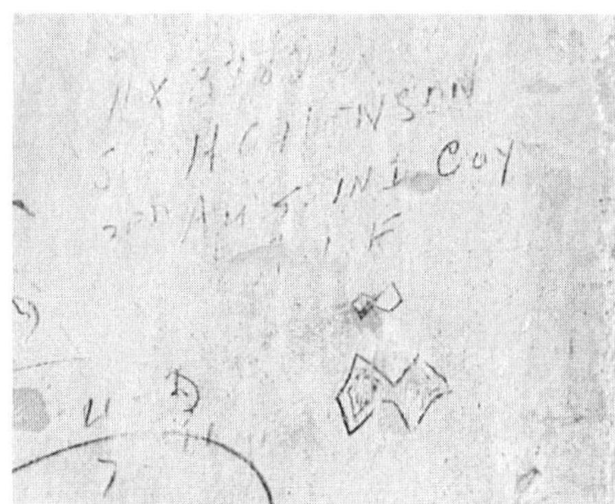

NX38826, Sig. H.G. Henson, 3rd Aus Ind Coy, AIF. *(Image Copyright Brisbane City Council)*

Similarly, Signalman Street included the heraldry of his militia unit, Brisbane Fortress, at Fort Lytton.

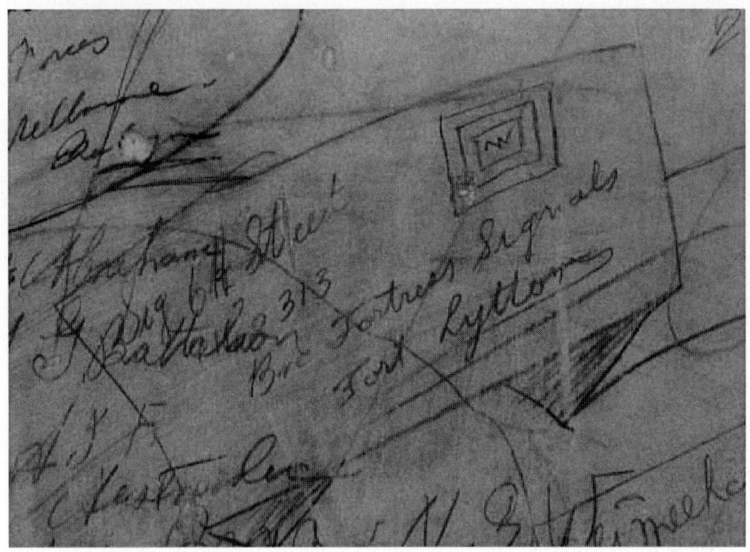

Sig C.H. Street, Q140313, Bne Fortress Signals, Fort Lytton. *(Image Copyright Brisbane City Council)*

Not to be outdone, musician Corporal James Fletcher of the 3rd Division Entertainment unit drew a picture of his saxophone.

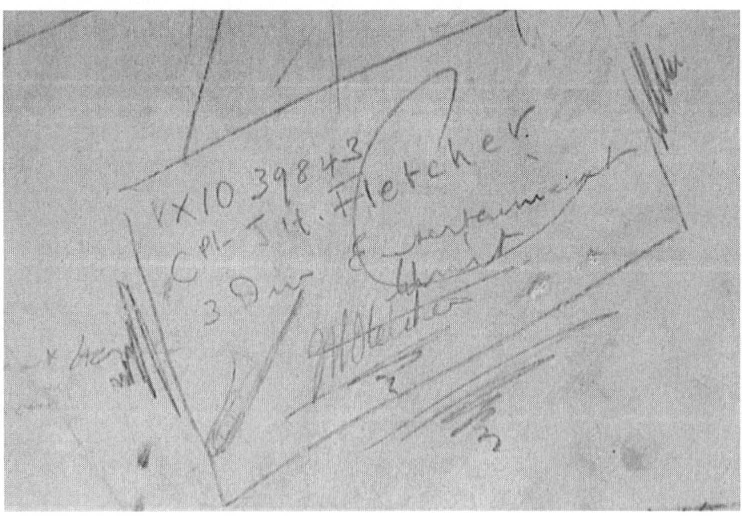

Vx1039843, Cpl J.H. Fletcher, 3 Div Entertainment Unit. *(Image Copyright Brisbane City Council)*

Politeness

This was an age when it was customary for people to be polite to one another. It was seen as a virtue. Despite being a wall of graffiti in a men's room, only one swear word has been found, and that was part of a quote provided by Sapper William Solomon.

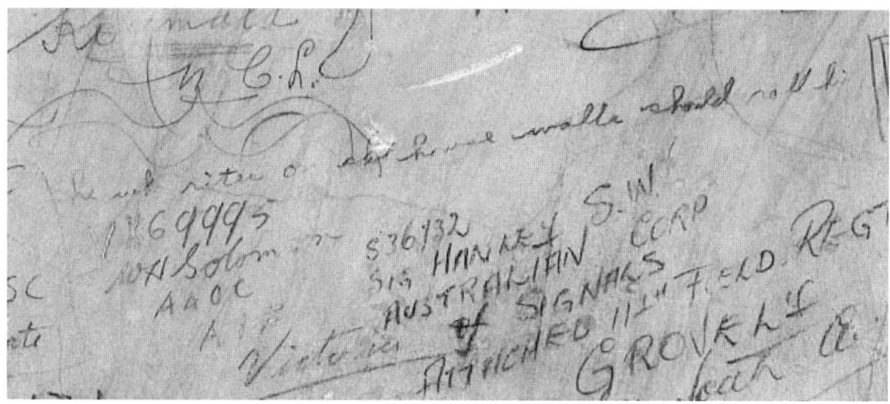

"He who rites on (bleep) house walls should roll him (in it?). VX 69995, W. H. Solomon, AAOC, AIF, Victoria". *(Image Copyright Brisbane City Council)*

The men were also polite regarding women. There is barely a mention of a female on the wall. Gentlemen did not do this, especially in such a place. It would have been considered vulgar to do so. Nevertheless, there are three females who were included as part of the graffiti. "Patsy" was written separately and does not appear to be attached to any particular soldier. "Loretta" was crossed out, which may give some indication about how the author felt about her. The American contribution, "Flatbush Floogie", could be viewed as a gentle dig to a girl in New York. Robert Friend, casting modesty aside, wrote very frankly about his relationship with women.

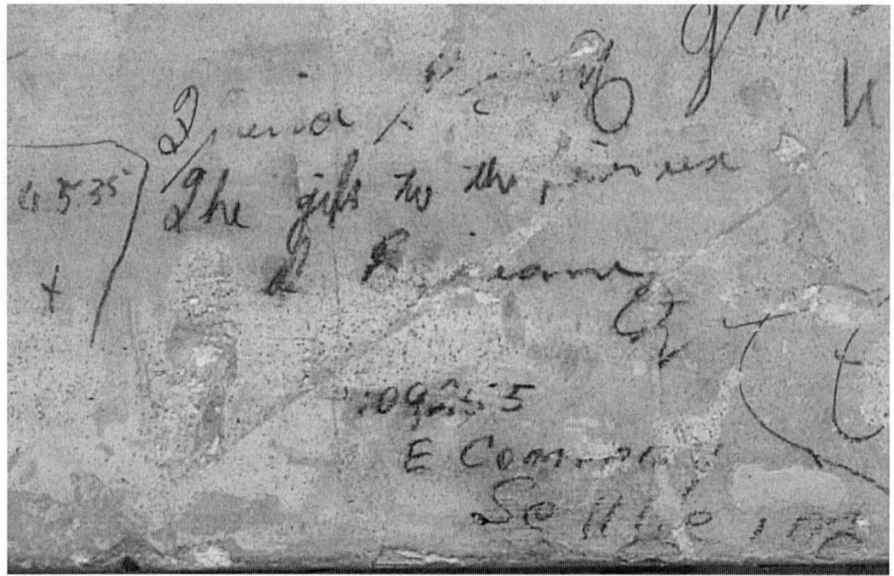

"Friend R.E.M., The gift to the fair sex of Brisbane, 109255, E Company, Sellheim". *(Image Copyright Brisbane City Council)*

When considering the graffiti of today, this wall would have to be described as *ultraconservative.*

Frustration

When the men enlisted during the war, duty or the desire to "do one's bit" was seen as a prime motivator *(Mark Johnston, Journal of the Australian War Memorial, Issue 29, November, 1996*). To many this would mean being involved in the actual fighting or at least being close to the front line in some capacity. During the war, 993,000 people served in the military. Of these, 400,000 did not serve overseas, but remained in Australia maintaining the services, supply and home defence. This vital work was viewed by many as being less glamorous, unexciting, mundane and far less heroic than their counterparts in combat. Some of the comments on the wall reflect this attitude. Several men had written "Lost Legion", which referred to the fact that they felt they had been forgotten like the men in the French Foreign Legion who had were considered *lost to the world.* This is particularly true for some of the men who were stationed at Woolloongabba and Redbank.

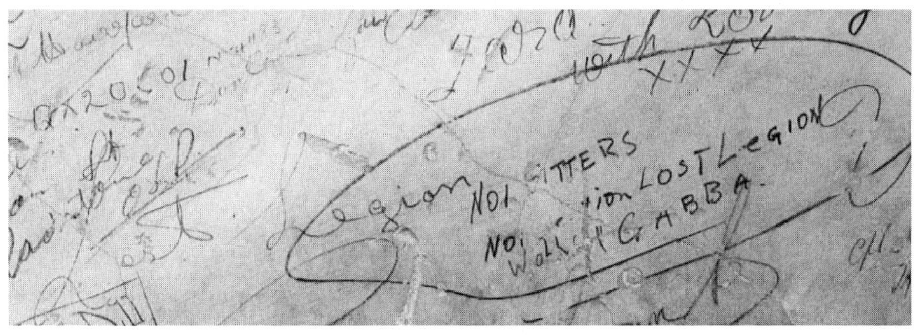

Lost Legion. *(Image Copyright Brisbane City Council)*

Two unidentified men, including a No. 1 Fitter from Woolloongabba, have shown their frustration and have written "Lost Legion" on the wall.

Onwards and Upwards

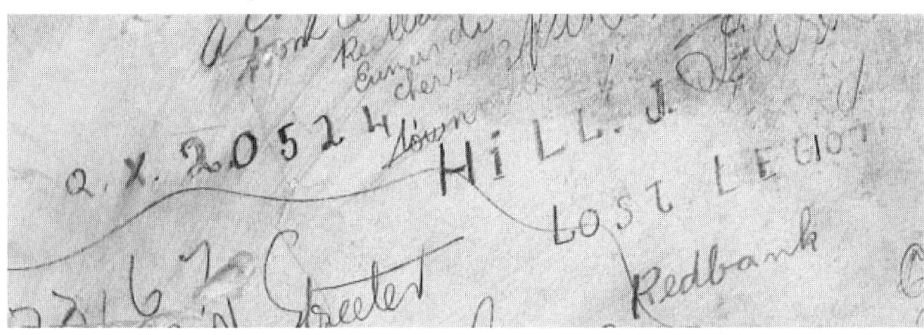

QX20524, HILL. J., Lost Legion, Redbank. *(Image Copyright Brisbane City Council)*

Private John Hill was at Redbank when he wrote "Lost Legion" along with his signature. He was eventually placed with the 31st Employment Company.

"--- Cross, --- QX27537, Lost Legion, Redbank". *(Image Copyright Brisbane City Council)*

Another of Redbank's "Lost Legion", James Cross, must have felt he was not in the right place or doing the right job. His record reveals many problems with discipline until he transferred to the 2/4th Docks Operating Company. Here he underwent extra training and was so well suited to the position that he attained rapid promotions. This was followed by a transfer to New Guinea. As Warrant Officer Class 1, he was to become the most senior man identified on the wall.

It is understandable that these Australian soldiers could feel frustration and wished they could be doing something more active and, in their eyes, more constructive for the war effort. This is despite the fact that the role of the men who stayed in Australia was so important that the war would have been lost without them.

Discipline

During World War I, Australian soldiers were reputedly notorious for their lack of respect for their commanding officers and for their lack of discipline, although it was agreed that they were extremely good soldiers. During World War II, the discipline had improved, but it was still a problem for many of the men.

Examples of breaches in discipline found in the men's records include "not wearing a shirt", "conduct to the prejudice of good order and military discipline" and for bringing "intoxicating liquor into the precincts of the camp" for which the culprit was fined £2. The majority of the breaches in discipline were due to the men being Absent Without Leave (AWL). One soldier even managed to be AWL while on board a ship for two days. For the number of days that they were absent they lost pay and allowances, and had to pay a fine. The punishment, referred to as an "Award", was usually automatic, so the men knew what to expect.

However, the 2/16th Battalion managed to surprise everyone. This Western Australian unit included many tough and hardened men from the goldfields. The Battalion was returning from the Middle East where it had sustained heavy losses, when the ship docked at Fremantle for a short stay. The men were given 36 hours leave on 16/3/42, but by the time this period ended 395 men, of whom 350 belonged to the 2/16th Battalion, had not returned. They were all officially AWL. The ship, the TSS *Kosciuszko*, had to leave with its convoy for Adelaide and so left the men behind. By the end of March, 232 men had rejoined the ship in Adelaide. It is not known whether the wall signatories Cook and Robinson, who were members of the 2/16th Battalion, took part in this mass AWL exodus, but it would have provided a lot of interesting stories for later conversations with their mates.

For more serious breaches of discipline, more severe action was taken. This was usually in the form of a court martial, which is the military form of a trial. There are at least 11 men on the wall who faced a court martial, some of them twice. The main reason was for being AWL for extended periods. One soldier was subjected to one court martial for being AWL for five months and then had another hearing for escaping from detention, although he was caught immediately. If found guilty the men incurred not only financial punishments, but were often given a period of detention during which time they received no pay or allowances.

Army discipline was difficult for many men to observe. Some had more difficulty with it than others. Private Ronald Greenhalgh had an interesting military career.

CASE STUDY NUMBER 22

GREENHALGH, GORDON RONALD, NX6170 (N130986), PRIVATE.

Private Greenhalgh, a lorry driver, enlisted into the AIF on 3/5/41 at 21 years of age. He was placed in the Australian Army Service Corps Training Corps in Sydney where he trained as a Driver. In September he went to the Middle East and joined 2/1st Field Ambulance, and in March 1942 the unit went to Ceylon (Sri

Lanka). From October 1941 until July 1942, when he left Ceylon, he committed numerous offences including "conduct prejudicial to good order and military discipline" and for being AWL. Now in the 2/1st Company AASC, he returned to Australia in August.

He was transferred to Brisbane in November where he served 20 days' detention at Grovely Barracks for being AWL. Throughout 1943 he was AWL several times and incurred numerous fines and detentions. He even managed to escape from detention at one point. In February 1944, with legal help, his fines and sentences were reduced. He was transferred to the 2/1st Butchering Platoon in July 1944.

In March 1945, as part of the 2nd Army Troops Company, he sailed to Lae in New Guinea. There were no fines or detentions while he was in Lae and he was given proficiency pay. He returned to Brisbane in July. The Army discharged him on 20/9/45, just a few weeks after the war had ended, citing that as a butcher he was in an essential occupation.

He was in Brisbane in late 1942. Gordon Greenhalgh's name is on the wall with his mate, Private Lionel Pascoe, from the same unit. The handwriting is not Private Greenhalgh's, so it was most probably written by Private Pascoe. The writing states "NX6170, DVR Greenhalgh, 6th Aust. Div. AASC, AIF". His mate also wrote his own name "NX9389, DVR Pascoe, 6th Div. AASC, AIF".

Like Warrant Officer Cross, Private Greenhalgh had felt *lost,* with no clear objective in sight. However, his misconduct was seen as the overwhelming factor in his career and it held him back from making the contribution to the war effort that he could have made. He eventually found his niche as an army butcher in Lae. His mate and fellow driver, Private Lionel Pascoe, wrote Gordon Greenhalgh's name on the wall as well as his own sometime in late 1942

Drinking

Drinking alcoholic beverages, especially beer, was an integral part of the Australian culture during World War II, just as it is today. The army had strict regulations about where and when alcohol could be consumed. There is frequent mention in the War Diaries *(Courtesy of the Australia War Memorial)* of alcoholic beverages being provided and sold at the canteens. Sometimes the canteens opened and remained "dry", but they remained places where the men could relax with their mates.

Brisbane, August 1942: Barman pouring beers at the Army Service Club wet canteen. A feature of the bar is the patented dispenser, which eliminated the head on a beer. The trading hours were limited to 11 am to 2 pm and 4 pm to 8 pm. *(Courtesy of the John Oxley Library, State Library of Queensland 165383)*

Mateship

Of all of the human feelings that have been exhibited by the men on the wall, it is mateship that stands above the rest. Mateship is seen as a military virtue, a cultural icon that maintains solidarity in the face of opposition. Loyalty to one's mates is the 'cement that binds'.

> *The camaraderie that I experienced in the defence force is like nothing else that I have ever known. I have never felt it so much before or since that time. In the military, good mates and good*

teamwork were vital for survival. They provided a sense of security because it meant that you were not on your own. Mateship is also fun.

John Klazema, Sergeant, Australian Army Reserve 1987-1997, June 2011

Wall signatory Walter Huggonson agrees and goes one step further.

Mates are everything. It would be tragic to try and live without a group of mates.

Wall Signatory Walter Huggonson, AIF 1941-1944, April 2012

It is more than just a dependency. It is a code of conduct towards comrades and a brotherhood that provides confidence and security. This is essential in a warzone.

Mateship takes on a new meaning when you are near the front lines. Your lives are dependent on each other.

Ron Archer, 2/2 Independent Company Commando, AIF 1941-1946, July 2011

Nothing is sacred where mateship is involved. The men get to know each other far better than they could ever have expected.

Brothers in Arms

In the New Guinea mountain country where a lot of fighting took place, two men went on a patrol to collect information close to a Japanese front-line group. One Australian soldier was answering the call of nature while the other man watched for enemy movement. Suddenly a bullet flew near them and both men took off, one still hitching up his trousers. You get to know each other really well. It can be closer than two brothers in a family. Fortunately the Japanese were not good marksmen and neither man was hurt.

Ron Archer, 2/2 Independent Company Commando, AIF 1941-1946, July 2011.

Boys will be Boys – Where the Digger Character Begins.

Mateship, larrikinism and breaches in discipline all form part of the Digger character. Wall signatory Corporal George Edwards had two sons who showed

early promise of this typically Australian trait. They were literally "Brothers in Arms".

> *We lived close to the Australian Camp at Kalinga Park. As children we used to go there and steal bayonets.*
>
> Thomas Edwards, son of Wall Signatory Corporal George Edwards, AIF 1942-1945, June, 2011

> *At one time while on leave, my father brought his rifle home. My brother, aged about six, and myself, aged about four, decided to load it. The only ammunition that we had was a machine-gun bullet, which would not fit into the chamber so we decided to use a hammer to ram it in. My father was not happy as he had to take his rifle to ordnance to be replaced. After our spanking, my brother and I never touched his weapon again.*
>
> Thomas Edwards, son of Wall Signatory Corporal George Edwards, AIF 1942-1945, June 2011

Boys Become Men

The men also used the wall to leave messages for their mates. On 15/8/41, Private Chadwick wrote "Nothing Yet" which presumably shows this ordnance craftsman had been waiting for news, perhaps of a posting to an army location, and wrote this message for his mates to read. Private William Johnson left instructions for his mates to "Return Man to 101 Con Dep, Copooroo" once he had finished his night out on the town.

The men often came into the city in groups. The various sets of mateship signatures are sometimes very obvious as the names within each set were often written in the same handwriting and are situated very close to each other on the wall. Several are enclosed together within a boundary. Most of the soldiers' friendships appear to be from men in the same unit or area of work, but with others, the relationship seems to have been formed at an earlier time and the friends have met up at City Hall.

Thomas Newman and Roderick McLeod have made it very easy to see their relationship. They were one month apart in age, and had both enlisted at Tara on the same day. They belonged to separate units, but had obviously come to City Hall together as their graffiti contributions were enclosed in a circle with the words "Tara" and "Mates". There was no doubt as to the friendship of these young men and they displayed it proudly.

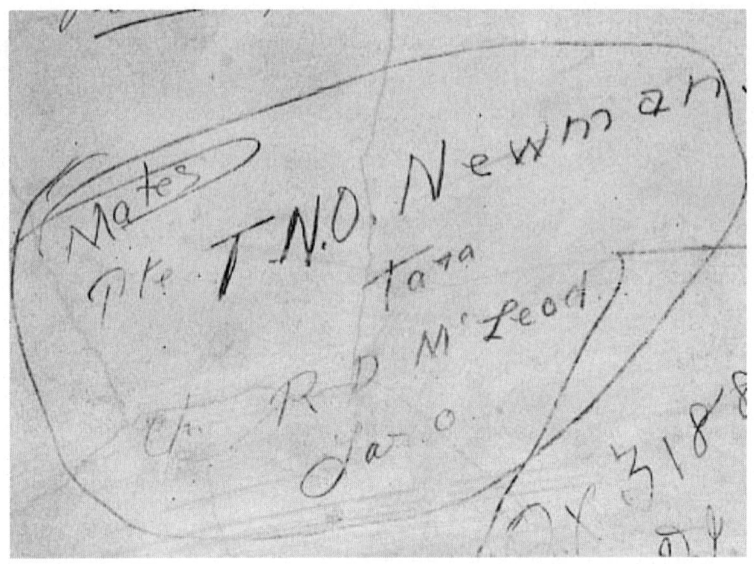

Mates Pte T.N.O. Newman and R.D. McLeod, Tara. *(Image Copyright Brisbane City Council)*

Gnrs Allan Werner and Herbert Drew, Grovely. *(Image Copyright Brisbane City Council)*

Similarly, Gunners Werner and Drew have written their names in a circle as well as the word "Grovely". Although there was more than 20 years' difference in age between them, both of these men served together in the artillery section at Grovely Camp and had obviously formed a friendship.

Sometimes the presence of mates on the wall next to each other helped in the identification of the men. Private Harvatt and Private Bowman have two sets of graffiti where both of their names are close together. In one case, Mr Harvatt's name and number are easy to read, but Mr Bowman's was not. In the second case, Mr Bowman's graffiti was fairly clear, but Mr Harvatt's was not. By combining the information on these two contributions the identification of both men became clear.

Corporals Harrison and McNaughton's names were written side by side and in different handwriting. They were both from Victoria and had only 22 days difference in age. They had both been in the militia in Victoria and now belonged to the 29th Infantry Battalion (East Melbourne Regiment), which was stationed in Queensland in March 1942. The men probably visited City Hall sometime between this date and August 1942 when the 29th Battalion merged with the 46th Battalion to become the 29/46th. This was helpful when dating the signatures on the wall. Both men drove carriers. These mates remained together in the 29/46th Battalion until their discharge in 1946.

A Budding Friendship

CASE STUDY NUMBER 23

BEUTEL, LAWRENCE ROY, QX41007 (Q11931(6)), CORPORAL

Lawrence Beutel was born in Lowood on 20/1/1910. He was a labourer and a farrier. On 24/9/41 he enlisted into the militia in Brisbane at the age of 31, after previously being a driver with the 1st Auxiliary Horse Transport Company at Enoggera. He continued his work as a farrier, i.e., a blacksmith who specialises in shoeing horses, while in the militia and stayed in the same unit. In December he was classified as a Driver of Horse Transport. "Drivers" refers to the men who actually handled and rode the horses, donkeys and mules of the unit. He was sent to Gatton and Toowoomba. In September 1942 he was transferred to the 2nd Pack Transport Company, which was an equine unit in the Australian Army Service Corps. In October he officially enlisted into the AIF while in the Field.

In November he was sent to 3rd Camp Hospital at Enoggera with an unknown diagnosis. After numerous visits to several different medical facilities he was finally diagnosed as having an anxiety state. He was promoted to corporal in June 1943 and in August

he was sent to the Atherton Tableland. Upon being admitted into hospital in January 1944, his medical classification was reassessed by the Medical Board and he was discharged from Redbank on 2/3/44 for medical reasons.

He had three signatures on the wall.

Corporal Lawrence Beutel very helpfully included the date 25/8/41 with his first signature. At the time, he was in the militia as an auxiliary horse driver at the Enoggera Camp. Meanwhile, another soldier, Private Mervyn Dawson, who was also in the auxiliary horse transport company, simply wrote his name and service number on the wall. It is set apart from Mr Beutel's signature. With their next two signatures they were together. One was dated 17/9/42 and was written by Mr Beutel. It appears that this visit to the city was to celebrate Mr Beutel's transfer to the 2nd Pack Transport Company in the AIF. By now they would have been true mates despite the 12 year difference in their ages. With their third graffiti, written by Mr Dawson, both men listed their separate horse transport units, and this time they added their own version of the unit name "N.G.Specials". They had worked together and obviously enjoyed a night out together on occasion, sharing "Graffiti Duty" on the wall.

The Gunalda Boys

Gunalda Boys. *(Image Copyright Brisbane City Council)*

Three young men were enlisted in the Number 1 Platoon of the 8th Pioneer Company, AIF when they visited City Hall. The first young man was Leonard Chaplin, who had been born in Cooroy. His mate was Henry Jacobson, who lived in Gunalda. The third man was Vivian Snell, who had also resided in Gunalda.

They had written their signatures below the board in the same format as each other. Private Jacobson and Private Snell are the only two men on the wall who were connected to Gunalda, so presumably these are the "Gunalda Boys". The Pioneer units tended to recruit men who were both very fit and capable of doing hard work as well as being able to fight as riflemen. It is not surprising that these three young men from rural South East Queensland were friends.

The Five Amigos

These men were all part of the 41st Field Training Battery at Grovely. Their names are close to each other on the wall and were all written in the same handwriting. Gunners John Ham, Eric McLeod, George Weston and Thomas Draper as well as an unidentified Gunner R.E.M. visited City Hall together. What is known about the four identified men is that they had all enlisted into the AIF prior to November 1941. Three of the men transferred to Australian Docks Operating Companies and Gunner Ham went to Northern Territory Canteens and was eventually discharged in January 1946 with the rank of Warrant Officer Class 2. His name was first on the list of these mates, so presumably he took the lead in the graffiti writing, just as he later took the lead in his duties.

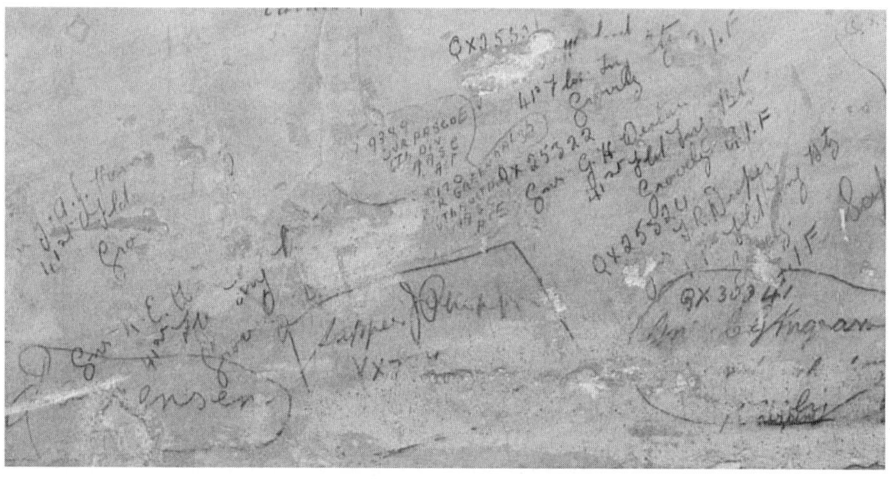

The Five Amigos from 41st Field Training Battery at Grovely – from left to right: Gunners Ham, Unidentified Gunner, then McLeod, Weston and Draper. *(Image Copyright Brisbane City Council)*

A Lifelong Friendship

From George Weston's records it is possible to determine that these signatures were made during the period 29/1/42 until 13/3/42 while Gunner Weston was training at Grovely with the 41st Field Training Battery. His relationship with at least one of the men was to become very permanent. During this period, Tom Draper took George Weston home to Beaudesert to meet his family. George met Tom's sister, Alice, and they fell in love. They married after the war ended.

George Weston AIF 1940-1946. *(Courtesy of Judith Grant née Weston)*

From left to right: George's sister Jean, Alice Weston *née* Draper, George Weston, Tom Draper. *(Courtesy of Judith Grant née Weston)*

CASE STUDY NUMBER 24

WESTON, GEORGE HENRY, QX25322 (Q90210), ACTING SERGEANT

George Henry Weston was a 25-year-old plumber from Annerley in Brisbane when he enlisted into the Australian Military Forces on 23/8/40. He joined the AIF in December 1941 and trained as a Driver Mechanic at Gaythorne before transferring to the 41st Field Training Battery at Grovely where he underwent gunnery training. He was sent to the 2/1st Docks Operating Company with the Royal Australian Engineers and then sent to Darwin for training as a specialist Winchman. He returned to New South Wales in March 1943 and embarked for New Guinea in July. He was promoted to corporal in March 1944 and returned to Sydney in April.

In May he was hospitalised for two days with a lacerated buttock due to an accident falling down the stairs, and a few days later was readmitted to hospital with pterygium of the right eye, caused by prolonged exposure to wind and weather. Upon his release he was transferred to the 2/10th Docks Operating Company and was sent to Darwin until October when he returned to Queensland. He left for the Dutch East Indies from Cairns, arriving at Morotai Island in March 1945, and then in the following June went to Labuan Island in Borneo managing the storage supplies. He returned to Morotai in September after the war ended. He was promoted to Acting Sergeant in October and returned to Brisbane In January 1946 for discharge from Redbank. He then resumed his civilian role as a plumber.

George Henry Weston died on 23/9/2003 aged 88. He has been described as a "real party goer" and someone who enjoyed the family trait of "joking around". It is therefore very appropriate that he is joined on the wall by his army mates from Grovely as they came into the city to enjoy some recreational time. "QX25322, GNR G.H. Weston, 41st FLD TNG BTY, Grovely, AIF."

The Graffiti Gang

Some of the entries on the wall were written in true graffiti-style. This refers to a type of script that is convoluted, turns back upon itself and, despite being very neatly done, is hard to read. This is an artistic way of being able to leave one's mark and of not being caught. Once the secret to unlocking the script had been discovered identifications could be made.

There are five such entries on the wall that were all written in the same handwriting. They each included the word "Gabba", which meant the Woolloongabba Army Camp. Two entries are in the name of Signalman Norman Francis, who ultimately became a sergeant in the 1st Multi Channel Wireless/

Telegraphy Section. He had also included his service number, which made identifying him easy. One of his entries was particularly large and was possibly made during an earlier visit to City Hall. This would make Mr Francis the prime candidate as the true graffiti artist.

Theoretically, with his next visit, his mates accompanied him. The names of Sappers Herbert Dull and William Melrose are present along with another signalman whose identity is less certain. Signalman R. Rice has been tentatively identified because not only was he a young South East Queenslander like the other members of the Graffiti Gang, but he is also the only R. Rice listed in the records as being a signalman. His records reveal that he was stationed at Fort Lytton from 7/1/42 until 25/5/42, which would have given him access to the Woolloongabba Camp and to the other signalman, Mr Francis. However, Mr Rice's story does not end there.

The 'Z' Special Unit–More than Coincidence

It is the location of his signature on the wall which provides further clues to Mr Rice's identity. Next to his entry is the name of Private Colin Doolan, a young South East Queenslander. According to his records, Mr Rice's former addresses were at schoolhouses in this region, so it is highly likely that Mr Rice's father was a schoolteacher who transferred to different locations. It is therefore possible that the two young men met as schoolboys. This is not a great coincidence in itself, but the next part of the story certainly points to the men having a connection.

The men were only a year apart in age when they joined up as teenagers in December 1941. Mr Rice went into the militia until 17/2/43 and then joined the AIF as a skilled radio and telephone mechanic. He underwent extensive training, which included, among other things, a course on the use of carrier pigeons. He eventually transferred to the 'Z' Special Unit on 7/8/43.

Mr Doolan, on the other hand, had enlisted straight into the AIF, and at the time that he wrote his signature on the wall he was a member of the 7th Pioneer Company, where strength, physical fitness and the ability to handle firearms were very important.

Both men became non-commissioned officers in the 'Z' Special Unit. This was a small raiding and commando unit that specialised in reconnaissance and sabotage behind enemy lines in South-East Asia. With more than 993,000 people in uniform, and only 155 identified on the wall, the odds of these two men having their signatures side by side could be seen as more than a coincidence. It is just possible that one man may have recruited the other into this small elite unit, having known him previously. Sergeant Ronald Rice's identification now seems more secure, thanks to his mate, Corporal Colin Doolan.

Sig R. Rice, Gabba and QX29349 Pte Doolan, C., 7th Pioneer Coy, AIF.

(Image Copyright Brisbane City Council)

The Legacy

Mateship often lasted long after the war had ended. Reunions, memorials and parades helped to bring the men together again.

> *My father, Captain Donald Hill Coop, was a member of the 'Z' Special Unit. For many years after the war he did not talk about his service years to his family. He attended all of the reunions and kept close contact with his fellow servicemen. He said that he was able to talk about it then.*
>
> Jenny Middleton *née* Coop, daughter of Captain Donald Coop, 'Z' Special Unit, AIF 1939-1946, October 2010

One of the most popular places for meeting old mates is the Returned Services League. There are many former soldiers like George Weston whose name appears on Honour Boards, in this case at the Annerley RSL, where over the years he met many of his old friends. On Anzac Day, after the marches and formal proceedings are over, it is at the RSLs and places like them where the more human aspects of servicemen are celebrated.

George Weston, AIF 1940-1946 *(Courtesy of Judith Grant née Weston)*

George Weston in retirement. *(Courtesy of Judith Grant née Weston)*

CHAPTER 12

OUR AMERICAN VISITORS

There are several contributions from Americans written on the wall alongside their Australian counterparts. It is estimated that there were approximately one million Americans who visited Australia from December 1941 until the end of the war. They made a sizeable impact. The reason why they were here, although fortuitous for Australia, had very sad beginnings for America.

Prior to December 1941, the Japanese in the South West Pacific region were seen as an increasingly aggressive force and war appeared to be imminent. Japan had a very large population, but lacked many of the vital raw materials to support it. The initial aim of the Japanese had been to seize territories rich in natural resources such as oil, tin and rubber. They wanted to extend their empire into the Pacific Ocean regions and Asia to obtain these territories and to establish strategic military bases to defend them. Fearing that the British and Americans would oppose them, they regarded neutralising these forces in the region, particularly the US Navy, as an important factor in their plan.

The war in the Pacific began just after midnight on 8th December 1941 when the Japanese invaded Kota Bharu in British Malaya. About 90 minutes later, the Japanese attacked Pearl Harbor in Hawaii. Due to its location east of the International Dateline, this occurred at 7.48 a.m. Hawaii Time on the 7th of December. The Americans were now drawn into the war.

On the following day the American Army Air Force bases in the Philippines were bombed and most of the planes were destroyed. The Japanese had achieved a complete tactical surprise. They were now in a position where they could invade the Philippine islands. The commander of the US Forces in the Far East, Lieutenant General Douglas MacArthur, mounted a defence of the islands, but the Japanese prevailed. With defeat imminent, in March 1942 President Roosevelt ordered MacArthur to leave the Philippines and to locate to Australia where he could create a base. The General is well remembered for his famous comment concerning the Philippines, "I shall return". He was appointed Supreme Commander of the South West Pacific Zone in charge of American, Australian and all other Allied land forces. His General Headquarters were initially in Melbourne, but he moved to Brisbane in July to be closer to the war zone and to maintain communications with the forces located there.

Hundreds of American servicemen, including the United States Navy, arrived in Australia, as well as ships, planes, equipment and supplies. As the war progressed, these numbers increased dramatically. There was a large American contingent that remained in Australia throughout the war as part of General Headquarters, supervising training, providing supplies and repairs, etc. Many other Americans were passing through on their way to the front lines or they were returning from the war zones on leave or for medical care. The presence of the Americans in Australia was to have a profound influence on the military, political and social structure of Australia.

The Military Situation in 1942

After Pearl Harbor and Darwin had been attacked, all of my friends were very frightened. Things only started to get better after the Americans arrived.

Anonymous lady, August 2011

Australia had been in a vulnerable situation. The bulk of the AIF was overseas. Australian troops were coming home from the Middle East and until they arrived it had been the militia that provided Australia's only protection from what had been perceived as an imminent Japanese invasion. With the successive victories by the Japanese and the fall of Singapore on 15th February, most of the entire Australian 8th Division and the British land forces stationed in the region had been either killed or captured. The British Royal Navy forces, without supporting air cover, had been destroyed. This emphasised the fact that the British would not be able to defend Australia and that a new ally was needed. Australia looked to the Americans for aggressive military action against the Japanese. The Americans in turn, needed Australia as a supply and staging area for its war effort.

From December 1941, American troop ships, supply ships and naval forces that had been heading to the Philippines and other parts of the Pacific were diverted to Australia. The American presence was welcomed and they were seen as our protectors. One mother informed her 11-year-old son of this during 1942 as they witnessed the American troops marching up Racecourse Road at Hamilton towards the Eagle Farm Racecourse where they were camped.

The Americans are here to save us!

Anonymous, November 2009

This was the prevailing feeling among the population. MacArthur's policy was to take the war to the Japanese in New Guinea rather than fighting them on Australian soil. His overwhelming goal was to liberate the Philippines before invading Japan. The Japanese policy was to take Rabaul in New Britain, in which they succeeded, and then to take Port Moresby, which was to be used as part of their network of strategic bases for air and sea dominance as well as to launch attacks on Australia. They had decided to isolate Australia and New Zealand from the Americans and other Allied forces. The bombing of Darwin on 19th February formed part of this plan. This attack on the Australian mainland and all of the others that followed were meant to be a deterrent to the Americans establishing a base there. They were also meant to tie up Australia's military resources.

The conquest of Port Moresby was therefore central to their plan and they were determined to have it. Rabaul was the major Japanese army and naval base in the South West Pacific. The decision was made to capture Port Moresby from the Australians by a naval invasion launched from Rabaul, but American and Australian naval forces prevented this during the Battle of the Coral Sea from the 4th to the 8th of May. The Japanese Navy had been weakened and this was one of the factors that caused it to sustain a major loss fighting the Americans in the Battle of Midway in June. This was an important turning point in the war. Afterwards the Japanese carrier fleet was never able to fully recover. Without a fully functioning navy, the Japanese would find it difficult to launch an invasion of Australia.

The next time the Japanese tried to take Port Moresby was by land from the north in July, using the Kokoda Trail, but they were again unsuccessful. Another attempt to take Port Moresby came from the east. Milne Bay was a strategic target on the eastern tip of New Guinea. It was manned by Australians and also present was a contingent of Americans from the U.S. Army Corps of Engineers building airfields and wharves. It was attacked on the 25th August by the Japanese, who were preparing to use the airfields to launch attacks on Port Moresby. Once again they were unsuccessful. The Americans and Australian soldiers working together also beat the enemy at the Battle of Buna in November, which they won convincingly, but with a high cost in casualties.

The two nations had fought together in the Guadalcanal Campaign, which began on 7th August 1942 with an American and Australian naval force, and a large contingent of American Marines, US Army and other Allied troops. During the Battle of Savo Island on the 9th August, the Australian cruiser HMAS *Canberra* was one of the ships that sank. The Americans later honoured their Australian allies by naming a new American naval cruiser the USS *Canberra*, which is the only American warship ever to be named after a foreign warship or a foreign capital city.

Guadalcanal was a long campaign that culminated in a victory in February 1943. It marked the end of the Japanese expansion into the Pacific and the beginning of the Allied offensives to remove the Japanese from the South West Pacific Zone.

1943 – The Beginning of the End

Douglas MacArthur had used the strategy of moving from point-to-point along the northern side of New Guinea and then on to the islands, leaving some pockets of Japanese isolated and cut off from their supply lines. This was the case in Rabaul, for example. This saved the Allies men, resources and time. The Australians, often in conjunction with the Americans, fought these isolated pockets of resistance in order to remove any potential threat.

The major base of Lae was captured in September by a joint American and Australian force. There were more Allied victories to come in 1943, and with each of these victories, the threat of an Australian invasion diminished. Finally, there was an announcement, although many considered that it could have been made more than 12 months earlier.

The threat of invasion has receded.

AMF Headquarters, October 1943.
(Courtesy of the Australian War Memorial)

Throughout the entire New Guinea Offensive Campaign the Americans had continued to work with the Australians to defeat the enemy. This was the first major phase before they were able to achieve their own goal in 1944 as they advanced towards the Philippines.

20/10/1944 Douglas MacArthur lands at Leyte in the Philippines. *(Courtesy of the United States Government)*

After the Battle of Leyte in October 1944 General MacArthur was able to fulfil his promise to return to the Philippines and eventually retake the islands. At the same time, during the largest sea battle of World War II, the Battle of Leyte Gulf, American and Australian naval forces defeated the Japanese Navy, rendering it an ineffective fleet. Japan was now isolated from its source of raw materials that it had previously obtained from its captured territories. In

addition, the Japanese forces in these territories became isolated from support from their homeland.

Although they had no chance of winning the war, the Japanese continued fighting and refused to surrender. After two atomic bombs had been dropped on the Japanese mainland in August 1945 they eventually surrendered unconditionally on the 15th. On 2nd September, as Supreme Allied Commander, Douglas MacArthur accepted the formal surrender of the Japanese on board the USS *Missouri* in Tokyo Bay.

The Americans had remained in Australia for the duration of the war, continuing with the fighting and providing reinforcements, equipment and supplies as well as transport and escort to the war zones.

Political Influence

Many of the US servicemen who arrived here had been conscripts who, unlike the Australia conscripts in the militia, were expected to serve anywhere in the war zone in the defence of a country that was not their own. Many of them made the ultimate sacrifice. They died here either from illnesses or accidents or from failing to recover from their injuries incurred during the fighting.

> *I was a child living in Ipswich during the war. On Cemetery Road, I used to see funeral processions for the American servicemen. The cemetery was very well kept with rows and rows of little white crosses. It was very sad as there was so many of them. After the war, they took the remains back home to America.*
>
> Beryl Savage, June 2011

This disparity in the deployment of conscripts was one of the factors leading to changes in the Australian Defence Act of 1943 whereby the area where the Australian militia could now be sent was extended to anywhere south of the equator within the South West Pacific Zone.

There were other problems. Douglas MacArthur had met often with the Prime Minister, John Curtin, who relied on him for military expertise. Australian General Blamey was rarely consulted. To some, this reliance on the American general was seen as giving up sovereignty to a foreign power. One example of this is censorship. Under the National Security Act of 1939, the Government had the power to impose censorship on all media and private correspondences to protect not just the military, but also to maintain the public morale. This meant, for example, that the real extent of the death and destruction of the bombing of Darwin was withheld from the public. There was a suppression of anything contrary to national security.

After the arrival of General MacArthur, greater demands were made of the censoring authorities, especially in relation to military matters and the media. Eventually, war correspondents could only limit their reports to information supplied from General MacArthur's headquarters. Consequently, in the later part of the war, reports contained mainly material about American operations and very little about the Australian war effort.

Social Impact

For the Australian public, the arrival of the Americans was an invasion of the very best kind. Their presence had a profound impact on the social life of Australians and improved the economy greatly. There were so many American troops stationed in Brisbane during the war that they appeared to dominate the population.

> *The Americans were everywhere, thousands of them, but I only knew a few personally.*
>
> Roy Woolley, March 2011

The American camps could not cope with the numbers and the overflow had to be boarded privately with families. This meant that many Australians came to know individual Americans very well.

> *SP (Shore Patrol) Harry Bailey was a US Naval Police Officer who boarded with my grandmother because there was a lack of lodgings. After my stay in hospital, he bought me a dog to comfort me. I named the dog "Bailey" and he lived with us at Woody Point for many years.*
>
> Marjory Woolley, March 2011

The Generosity of the Americans

They were known to be extremely generous and this was greatly appreciated by a population who had been living with rationing on luxuries for several years.

> *The Americans were especially generous to Aussie children. They gave us lollies in pink tins, which came from their own canteens. We had not seen lollies for a long time.*
>
> Marjory Woolley, March 2011

The Americans could purchase items from their own PX stores to which Australians did not have access. Items such as chocolates, lollies and highly sought after chewing gum were shared with many Australians.

> *There was a US camp at Moorooka near where we lived. The Americans passed by our house every day. For some reason they did not like Australian pennies so they threw them to the kids. They also threw Hershey bars. It was great!*
>
> Anonymous lady, August 2011

Many children were to benefit from their generosity, and it was not just the children in Brisbane. There were large American camps in many parts of Australia, especially Queensland.

> *In Toowoomba during the war, there was a large US camp at Laurel Bank in Herries Street. They walked past my house on their way to the fair next to the Town Hall. I was about seven years old and I used to sit on the front gatepost and say to the US troops "Have you got two bob (shillings), mate?" and they would give it to me! I needed sixpence to get to the movies and three pence for an ice cream, so I had some money left over.*
>
> Bill Carmichael, April 2011

Their generosity was not just limited to the lower ranks. The son of wall signatory Corporal George Edwards had a lucky encounter.

> *My uncle was a bootmaker at Downes Boot Shop in George Street. They often repaired officers' boots. I was four years old when I visited him with my mother. An American officer came in and spoke to me. He gave me two shillings. I was told later that he was General Douglas MacArthur and he was living at Lennon's Hotel in Queen Street at the time.*
>
> Thomas Edwards, son of Wall Signatory Corporal George Edwards, AIF 1942-1945, June 2011

Lifestyle Changes

One of the areas that changed very quickly with the advent of the Americans was the food sector. In order for the food industry to be able to cater for all of the population, including the Americans, new technologies were introduced by their scientists, especially in the canned and dried foods area. Not only were these technologies more efficient in order to feed the increasing number

of visitors, but they also led to a change in types of food that were consumed. Americans enjoyed a large variety of tinned fruit, vegetables and meat. Australia started to shift from English diets like Bully Beef (tinned corned meat) to American styles like hot dogs and hamburgers. The Americans loved ice cream and consumed a lot of it. Restaurants catering to the well-paid Americans were common and now had much longer opening hours.

Entertainment venues, such as cinemas and dance halls, also stayed open longer. Australian cities were now offering entertainment to cater for the servicemen, especially the Americans, who were in the city on leave and often had only limited time in which to relax. The style of entertainment was different for the Americans. One type of music that both the Australians and Americans loved was Big Band and there were many musicians who were happy to provide it.

> *I was a young woman during World War II. I remember dancing the night away with the American G.I.s to the sound of the orchestra playing Glenn Miller's music. You could barely move in that large auditorium at City Hall because there were so many people dancing. It was a magic night!*
>
> Jeanie Griffin *née* Turnbull, November 2011

The Americans introduced Australians to the jitterbug, which was so much livelier than the old fashioned dances. They were regular visitors to City Hall where they could enjoy their dancing and other entertainments while on leave.

> *My three unmarried aunts met a lot of American military men at City Hall where they volunteered in the Red Cross rooms several evenings a week. They volunteered their time to assist the Australian Comforts Fund, which provided meals, dances, outings and other entertainments. The dances were open to all visitors and attracted a lot of American personnel in particular. There were usually more Americans than Australian servicemen visiting City Hall because most of the Australians were stationed outside of Brisbane. On the other hand, there were a lot of US camps in the Brisbane area because Douglas MacArthur had his headquarters here. The Americans were very generous and had lots of money.*
>
> Marjory Woolley, March 2011

Dating the Americans

Many Australian women found the American men very appealing. Their conduct towards the women was regarded as respectful. They were not afraid to show

their regard in public, which was something Australian men would have been reluctant to do.

> *A lot of American soldiers and sailors came to the city. Many young women would go out with them to places like dances, restaurant, zoos and parks. They were absolute gentlemen, nice and considerate, and were better behaved towards the girls than the Australians. They also had a lot of money, but did not spend it on alcohol for the girls as most young women in those days did not drink alcohol. We took a lot of photos of them and gave them little toy koala bears, which they loved. I was asked by one of the men to marry him, but I was too young and too frightened to leave Australia.*
>
> Anonymous lady, May 2011

Many young women did marry American servicemen and after the war followed their husbands to the United States as war brides. The Australian men viewed the Americans as competition and resented the Australian women who dated them. Australian men, although they were often brash, red-blooded and outspoken themselves, maintained a conservative image where women were concerned.

> *Mum recalls that during the war the American troops were in the streets of Brisbane. They were very popular with Aussie girls as they brought gifts of chocolates and stockings. There were often brawls in the city streets between the Americans and the Aussies.*
>
> Rosalind Newlands née Dulley, October 2010

Fighting the Americans

From the moment they arrived the differences between the American and Australian servicemen had been apparent. Marjory Woolley was 10 years old when the Americans arrived in Brisbane in 1942. Her mother would take her to the parades as the Americans marched through the streets of the city.

> *There were great marches of Americans down Adelaide Street past City Hall. The numbers of military men was massive. It was very exciting. We looked in wonder at their beautiful uniforms, which were so different to the baggy khaki uniforms worn by the Australians. The Australians wore thick, baggy uniforms that were very hot. They even wore them in summer. The boots were heavy and cumbersome and clunked as they marched.*
>
> Marjory Woolley, March 2011

Brisbane, undated. American sailors marching in Queen Street. *(Courtesy of the John Oxley Library, State Library of Queensland 81239)*

The Americans were resented not just for their effect on women or for their better uniforms, but also because they were better paid and given preferential service in shops and hotels. By the middle of 1942, for some of the military, this resentment had turned to violence.

> *There were fights between the Americans and the Australians every night in the Valley. On Saturday nights I used to go with my mates to Queen Street in the city. It was also a popular spot for the Americans to gather because this was where MacArthur had his headquarters. A lot of fights happened there between the Australians and the Americans mainly over women, so military police from both armies were constantly on patrol nearby. The main difference between these two groups of police was the fact that the Americans carried batons while the Australians did not. I remember very well running up Queen Street as fast as I could as a young 19-year-old in order to get away from those batons.*
>
> Veteran Peter Lahanas, AIF 1942-1944, October 2010

Brisbane, 1942: Two American military policemen with their batons lean on saltwater pipes used to provide water in case of possible bombing attacks.
(Courtesy of the John Oxley Library, State Library of Queensland 107852)

The men who signed the wall were not immune to fighting the Americans. As his son recalls, Corporal George Edwards had obviously participated in a street fight.

> *My father arrived home one night with his hand in plaster. The family was really worried until we found out how he did it. He had broken it on "some Yank's jaw".*
>
> Thomas Edwards, son of Wall Signatory Corporal George Edwards, AIF 1942-1945, June, 2011

In November 1942, the tensions culminated in a major fight between the two forces, known as the Battle of Brisbane, where one Australian soldier was killed and many others were injured, some seriously. This event, which involved thousands of servicemen from both countries, was heavily censored in the press.

On Racial Segregation

There were many African American servicemen who came to Australia. They were subject to discrimination and often their duties were to provide labour for occupations such as medical sanitation and air base-security. They had their own recreational bands but did not participate in official ones due to segregation. Although they had certain freedoms, their movements were strictly controlled by city authorities.

> *The black US troops were only allowed south of the Brisbane River. They were not allowed into the city.*
>
> Marjory Woolley, March 2011

Australia's Indigenous population had been involved in both the military and the civilian war effort. However, they were influenced greatly by the better skills, higher pay and greater civil rights of the African Americans and saw possibilities for their own future. The American presence would have a lasting effect, especially in this area.

The American Signatories

There are at least nine American contributions to the graffiti on the wall. In common with the Australians contributions, many of the American signatures are hard to read.

C. J. Earl? USA, in American Cursive. *(Image Copyright Brisbane City Council)*

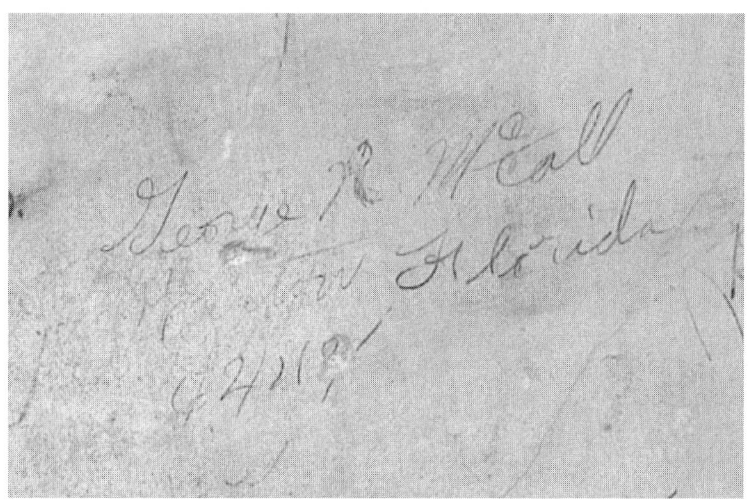

George R McCall,----ow? Florida, 6/2/42. *(Image Copyright Brisbane City Council)*

Ralph Pieck, Ruthven, Iowa. *(Image Copyright Brisbane City Council)*

Daniel Harris, Tampa, Florida, USA. *(Image Copyright Brisbane City Council)*

Some Americans left drawings.

This drawing may be a self-portrait of the man from Fort Monmouth, New Jersey, or could it possibly be "Uncle Sam"? *(Image Copyright Brisbane City Council)*

This is a drawing of an American soldier with the initials E.D.H. beneath the name of Pvt. Ralph Bolio, SCPC, Aug 22/42 of Long Island, New York. *(Image Copyright Brisbane City Council)*

Sometimes the meanings are a little unclear.

Flatbush Floogie *(Image Copyright Brisbane City Council)*

The term *Floogie* was a convenient alternative to the word *Floosie*. In 1938, a very popular jazz song called Flat Foot Floogie was released in America and was played constantly into the 1940s. It was originally called Flat Foot Floosie but the name was modified in order for it to be permitted to be played on radio. Floosie is an American colloquialism for a woman of indeterminate morals and this word was not allowed to be aired in public. This particular Floogie comes from Flatbush which is an area in New York.

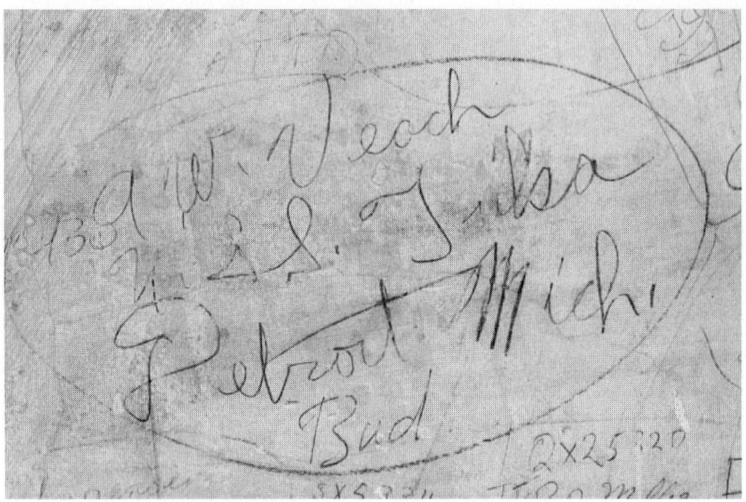

A.W. Veach, USS Tulsa, Detroit Mich. Bud. *(Image Copyright Brisbane City Council)*

Mr Veach has provided the largest American signature on the wall and also the most information. By using computer sources, he is thought to be Aldon Wardell Veach from Detroit, Michigan. His nickname is "Bud". He has provided the name of his ship, the USS *Tulsa*, which first visited Brisbane in March 1942 for repairs at South Brisbane's dry dock.

The USS *Tulsa* and the *PT-109*

The USS *Tulsa* was a veteran gunboat and one of only three American surface ships to arrive safely in Australia from the Philippines at the beginning of the Pacific War. She was equipped as a convoy escort vessel and also as a towing vessel for practice targets for submarines. She was based in Brisbane at the end of 1942, and later returned to the war zone providing escort duty and supplies to Buna and Milne Bay and other places in Papua New Guinea.

USS Tulsa: April 1941 *(Courtesy of the United States Navy)*

In 1943 the *Tulsa* served as the flagship of the 7th Fleet and tendered PT boats. One of these Patrol Torpedo boats was the *PT-109,* which was commanded from the 23/4/43 by Lieutenant John Kennedy. It performed mainly night-time operations sinking Japanese supply barges in the waters east of New Guinea. On the 2nd of August 1943, the *PT-109* was rammed and sunk by a Japanese destroyer. Most of the crew were eventually rescued from a nearby island. Many years after the war, the captain of the *PT-109* went on to become the American President, John Fitzgerald Kennedy.

The American Legacy

From a military standpoint, the Americans were here when Australia needed them. Australia and America's goals, such as maintaining liberty, equality and freedom, had been the same. The two countries have fought alongside each other in many instances since World War II in order to protect these ideals. In September 1951, a formal military alliance known as the ANZUS Treaty was signed, which provided for military assistance should either Australia, New Zealand or the United States need it. In 1985, the United States suspended its treaty obligations to New Zealand, but has maintained a close co-operation with Australia. Australia supported the Americans in Afghanistan and became the largest non-NATO contributor of troops to fight the Taliban. Every year both nations commemorate the Battle of the Coral Sea in celebrations organised by the Australian-American Organisation and many Americans visit Australia at this time. Recently, American Marines have been involved in joint training exercises in the Northern Territory with Australian soldiers. General Douglas MacArthur's Brisbane Headquarters have now been made into a museum.

The political ties with the United States have remained stable since World War II. During the war, Eleanor Roosevelt, the Head of the American Red Cross

and wife of the American President, came to Brisbane's City Hall and thanked the people for their contribution to the war effort. Four American Presidents have visited Australia since then. In 2011, the Australian Prime Minister, Julia Gillard, was given the honour of being invited to address the American Congress. She emphasised the strong ties between the two countries.

Brisbane, 1943: Eleanor Roosevelt is welcomed at the steps of City Hall.
(Courtesy of the John Oxley Library, State Library of Queensland 444907)

The social legacy is also very strong. Australia's experience with the Americans during the war had opened up new ideas for lifestyle changes and there were now many more choices available. The population had been quite prepared for the American cultural onslaught in the 50s when television was introduced with so many American programs. American culture was here to stay.

The American presence during the war had facilitated the move that Australia made from being a primarily conservative society to becoming a more liberal one. This paved the way for the multicultural society that was to come in later years.

CHAPTER 13

HOMECOMING AND DISCHARGE

I was overjoyed when I knew that I was going to be discharged. It meant that I could go home.

Wall Signatory Ronald Hughes, AIF 1940-1944, as told to his wife, Florence. January 2012

The war in Europe had ended on the 8th of May 1945 when the German High Command surrendered unconditionally to the Allies. This has been referred to ever since as VE Day, meaning Victory in Europe. There were scenes of rejoicing all over the world, not the least in Australia. However, the Australian people's joy was moderated by the fact that the war in the Pacific was still very active.

The Japanese had continued fighting despite their heavy losses in terms of both men and territory. They did not surrender until after atomic bombs had been dropped on Hiroshima and Nagasaki in early August 1945. The devastation caused by the bombings showed all too clearly that their only option was to surrender. To the Japanese, surrender was an anathema, an accursed thing and a cultural taboo. During the fighting, many Japanese had chosen death rather than surrendering to the Allies. It was therefore viewed as humiliating to the nation when Emperor Hirohito broadcasted Japan's unconditional surrender on the 15th of August 1945, using the words "a settlement has been reached". This day is now called VP Day for Victory in the Pacific, but many people refer to it as VJ Day for Victory against Japan.

Brisbane, August 1945: Group of soldiers, three men and two women celebrating, VJ Day in the Botanic Gardens. *(Courtesy of the John Oxley Library, State Library of Queensland 67959)*

The formal act of surrender was signed on board the American battleship USS *Missouri* in Tokyo Bay on 2/9/45 by the Japanese Foreign Minister, Shigemitsu, and the Supreme Commander of Allied Powers, General Douglas MacArthur. General Thomas Blamey also signed as Australia's representative. This day is celebrated by the Americans as VJ Day.

It took several weeks for the individual pockets of Japanese forces in outlying areas to surrender officially. In some places there was no surrender at all as the Japanese refused to accept that defeat was a reality.

> *My father, Sergeant George Noffke, told the family how the Japanese in isolated areas such as Bougainville kept fighting for many weeks after the war had ended. They had thought that the Emperor's speech telling them that the war was over was an Allied trick. They could not believe that Japan had really surrendered.*
>
> Robert Noffke, son of Sergeant George Noffke, AIF 1941-1946,
> April 2012

General Blamey accepted the surrender of the Japanese forces on Morotai Island on 9/9/45. He made a very famous speech that summed up how Australians viewed the preceding four years. He had listed the role that Japan had played and the atrocities that had been committed as well as pointing out that the Allies would treat them fairly. This is an excerpt from his speech.

> *In receiving your surrender I do not recognise you as an honourable and gallant foe, but you will be treated with due but severe courtesy in all matters.*
>
> General Thomas Blamey, Morotai Island, 9/9/45
> (Courtesy of the Australian War Memorial)

The Australian people had waited for a long time to hear such a speech.

The Long Wait

The war had lasted for six long years. Australians had endured more hardships than they could ever have expected.

> *Life had been suspended during the war. It had been very rough with the shortages and rationing of everything.*
>
> Gloria Brosnan *née* Sherriff, August 2011

One of the worst aspects was the lack of knowledge about what was happening. For the people at home who were waiting for news of their loved ones, any news had been welcomed.

> *As a child, I was not told a great deal about the war. All I really knew was that my father had gone away to join the fighting. He had been with the Light Horse in Eidsvold, and then in July 1941 he and the other men from his unit went to Gympie and joined the Army (AIF). After he left we worried about him a lot as there was very little news about him. We had no idea where he was, but sometimes he would just turn up on our doorstep without any warning. His leave was unpredictable and communication was poor. We found out later that he had been with the Paga Battery in Port Moresby and then in the Lae region of New Guinea.*
>
> Marjory Woolley *née* Johnson, daughter of Corporal Robert Johnson, AIF 1941-1945, March 2011.

For wives and sweethearts, the long separations posed extra difficulties. The wife of wall signatory Ronald Hughes explains:

> *For the last years of the war the family did not know where my husband Ronald was stationed. We had letters from him, but he never told us where he was. We found out later that he had been on Horn Island in the Torres Strait protecting the airstrip. When he finally came home we were like strangers because we had not seen each other for so long. We had been married since 1942.*
>
> Florence Hughes *née* Keir, wife of Wall Signatory Ronald Hughes, AIF 1940-1944, January 2012.

For some the waiting for news lasted long after the war. Madeline Blyth lost two brothers in very sad circumstances.

> *My brother, Leading Aircraftman John Eagar, died on 11/11/1940 when an old balcony gave way while he was celebrating with his mates at a local club. They had just finished a RAAF training course at Narromine in New South Wales. My other brother, Acting Sub Lieutenant Alexander Eagar, died one year later on 20/11/1941 when the HMAS Sydney disappeared off the West Australian coast. He was declared MIA (Missing in Action) and presumed dead. We did not know where the ship was until the wreck was discovered in 2008. The waiting had been awful, but at least we finally knew what had happened.*
>
> Madeline Blyth *née* Eagar, sister of Kingsley John Eagar, RAAF 1940, and Alexander Eagar, RAN 1939-1941, November 2011

For the thousands of men overseas, the waiting had also been extremely hard. They found ways to occupy their time.

> *As part of the trench art, the men made Sweetheart Badges from their uniforms or anything else they could get their hands on. These badges were modelled on the Rising Sun images on their hats. They sent them to their female loved ones back home, especially if they thought that they would not be returning.*
>
> Edna Bate, November 2011

A Day of Uncontrolled Jubilation

Whether civilian or in the military, at home or overseas, there were scenes of jubilation when the war finally ended. Those who were very young at the time remember it clearly.

> *The happiest day of my life was VJ Day when the Japanese surrendered. I was 10 years old. We were at Deception Bay and my family joined with other families on the beach to celebrate. We lit a huge bonfire from bushes and old tyres and anything else we could find. It could be seen from as far away as Moreton Island. Afterwards we had a sing-song.*
>
> Viv Tucker, November 2011

A schoolgirl remembered coming into the city and witnessing the elated crowds.

> *On VJ Day, I came into Brisbane after school by tram. I was about 10 years old and had a relative with me. I remember seeing Evie Hayes singing from the Adelaide Street corner balcony of City Hall. The street was filled with an ecstatic crowd and they were all so excited and singing together. Everyone was kissing and hugging each other. It was a really big day.*
>
> Anonymous lady, August 2011

Queensland rural centres were not left out of the celebrations. Many of the coastal towns had once been in danger of a Japanese attack.

> *On VJ Day, I was a student at the Yeppoon Boarding School. The whole school celebrated by taking the day off and going on a huge picnic in the park. We had a really good time.*
>
> Anonymous Lady, August 2011

Townsville had been a major military centre and had been attacked on several occasions. There were thousands of Australian and American servicemen stationed there. The celebrations were enormous.

> *In Townsville on VJ Day, I was a teenager working in an office. All of the workers streamed out of the offices and shops and went to Flinders Street. Workers, soldiers, sailors and perfect strangers joined together for singing and dancing. Strangers were kissing strangers. There were a lot of American soldiers who joined in.*
>
> Gloria Brosnan *née* Sherriff, August 2011

There were victory marches organised all over Australia on VJ Day as well as for many months afterwards. The people turned out in their thousands to watch the parades as hundreds of men and women in uniform marched to the beat of military bands. This is a part of military tradition that the public really enjoyed no less then as they do today.

Brisbane, August 1945: Army band leads a procession of soldiers on VJ Day.
(Courtesy of the John Oxley Library, State Library of Queensland 151455)

As well as music, it was inevitable that food would play a large part of the celebrations. For soldiers who had lived on basic army rations for the past few years, there would be no better way to celebrate than by enjoying a feast. Rationing was forgotten for a short time as cooks provided the best they could from what was available. Men on Tarakan Island, for instance, dined on suckling pig on a spit, chickens and fish *(Courtesy of the Australian War Memorial).*

Throughout all of the victory celebrations, there was a sombre note. A sapper from the Royal Australian Engineers who was in New Guinea on VJ Day has his say:

> *I couldn't believe it! I just couldn't believe it! Bloody marvellous! I just wished it had come sooner.*
>
> Anonymous Veteran, AIF 1939-1945, April 2012

Comments from other veterans are also tinged with sadness. Wall signatory Walter Huggonson revealed how he and his mates felt:

> *Everyone was absolutely delighted of course, but we remembered that there had been lots of tragedy.*
>
> Wall Signatory Walter Huggonson, AIF 1941-1944, April 2012

Another wall signatory gave his honest opinion to his wife:

> *My husband told me that the war was a very sad time, but a good time for being with his mates. His mates were wonderful. They were everything. Some of them did not come home and he missed them very much.*
>
> Iris Veigel, wife of Wall Signatory Private James Veigel, AIF 1942-1945, February 2012

So many Australians had been killed during the war and there were many who had been injured or succumbed to illnesses and diseases. Services were conducted wherever possible to give thanksgiving for the victory and to remember the men who had fallen. Thankfully, all of the 155 men identified on the wall had come back alive.

HOMECOMING

Now the troops could start coming home. For some the homecoming was especially emotional, as seen through the eyes of a 13-year-old girl:

> *The ship Largs Bay carried my brother, Geoffrey Harris, and other men from Changi home to Brisbane. The ex-prisoners of war were taken through the streets in any available vehicle. Open cars were the best as then people could throw flowers into the vehicle and try to reach them to touch the men. My family raced to the car to hug my brother. When he looked at me he said, "Who's the girl?" I*

had been just a small child when he left and we had not seen each other for so long.

Myra O'Shea *née* Harris, sister of Private Geoffrey Harris, AIF 1940-1946, August 2011

It was only to be expected that the war had made changes to the men.

When he came home, it was apparent that he was not the same man who went away to war. He said that seeing his mates being shot and falling down changed him. There was no counselling in those days. We were married six months after he returned.

Irene Kastrissios, wife of Lance Corporal Charles Kastrissios, AIF 1944-1945, July 2012

My family told me that Dad never smoked or drank before the war, but he did by the time he returned home from New Guinea.

Ann Rammerath *née* Kastrissios, daughter of Lance Corporal Charles Kastrissios, AIF 1944-1945, July 2012

For some of the families, the thought of any further separation was too hard to bear.

Dad (Flight Lieutenant William Dulley) returned from England in 1944, but stayed on the Active List with the RAAF until August 1945. He was then offered the chance of training with KLM Royal Dutch Airlines, which was reaching out into South-East Asia, and I assume establishing a base in Indonesia. Mum won on that one, as she didn't want him leaving home or flying overseas any more.

Ros Newlands *née* Dulley, daughter of Flight Lieutenant William Dulley, RAAF 1941-1945, September 2010

DISCHARGE

In World War II, more than 993,000 people served in the military. The enormous task of discharging so many personnel soon became apparent. In this non-computer age, processing was done manually and was extremely time-consuming. A lot of details had to be obtained, which included rank, unit, number of dependants and other personal information. Length of full-time service in either the AIF or the militia, time spent in active service both within and outside of Australia, and the whereabouts of their operational service

overseas were all included. These details contributed to the eventual payout at discharge and the issuing of medals and badges.

Early Discharge

There were 55 men on the wall who had been given an early discharge (35.48%). The reasons for the timing of an individual soldier's discharge were based on many factors. The most obvious reason for early discharge while the war was still in progress was based on medical grounds. Any soldier who was severely injured, disabled or regarded as medically unfit was eligible for early discharge. The reason for Private Martin's early discharge on 6/2/42, nine days prior to the fall of Singapore on the 15/2/42, is unknown, but his unit (2/26th Infantry Battalion, 8th Division) had been fighting the Japanese in Malaya just a few weeks previously. He had possibly been severely injured or was perhaps suffering from an illness. If he had stayed in Malaya he most probably would have been killed or captured like most of the 8th Division.

Craftsman Harrington was found to have seizures and was discharged on 21/3/44 with a medical classification of D, i.e., *permanently unfit for military service*. He was considered a suitable case for repatriation, so his pay and conditions were extended until 17/5/44. Similarly, Walter Huggonson was put into repatriation and given an early discharge on 24/11/44 after being severely burnt in an accident. Thomas Newman, who had been shot in the shoulder, was unable to return to his infantry unit due to his injury. He applied for an early discharge to work on his father's cattle property, which was considered an essential industry, and was discharged on 25/11/43.

CASE STUDY NUMBER 25

NEWMAN, THOMAS NEVILLE ORCHARD, QX29353, PRIVATE

Thomas Newman, 21, was employed as a grazier on his father's property at Tara in Queensland when he enlisted into the AIF in January 1942. He was sent to the 7th Training Battalion at Redbank and then transferred to the 7th Pioneer Company. In June he went to Goondiwindi as a volunteer for the RAAF Air Crew for three weeks. He transferred to the 2/25th Infantry Battalion in October and in December he went to the Advanced Reinforcement Training Camp (ARTC) at Canungra. This was followed by more training in February 1943 with the New Guinea Advanced Reinforcement Depot (NGARD). He was then sent to New Guinea and was transferred the 2/7th Infantry Battalion.

On 29/4/43, while the battalion was participating in the push towards Salamaua in the Huon Gulf in New Guinea, Private Newman was wounded in action. He sustained a gunshot wound to his right shoulder joint. He was evacuated by the 2/2nd

Field Ambulance and taken overnight to the 2/9th Australian General Hospital in Port Moresby. He was then evacuated by air to Townsville, Queensland and then to hospital in Brisbane. His medical classification was assessed by the Medical Board on 12/10/43 as being B which meant restricted medical fitness. He was sent to Redbank in November and was discharged on 25/11/43. The reason given for his early discharge was "To enable him to take up employment in an Industry or Occupation". The production of food, in this case, meat, was seen as an essential industry. He stated on his Release to Industry Form on 10/11/43 that he desired to return to manage the property due to his father's age (72 years).

Private Thomas Newman was in Brisbane initially from 31/1/42 until 8/6/42. He wrote on the wall "Pte T.N.O. Newman, Tara" in an oval with the word "Mates" and the name of his mate, "Pte R.D. McLeod, Tara".

Towards the end of 1943 when the immediate threat of a Japanese invasion had abated, men considered to be in essential industries were often given an early "Discharge to Industry". Many of the men listed on the wall had worked in the food-production industries prior to the war. Cyril Jorgensen, who had worked in the sugar industry, was discharged on 7/3/44. Mervyn Streeter was discharged on 12/4/44 to continue with his dairy farming, and Gordon Greenhalgh, a butcher, was discharged on 20/9/45 just a few weeks after the war ended. This provided manpower and helped to relieve the pressure on the civilian population, who had undergone severe wartime rationing.

CASE STUDY NUMBER 26

JORGENSEN, CYRIL EDWARD, QX29624, GUNNER

Cyril Jorgensen, a labourer from Esk in Queensland, enlisted in the AIF in Brisbane on 27/12/41 at the age of 18. Originally classified medically as Class I, he was later classified at the Redbank Reinforcement Depot as Class II, which meant that he was fit for specified duty for which a particular disability was no bar. The reason for this change is unknown. He was attached for duty to the 101st Convalescent Depot at Coorparoo. In February, he was admitted to the Camp Hospital at the Exhibition Grounds for nine days suffering from influenza. Upon his release he was sent back to the 101st Convalescent Depot for one week, but this time it was for his own convalescence. In March he was sent to Grovely, where he underwent gunnery training with the 17th Field Regiment.

On 21/9/42, Gunner Jorgensen was granted leave without pay from his regiment in order to do "sugar work", which as a labourer,

this most probably meant cane cutting and general fieldwork. He was placed on the X list until he returned to duty on 28/1/43. In June he was transferred to the 5th Field Regiment and was sent by train, arriving in the Northern Territory in July. In early January 1944 he spent several weeks at the Headquarters of the Northern Territory Forces until February when he returned to Queensland.

While in Brisbane he was given an early "Release to Industry" and was eventually discharged at Redbank on 7/3/44. The sugar industry was seen as one of the vital and essential industries that provided food to the nation and it needed manpower. Cyril Jorgensen had been working in the Bundaberg area at the time of his enlistment and could now return to his former employment.

He had been stationed at Grovely for a period from 20/3/42 until 6/5/42, during which time he most probably signed the wall. He wrote "Gunny Cyril Edward Jorgensen, QX 29624, Grovely, Bundaberg". At a later date, he wrote his name for a second time, simply adding "Grovely" to his signature.

Fifteen of the soldiers who had been discharged early had been born in 1913 or earlier, so age may have been a contributing factor. At the other end of the scale, one of the youngest men on the wall, Private Sansky, was also given an early discharge on 15/4/44 but the reason is unknown. He was 19 years old. Sergeant Scott had enlisted early in the war on 27/11/39 and therefore had a very long service record, which was most probably a factor in his early release on 31/7/45.

General Demobilisation Process

After the Japanese surrender on 15/8/45, the task of general demobilisation began. The Volunteer Defence Corps was disbanded immediately and its members waited to be demobbed. There were often long delays while the men and women waited for their turn to be demobilised. They needed to make out an application for discharge and to wait for the determination of demobilisation priority. Discharges were conducted on this priority basis and according to a strict set of criteria.

Many soldiers who had specialist war qualifications, such as parachutist Private Jones, were transferred to other less-specialised units with a subsequent loss of proficiency pay. The normal process was for men to be gradually transferred to other units, sometimes to several other units, until it was their turn to be demobbed. In each State, the Leave and Transit Depot (LTD) and the General Details Depot (GDD) arranged for most of these transfers. Staff Sergeant Hanley was sent to Sandy Creek in South Australia to assist with the prisoners of war before he was eventually demobilised at Hampstead on 27/11/45. Sergeant Rice became a staff member for the Queensland Lines of

Communication before his discharge on 27/3/46. In Queensland, most of the demobilisation process was conducted at Redbank Camp.

Some men were kept on for many months during 1946, especially the NCOs, to supervise the men who were waiting to leave and to oversee the clean-up operations in Australia and overseas. This was referred to as occupational duties. They also helped to re-establish former battle zones to return them to normal as soon as possible. Warrant Officer James Cross remained at Lae until 20/05/46 for this reason.

From 15/8/45 until the end of 1946, 93 of the men on the wall (60%) had been demobilised. Except for five men who elected to stay with the army, the rest were demobbed by the end of 1947. Private Bancks elected to stay with the CMF for many years after the war.

From 1945 until 1952, Australia supplied a contingent to the occupational forces in Japan. At its peak, this contingent was 12,000 strong and was responsible for the military operations mainly in the Hiroshima Prefecture. This number decreased in 1950 when the United Nations directed Australian forces to operations in Korea.

Medals and Badges

The entitlement of medals and badges was also listed at discharge. Medals were of two types. The first were medals issued in recognition of gallantry or conspicuous acts of bravery. There is no mention of any of the men on the wall having been issued with these medals, although many of their units were given Battle Honours.

The other type of medal was the Campaign/Service Medal. Every man on the wall should have received one or more of these. There are strict conditions for the issuing of these medals based on time spent in specific areas and the type of service. There were 11 types of World War II Campaign/Service Medals issued. These are the 1939/45 Star, the Atlantic Star, the Air Crew Europe Star, the African Star, the Pacific Star, the Burma Star, the Italy Star, the France and Germany Star, the Defence Medal, the War Medal and the Australian Service Medal. Clasps and emblems which signified additional service were also listed at the time of discharge.

Acting Sergeant George Weston had problems claiming at least two of his medals. After the war ended and while he was still serving in the Dutch East Indies, he made an application to the Defence Department for the 1939/45 Star and the Pacific Star. He was eligible for both medals and was eventually issued with them. Altogether he received five medals, including the Defence Medal, the War Medal and the Australian Service Medal. One of the other men on the wall, Gilbert Myers, received a total of six medals, including the African Star because he had served in Egypt and the Middle East as well as the South West

Pacific Area. He is listed in the Nominal Roll as being a private in the 26th Field Baking Platoon, yet he had earned most of his medals while in combat with the 2/33rd Infantry Battalion. Like so many soldiers, his records do not give a true indication of his contribution to the war effort.

There were two main type of badges issued. There was the General Service Badge for personnel who did not go into operational areas overseas, and the Returned from Active Service Badge for those who did. It was normal procedure to calculate Active Service in an operational area from the date that the soldier left Australia to when he returned. The Northern Territory was also considered to be an operational area because of the frequent attacks by the enemy and its proximity to the war zone. These badges were issued directly upon discharge and were inscribed with a number that was specific to the recipient. Medals generally took longer to be issued than badges.

All military decorations were worn or displayed according to strict guidelines. These rules are still followed today.

As was the case in World War I, the wife and the mother (or the nearest female relative) of military personnel on active service overseas could ask to be issued with a Female Relatives Badge. These badges were inscribed with "To the Women of Australia" and, in the case of mothers, had stars attached that denoted the number of their children on active service. Both Sergeant Loveday's wife and mother applied for this badge, which had one star. George Weston's mother was issued with a badge with two stars as George's brother Ken was also on active service.

> *When I was a kid during the war I used to see the mothers and wives of servicemen in the bus on their way to the city. They were knitting mittens and socks for their boys overseas. They wore their Female Relatives badges proudly and chatted among themselves constantly about the war.*
>
> Viv Tucker, November 2011

After the War

As a result of their wartime service, veterans have been able to maintain contact with the numerous associations and services provided for their benefit. These include the Department of Veterans' Affairs, Repatriation, Pensions, Legacy, War Service Homes, War Service Loans, Remembrance Day and Anzac Day activities, Unit Associations and RSLs, to name just a few.

For the soldiers, life began to get back to normal, but they had to make up for lost time. Getting a job, getting married, starting a family and finding somewhere to live were all very high on the agenda. The era of the baby boomers was about to begin.

> *My sister was born in October 1945. Due to a shortage of accommodation they all had to stay with my grandmother who lived on the river at New Farm. In 1947 they moved into their new house at Wavell Heights, which was a new estate then and regarded as being "a fair way out". Mum recalls that it was hard to get light fittings, etc. in new houses due to shortages and there were few choices in style. Surrounding suburbs such as Stafford and Zillmere were set up as low-cost war-service housing estates as there was such a housing shortage. Apparently our home in Wavell Heights was obtained through a war-service loan but Mum was quick to add that it was it was not a war-service home. It was independently built.*
>
> Ros Newlands *née* Dulley September 2010

After the war, wall signatory Herbert Dull married and became the father of nine children. His granddaughter has supplied a copy of his memoirs where he had written that he had "a very fortunate army life".

He had fulfilled his commitment to his family life just as he had fulfilled his commitment to his country during the war. This was the pattern followed by many of the soldiers on the wall.

Herbert Dull AIF 1941-1944. *(Courtesy of Rebecca Dull 2011)*

"Sapper Herb Dull, Gabba". *(Image Copyright Brisbane City Council)*

CHAPTER 14

CONCLUSION

This wall is a really important find. At first glance it resembles a collection of unrelated names and numbers, but it is far more than it appears. Since its discovery in 2008 it has been a source of valuable information. It has provided a glimpse into an important period of Australia's history when lives were disrupted and the future was unknown. From the moment of their enlistment these men became part of history although many of them would not have realised it at the time. Some had already made history by the time they arrived in Brisbane. For others their contributions to history was yet to come. Each man had his own story to tell.

When they wrote on the wall they conveniently supplied a small and select list of men who could be researched in detail from army records and other sources. Extensive research has revealed several main aspects about themselves and about the war. The majority of them were young Queensland country boys who came to Brisbane to enlist. There is also a long list of experienced men who were in Brisbane to train or who were just passing through. Several of the men were born overseas, but decided to join the Australian Army to fight the enemy.

There is a very large depth of experience that is represented by these men. Their various military positions cover nearly all of the occupational areas available in the army. From their units and deployments, it can be seen that they were connected to practically every important event that involved Australian land forces during those six momentous years. The timeline has shown that several historic events were often running concurrently and in various locations on two fronts. The logistics of providing both men and supplies was a gigantic team effort requiring a very large section of the army. This is where the Lost Legion really shined.

Many of their activities were conducted in deprived or even primitive conditions where death and disease were prevalent. From the men in the 26 case studies it is known that three were shot by the enemy and one was wounded in a firearms accident. From these statistics alone it could be assumed that many more of the 155 men on the wall were also affected by gunshot wounds.

In the face of adversity, the men depended on each other. The famous Australian Digger character is well exemplified by the number of examples of mateship on the wall. It is easy to imagine them banding together to have a night out and being just a little bit daring. The fact that the wall exists at all can be attributed to this very human aspect of these alleged miscreants writing their graffiti. Unlike books, photographs and memorials, the writing is a tangible contact with real people, real places and real times. It is this direct connection to the past that is felt by many of the visiting public.

The American signatures written alongside their Australian allies could be classified as one of the earliest examples of the beginning of a special

relationship that continues today. Their presence not only provided security at the time, but also prepared Australia for the future.

The fact that only servicemen's names are written here shows that the civilian population had a great respect for the men in uniform and refrained from writing their own names, leaving it solely as the Soldiers' Wall. It remains as an unofficial and unintentional Honour Board for these men.

The Soldiers' Wall has provided a solid picture of the soldiers' world. The willingness of other veterans, their relatives and members of the public to provide information about the war has provided a true account of many of the aspects about civilian and military life. They endured a massive lifestyle change for six years to ensure that the Australian way of life continued in a free society. The fact that so many of the older contributors wished to remain anonymous demonstrates the humility of the age, when people did not put themselves forward but were content to remain in the background. Yet it was this humble generation that took on the awesome responsibility of defending first the Commonwealth and then Australia itself. They did not see themselves as heroes.

> *There are all kinds of heroes. By simply doing his duty, every soldier is a hero in his own way. They were all heroes, but not every act of heroism was witnessed or acknowledged.*
>
> Sally Iliff, October 2010

In the future, there are many more stories to be revealed as more of their records become available. These men are still serving their country, but in a very different way to anything they could ever have imagined as they continue to provide a glimpse of their world to new generations.

APPENDIX 1

SOLDIERS' WALL MAP

	← 46 CMS →	← 46 CMS →	← 48 CMS →	← 46 CMS →	← 46 CMS →	
	UPPER FAR LEFT	**UPPER LEFT**	**UPPER CENTRE**	**UPPER RIGHT**	**UPPER FAR RIGHT**	
UPPER ↑ 34 CMS ↓	Casey Miller,K.D. McGill O'Conner	Hobbs A. Jackson Hughes	Floyd	Huggonson Cook Harrington Newman Leigh McLeod Dendie	Beinke Freebury Werner Pemble	↑
MID ↑ 34 CMS	Drake **MID FAR LEFT** Cross Hill Streeter Wallace Vallis	**MID LEFT** Fletcher Spry Veigel Parkinson McEwen Harris's Rangers Davy,C	**MID CENTRE** N20688 Myers Marshall Abrahams McDonald	**MID RIGHT** Faulkner Edwards Gosper Davy,D. Melrose Francis Veach	**MID FAR RIGHT** Lawrence Dixon Rice/Doolan Scott Davie Beutel Davie Jones Reid Henson	1.02 METRES
LOWER ↑ 34 CMS	Dobbin **LOWER FAR LEFT** Beutel Dull McDuff Lee	**LOWER LEFT** Harrison McNaughton Greenhalgh Friend Jorgensen Weston	Nothing **LOWER CENTRE** Yet Caldow Loveday Sankey	**LOWER RIGHT** Miller, R Saxby Jorgensen Robinson Kurkowski	**LOWER FAR RIGHT** Hanley Large Face	
			BELOW BOARD (BB)			
↓	Harvatt Bowman	GUNALDA BOYS	Chaplin Jacobson	Chocolate Beutel Kid	Snell N. Smith	↓
	FAR LEFT	LEFT	CENTRE	RIGHT	FAR RIGHT	

← 2.32 METRES →

LIST OF SOLDIERS' IDENTIFICATIONS

Location of Signatures

The wall has been divided into five vertical sections in order to facilitate the finding of specific signatures. These are far left, left, centre, right and far right. There are also three horizontal levels – upper level, mid-level or lower-level. BB means the signature is located below the horizontal base board. The stated location of the signature is as close as possible to the relevant section, but may overlap into another section. Some soldiers have more than one entry.

Identity of Soldiers' Signatures

The actual place of enlistment is stated first, followed by the place of residence at the time of enlistment in brackets. NOK means next of kin. The National Archives of Australia bar code is provided as well as an indication of the availability of digital records.

ABRAHAMS, ARTHUR EDWARD, NX72282, SIGNALMAN MID CENTRE
DOB 27/3/20, CANDELO, NSW
ENLISTED 27/3/41, PADDINGTON, NSW (UNKNOWN)
NOK, ABRAHAMS, ARTHUR
DISCHARGED 11/1/44, 2/1st MACHINE GUN BATTALION
BAR CODE 4660395
WROTE "GUNNY A.E. ABRAHAMS, 2/1 A.M.G. BATTALION, BNE, C COY, AIF, AUSTRALIA, HOME STATE BEGA NSW" (CANDELO AND BEGA SHARE THE SAME POSTCODE).

ANDERSON, GORDON, Q122208, PRIVATE MID FAR LEFT
DOB 10/12/23, BRISBANE, QLD
ENLISTED 2/2/42, BRISBANE, QLD (UNKNOWN)
NOK, BOURNE, ARTHUR
DISCHARGED 26/10/42, 25th INFANTRY BATTALION
BAR CODE 4450396
WROTE "PTE G ANDERSON, Q122208, 25 BTY, A COY, FROM GAYTHORNE, REDBANK, EUMUNDI, CHERMSIDE, TOWNSVILLE". LOCATED LEFT OF HARRIS.

ARNOLD, LLOYD JAMES, QX29335, SERGEANT UPPER MID CENTRE
DOB 21/4/19, DALBY, QLD
ENLISTED 10/1/42, BRISBANE, QLD (TARA, QLD)
NOK, ARNOLD, JAMES
DISCHARGED 28/5/46, 2/2nd PORT OPERATING COMPANY
BAR CODE 4920233

WROTE "QX29335, L.J. ARNOLD, MOUNT PERRY, TARA---DALBY". VERY FAINT, LOCATED LEFT OF FLOYD.

BAKER, PERCIVAL WILLIAM, QX27531, GUNNER MID LEFT

DOB 25/9/22, MACKAY, QLD

ENLISTED 11/2/42, BRISBANE, QLD (MACKAY, QLD)

NOK, BAKER, ETHEL

DISCHARGED 22/6/44, 57th ANTI AIRCRAFT REGIMENT (COMPOSITE) LE

BAR CODE 4855496

WROTE "QX27531, GNR P.W. BAKER, AIF, GROVELY". VERY FAINT, LOCATED RIGHT OF McEWEN.

BANCKS, LINDSAY RONALD, Q147661, PRIVATE LOWER CENTRE, BB

DOB, UNKNOWN

UNIT – 22nd INFANTRY BATTALION, CITIZENS MILITARY FORCES

BAR CODE 8138673

LONG-SERVING CMF MEMBER, REMAINED IN THE CMF UNTIL LONG AFTER THE WAR HAD ENDED

WROTE "Q 147661, PTE L.R. BANCKS, WARWICK, 30.8.42". IDENTITY CONFIRMED BY NATIONAL ARCHIVES OF AUSTRALIA.

BEINKE, SIDNEY MERVYN, SX12050, PRIVATE UPPER FAR RIGHT

DOB 3/11/19, PT LINCOLN, SA

ENLISTED 31/3/41, WAYVILLE, SA (STIRLING NTH, SA)

NOK, BEINKE, FREAA

DISCHARGED 18/6/45, 9th DETENTION BARRACKS

BAR CODE 6402727

WROTE "S.M. BEINKE, SX12050, 2/10 CON DEPOT".

BETTS, HUGH BEN, QX24508, CORPORAL UPPER RIGHT

DOB 6/6/18, BUNDABERG, QLD

ENLISTED 13/11/41, BRISBANE, QLD (NORTH KOLAN, QLD)

NOK, BETTS, WILLIAM

DISCHARGED 8/4/46, 5th MOVEMENT CONTROL GROUP

BAR CODE 4483328

WROTE "QX24508, PTE H.B. BETTS, 1 AUST ARMOURED TRANS COY, A.A.S.C. AIF, AUSTRALIA, FROM YANDARAN VIA BUNDABERG".

First graffiti

BEUTEL, LAWRENCE ROY, QX41007 (Q11931{6}), CORPORAL LOWER FAR LEFT

DOB 20/1/10, LOWOOD, QLD

ENLISTED 24/9/41, BRISBANE, QLD (FERNVALE, QLD)

NOK, BEUTEL, MAY

DISCHARGED 2/3/44, 2nd PACK TRANSPORT COMPANY

BAR CODE 4475541 **DIGITAL COPY AVAILABLE**

WROTE "Q119316, FULL TIME DUTY, DRIVER, L.R. BEUTEL, 1 AUX H, ENOGGERA, 25/8/41" IN A RECTANGLE.

Second graffiti

BEUTEL, LAWRENCE ROY MID FAR RIGHT, NEAR FRAME

WROTE "17/9/42, L. BEUTEL, 2ND AUSTRALIAN PACK COY, M. DAWSON".

Third graffiti

BEUTEL, LAWRENCE ROY LOWER RIGHT, BB

WROTE "DVR M. DAWSON, L. BEUTEL, 1ST AUX. H.T. COY, 2ND AUSTRALIAN PACK. COY, N.G. SPECIALS" IN A SEMICIRCLE.

First Graffiti

BOWMAN, LESLIE ROBERT, QX31359, PRIVATE MID FAR RIGHT

DOB 26/5/13, GLADSTONE, QLD

ENLISTED 8/4/42, BRISBANE, QLD (YALBOROO, QLD)

NOK, BOWMAN, CATHERINE

DISCHARGED 22/6/45, 1st PERSONNEL STAGING CAMP

BAR CODE 4851891

WROTE "BOWMAN, QX31359". THE NUMBER IS VERY DIFFICULT TO READ.

Second Graffiti

BOWMAN, LESLIE ROBERT LOWER FAR LEFT, BB

WROTE "BOWMAN, L.R.". WRITTEN BELOW HARVATT.

BURR, RONALD LEO, NX192196 (N346795), SIGNALMAN UPPER FAR LEFT

DOB 6/4/22, BLACKTOWN, NSW

ENLISTED 7/3/44, THURSDAY ISLAND, QLD (BLACKTOWN, NSW)

NOK, BURR, MURIEL

DISCHARGED 9/8/44, TORRES STRAIT SIGNALS
BAR CODE 5584842
WROTE "SIG BURR, BLACKTOWN NSW". LOCATED ABOVE WARNER.

CALDOW, JOHN, QX29572, CORPORAL LOWER CENTRE
DOB 3/4/20, INVERELL, NSW
ENLISTED 11/1/42, BRISBANE, QLD (FOREST HILL, QLD)
NOK, CALDOW, MARY
DISCHARGED 11/1/46, 229th SUPPLY DEPOT PLATOON
BAR CODE 4920478
WROTE "QX29572, PTE J. CALDOW, ATTD" IN A RECTANGLE.

CAMPBELL, ROBERT, QX56335 (Q131129), PRIVATE MID RIGHT
DOB 25/5/02, LEEDS, ENGLAND
ENLISTED 23/7/43, PAPUA NEW GUINEA (WINTON, QLD)
NOK, CAMPBELL, MALCOME
DISCHARGED 19/11/45, 2/1st FIELD BUTCHERING PLATOON
BAR CODE 4466570
WROTE "Q131129, CAMPBELL, R. EXHIBITIONS, BRISBANE" IN A RECTANGLE.

BEST GUESS

CARDWELL, HAROLD REX, VX147917, PRIVATE LOWER FAR RIGHT, BB
DOB 28/10/20, TALLANGATTA, VIC
ENLISTED 2/2/44, IN THE FIELD, QLD (MITTA MITTA, VIC)
NOK, CARDWELL, THOMAS
DISCHARGED 7/6/46, 160th AUSTRALIAN GENERAL TRANSPORT COMPANY
BAR CODE 6668399
WROTE "V22604 (OR 9), H.R. CARDWELL, FROM THE BUSH".

THIS SOLDIER NEEDS TO HAVE HIS V NUMBER AND HIS VX NUMBER CONFIRMED THAT THEY BELONG TO THE SAME MAN. HE IS THE ONLY H.R. CARDWELL FROM VICTORIA.

CARNABY, WILLIAM ALLAN, VX141888, PRIVATE MID RIGHT
DOB 20/10/18, IVANHOE, VIC
ENLISTED 14/4/43, IN THE FIELD, VIC (HAMPTON, VIC)
NOK, CARNABY, LAUREL
DISCHARGED 15/2/46, 4th FIELD AMBULANCE
BAR CODE 6099807

WROTE "----, W. CARNABY, 4TH F. AM., HAMPTON" IN A SQUARE LEFT OF EDWARDS.

CASEY, THOMAS BAXTER, QX29949, PRIVATE UPPER FAR LEFT
DOB 17/6/15, CAPELLA, QLD
ENLISTED 10/2/42, BRISBANE, QLD (CLERMONT, QLD)
NOK, CASEY, MARY
DISCHARGED 25/1/46, 2/15th INFANTRY BATTALION
BAR CODE 4920836
WROTE "QX29949, CASEY". THIS SIGNATURE IS VERY HIGH UP ON THE WALL.

CHADWICK, ROBERT ABRAHAM, QX24183, CRAFTSMAN LOWER CENTRE
DOB 21/1/21, CAIRNS, QLD
ENLISTED 13/10/41, BRISBANE (GORDON PARK, QLD)
NOK, CHADWICK, GWENDOLINE
DISCHARGED 18/12/45, CRAFTSMAN, 113th AUST LIGHT AA ORDNANCE WORKSHOP
BAR CODE 4484999
WROTE "QX24183, 15/8/41, PTE R. CHADWICK, NOTHING YET" IN A RECTANGLE.

CHALMERS, WILLIAM JOHN, QX31886, PRIVATE UPPER RIGHT
DOB 21/2/21, MT MORGAN, QLD
ENLISTED 28/4/42, BRISBANE, QLD (BARALABA, QLD)
NOK, CHALMERS, ELLEN
DISCHARGED 31/5/46, 2/15th INFANTRY BATTALION
BAR CODE 4915529
WROTE "QX31886, PTE W.J. CHALMERS, BARALABA DVL, QLD, AUSTRALIA" IN A RECTANGLE.

CHAPLIN, LEONARD GORDON, NX43223, SAPPER LOWER MID CENTRE, BB
DOB 23/9/16, COOROY, QLD
ENLISTED 20/8/41 PADDINGTON, NSW (UNKNOWN)
NOK, CHAPLIN, MARY
DISCHARGED 9/1/43, 2/1st FIELD PARK SQUADRON
BAR CODE 4921633
WROTE "NX43223, PTE L.G. CHAPLIN, 2/8 PIONEERS, NO. 1 PLATOON, AIF, AUSTRALIA" IN A SQUARE.

CLARK, WILLIAM, QX51167 (Q136517), PRIVATE UPPER FAR RIGHT
DOB 1/12/14, SPRINGSURE, QLD
ENLISTED 5/4/43, WARWICK, QLD (SPRINGSURE, QLD)
NOK, RYAN, ANNIE

DISCHARGED 12/4/46, 2/9th FIELD COMPANY

BAR CODE 4465270

WROTE "PTE W. CLARK, Q136517, W'GABBA". VERY FAINT, LOCATED ABOVE NX9212 FREEBURY AND NEXT TO BEINKE.

CONNELL, WALTER, QX54442 (Q147591), CORPORAL UPPER LEFT

DOB 3/6/13, TENTERFIELD, NSW

ENLISTED 3/6/43, UNKNOWN (WALLANGARRA, QLD)

NOK, CONNELL, ALBERT

DISCHARGED 11/4/46, 58/59th INFANTRY BATTALION

BAR CODE 4887268

WROTE "PTE W. CONNELL Q147591 ASRF". VERY FAINT, LOCATED ABOVE THE A OF JACKSON.

COOK, CECIL ROY, WX5802, LANCE CORPORAL UPPER RIGHT

DOB 3/3/03, GUILFORD, WA

ENLISTED 22/6/40, NORTHAM, WA (YOTING, WA)

NOK, COOK, BETSY

DISCHARGED 31/12/43, 2/16th INFANTRY BATTALION

BAR CODE 6457848

WROTE "WX5802, C.R. COOK, WEST AUS, 2/16 BATT" VERY FAINT, LOCATED ABOVE LEIGH AND LEFT OF NEWMAN.

COOPER, JAMES KEVIN, VX148925 (V245948), PRIVATE MID LEFT

DOB 1/10/23, BENDIGO, VIC

ENLISTED CMF 18/1/41, RAYWOOD, VIC (TANDARA, VIC)
AIF 6/6/44, IN THE FIELD (TANDARA, VIC)

NOK, COOPER, JOHN

DISCHARGED 19/6/46, 22nd INFANTRY BATTALION

BAR CODE 6610519

WROTE "V245948 PTE J.K. COOPER, 101 CONVALESCENT HOSPITAL, COOPAROO".

THE NUMBER IS PARTIALLY OBSCURE. LOCATED LEFT OF FLETCHER.

CRANSTON, HENRY CHRISTIAN, QX31344, PRIVATE MID FAR LEFT

DOB 20/9/15, MACKAY, QLD

ENLISTED 8/4/42, BRISBANE, QLD (AJUKAN, QLD)

NOK, CRANSTON, H.

DISCHARGED 18/2/46, 2/14th INFANTRY BATTALION

BAR CODE 4838670

WROTE "PTE H. C. CRANSTON, AJUKAN, QX31344" IN AN ELLIPSE.

CREFFIELD, CLARENCE ROBERT, QX54230 (Q131589), SAPPER UPPER FAR RIGHT
DOB 26/2/23, TOWNSVILLE, QLD
ENLISTED 10/5/43, TOWNSVILLE, QLD (AYR, QLD)
NOK, CREFFIELD, NORMAN
DISCHARGED 22/10/45, 2/11th ARMY TRANSPORT COMPANY
BAR CODE 4887479
WROTE "C. CREFFIELD, Q131589, AYR" VERY FAINT, LOCATED IN THE TOP CORNER OF THE RIGHT SIDE OF THE WALL.

CROSS, JAMES EDWARD, QX27537, WARRANT OFFICER, CLASS 1 MID FAR LEFT
DOB 12/8/22, MACKAY, QLD
ENLISTED 11/2/42, BRISBANE, QLD (SARINA, QLD)
NOK, CROSS, ROBERT
DISCHARGED 14/6/46, 2/4th DOCKS OPERATING COY
BAR CODE 4855461 **DIGITAL COPY AVAILABLE**
WROTE "--CROSS, ------------, QX27537, LOST LEGION, REDBANK". SOME OF THE WRITING IS EITHER DAMAGED OR COVERED IN PLASTER.

DARE, LEONARD RICHARD, QX21015 (Q859), PRIVATE MID CENTRE
DOB 9/5/13, CHARLEVILLE, QLD
ENLISTED 8/1/41, LYTTON, QLD (BRISBANE, QLD)
NOK, DARE, BERTHA
DISCHARGED 1/11/45, 2/12 INFANTRY BATTALION
BAR CODE 4498332
WROTE "QX21015, L.R. DARE". DIFFICULT TO READ, LOCATED ABOVE SANKEY AND CALDOW.

DARLINGTON, CHARLES MAGNUS, QX24980, PRIVATE MID CENTRE
DOB 2/3/18, BUNDABERG, QLD
ENLISTED 31/12/41, MARYBOROUGH, QLD (YANDARAN, QLD)
NOK, GAHAN, ALICE
DISCHARGED 18/4/46, 2/1st INFANTRY BATTALION
BAR CODE 4483810
WROTE "QX24980, PTE C.M. DARLINGTON, A COY, 7TH I.T.B, REDBANK FROM YANDARAN, VIA BUNDABERG". VERY FAINT, LOCATED ABOVE CHADWICK.

First graffiti

DAVIE, MARCELLUS THEODORE JAMES, QX25037, CORPORAL MID FAR RIGHT
DOB 14/10/19, MUNGINDI, NSW

ENLISTED 10/12/41, TOOWOOMBA, QLD (TOOWOOMBA, QLD)

NOK, DAVIE, EILEEN

DISCHARGED 29/4/46, 2/33rd INFANTRY BATTALION

BAR CODE 4483873 **DIGITAL COPY AVAILABLE**

WROTE "QX25037, DRIVER JIM DAVIE, GROVELY".

Second graffiti

DAVIE, MARCELLUS THEODORE JAMES, QX25037, CORPORAL MID FAR RIGHT

WROTE "QX25037, DRIVER M.T.J. DAVIE, A I F, GROVELY" IN LARGE CURSIVE LETTERS.

DAVIS, WILLIAM HERBERT, QX30022, CORPORAL UPPER FAR RIGHT

DOB 1/6/17, MIRANI, QLD

ENLISTED 9/2/42, MACKAY, QLD (MOUNT MARTIN, QLD)

NOK, DAVIS, HENRY

DISCHARGED 9/4/46, 2/15th INFANTRY BATTALION

BAR CODE 4920909

WROTE "QX300--, PTE DAVIS, W.H., 2/15 BOGGABILLA NSW". PART OF THE NUMBER IS MISSING.

DAVY, COLIN, QX30922, GUNNER MID LEFT

DOB 15/2/23, PROSERPINE, QLD

ENLISTED 26/3/42, BRISBANE, QLD (PROSERPINE, QLD)

NOK, DAVY, GRACE

DISCHARGED 17/7/46, 235th LIGHT ANTI AIRCRAFT BATTERY

BAR CODE 4900463 **DIGITAL COPY AVAILABLE**

WROTE "QX30922, GNR DAVY, 101 A/TANK FLD TRG BTY, GROVELY AIF" AND "PROSERPINE" IN A SQUARE, NEXT TO "HARRIS'S RANGERS" LOCATED ABOVE McNAUGHTON.

DAVY, DOUGLAS WILLIAM, QX27471, STAFF SERGEANT MID RIGHT

DOB 27/5/15, KURILDALA, QLD

ENLISTED 19/2/42, BRISBANE, QLD (NEW FARM, QLD)

NOK, DAVY, HELEN

DISCHARGED 6/12/45, 102nd BRIGADE WORKSHOP

BAR CODE 4856098

WROTE "QX27471, DAVY, D.W., ORDNANCE, B. W." IN AN ELLIPSE.

First graffiti

DAWSON, MERVYN PHILLIP, QX58423 (Q128198), PRIVATE LOWER CENTRE, BB
DOB 4/7/22, IPSWICH, QLD
ENLISTED 13/10/43, IN THE FIELD, QLD (HARRISVILLE, QLD)
NOK, DAWSON, PHILLIP
DISCHARGED 19/6/46, 3rd INDEPENDENT FARM PLATOON
BAR CODE 4923745
WROTE "Q128198, M. DAWSON".

Second graffiti

DAWSON, MERVYN PHILLIP, QX58423 (Q128198), PRIVATE MID FAR RIGHT
WROTE "17/9/42, L. BEUTEL, 2ND AUSTRALIAN PACK COY, M. DAWSON", NEAR FRAME.

Third graffiti

DAWSON, MERVYN PHILLIP, QX58423 (Q128198), PRIVATE LOWER RIGHT, BB
WROTE "DVR M. DAWSON, L. BEUTEL, 1ST AUX. H.T. COY, 2ND AUSTRALIAN PACK COY, N.G. SPECIALS" IN A SEMICIRCLE.

DEAN, MERVYN ROY, QX27835, PRIVATE MID LEFT
DOB 2/1/16, MT PERRY, QLD
ENLISTED 3/3/42, BRISBANE, QLD (MOUNT PERRY, QLD)
NOK, DEAN, ALICE
DISCHARGED 11/1/46, 2/7th INFANTRY BATTALION
BAR CODE 4485055
WROTE "MT PERRY, M. R. DEAN, QX27835, 7TH PIONEERS, AIF, AUSTRALIA" IN A CIRCLE, VERY FAINT, LOCATED RIGHT OF McDERMID AND LEFT OF FLOYD.

DENDLE, ROY EDWIN, Q136523, SAPPER UPPER RIGHT
DOB 18/2/21, SPRINGSURE, QLD
ENLISTED 19/5/42, SPRINGSURE, QLD (SPRINGSURE, QLD)
NOK, DENDLE, GEORGE
DISCHARGED 7/2/46, 51st FIELD PARK COMPANY
BAR CODE 4452103
WROTE "PTE ROY E, DENDLE, NO 136523, W'GABBA, LATE OF SPRINGSURE".

DIXON, ALBERT JOHN STANLEY, VX736, SAPPER MID FAR RIGHT
DOB 16/1/16, OAKLEIGH, VIC

ENLISTED 26/10/39, EAST ST KILDA, VIC, (CARNEGIE, VIC)
NOK, DIXON, PERCIVAL
DISCHARGED 31/8/45, RAE PLUMBER
BAR CODE 6146345 **DIGITAL COPY AVAILABLE**
WROTE "VX736, A.DIXON", IN A CIRCLE, VERY FAINT. LOCATED ABOVE SX1150 NEXT TO THE FRAME.

DOBBIN, SYLVESTER, QX31052, PRIVATE LOWER FAR LEFT
DOB 12/5/22, MITCHELL, QLD
ENLISTED 31/3/42, BRISBANE, QLD (MITCHELL, QLD)
NOK, DOBBIN, FORBES
DISCHARGED 22/1/46, HEADQUARTERS 2nd AUSTRALIAN CORPS
BAR CODE 4855532
WROTE "QX31052, DOBBIN, MITCHELL". SOME WRITING IS COVERED IN PLASTER.

First graffiti

DOBSON, GORDON THORNTON, SX27714 (S11444), GUNNER LOWER RIGHT
DOB 4/7/15, CAULFIELD, VIC
ENLISTED 21/11/42, PORT MORESBY, PAPUA NEW GUINEA (HAMPTON, VIC)
NOK, DOBSON, LENA
DISCHARGED 14/11/45, 13th FIELD REGIMENT
BAR CODE 6405011
WROTE "GNR. G.T. DOBSON, SMX 11444, ADELAIDE, SA".

Second graffiti

DOBSON, GORDON THORNTON, SX27714 (S11444), GUNNER LOWER FAR RIGHT
WROTE "---444, G.T. DOBSON, ADELAIDE, SA".

DOOLAN, COLIN, QX29349, CORPORAL MID FAR RIGHT
DOB 30/1/23, ESK, QLD
ENLISTED 29/12/41, BRISBANE, QLD (IPSWICH, QLD)
NOK, DOOLAN, SIMON
DISCHARGED 15/1/46, 'Z' SPECIAL UNIT
BAR CODE 4920219
WROTE "QX29349, PTE DOOLAN, C, 7TH PIONEER COY, AIF", VERY FAINT, LOCATED BETWEEN GRAFFITI-STYLE SIGNATURE OF RICE AND SX1150, WHICH IS NEXT TO THE FRAME.

DRAKE, CLIFFORD CHARLES, QX 27326, PRIVATE UPPER FAR LEFT
DOB 7/3/22, MACKAY, QLD
ENLISTED 15/1/42 MACKAY, QLD (MIRIAM, QLD)
NOK, DRAKE, DOROTHY
DISCHARGED 14/6/42, 101st CONVALESCENT DEPOT
BAR CODE 4855481
WROTE "QX27326, PTE DRAKE, C.C., 6 GOLD ST, MACKAY". LOCATED NEAR THE FRAME.

DRAPER, THOMAS RODERICK, QX25324, (Q90239), CORPORAL LOWER LEFT
DOB 9/7/19 HARRISVILLE, QLD
ENLISTED 8/4/41, BEAUDESERT, QLD (BEAUDESERT, QLD)
NOK, DRAPER, HANNAH
DISCHARGED 13/7/45, 2/10th DOCKS OPERATING COMPANY
BAR CODE 4486154
WROTE "QX25324, GNR T.R. DRAPER, 41ST FLD. TRG. BTY, GROVELY, AIF".

BEST GUESS

DREW, HERBERT, QX38345 (Q89333), CORPORAL UPPER FAR RIGHT
DOB 4/5/1898, NAMBOUR, QLD
ENLISTED 18/7/41, BRISBANE, QLD (ROSALIE, QLD)
NOK, DREW, ELIZABETH
DISCHARGED 6/7/48, PAGA COASTAL DEFENCE HEAVY BATTERY
BAR CODE 4476505
WROTE "GNR H. DREW, GROVELY, QX" ALONG WITH HIS MATE'S NAME "GNR A. WERNER". VERY FAINT, LOCATED LEFT OF PEMBLE.

DULL, HERBERT ALFRED, QX41933 (Q108573), SAPPER LOWER FAR LEFT
DOB 6/3/17, ROADVALE QLD
ENLISTED 28/3/41, BOONAH, QLD (ROADVALE, QLD)
NOK, DULL, WILHELM
DISCHARGED 26/10/44, 12th ARMY TROOP COMPANY RAE
BAR CODE 4891891
WROTE "SPR HERB DULL, GABBA" IN GRAFFITI STYLE IN A RECTANGLE.

EDWARDS, GEORGE LEWIN, QX28722, CORPORAL MID RIGHT
DOB 23/5/11, BRISBANE, QLD
ENLISTED 15/1/42, BRISBANE, QLD (KALINGA, QLD)
NOK, EDWARDS, ESME
DISCHARGED 23/10/45, 2/15th FIELD COMPANY

BAR CODE 4485398
WROTE "G.L. EDWARDS, QX28722, ATTD".

FAULKNER, ROYAL, QX24982, PRIVATE MID RIGHT
DOB 25/11/22, BUNDABERG, QLD
ENLISTED 31/12/41 MARYBOROUGH, QLD (AVONDALE, QLD)
NOK, FAULKNER, HELENA
DISCHARGED 16/4/46, 56th COMPOSITE ANTI AIRCRAFT REGIMENT
BAR CODE 4483808, **DIGITAL COPY AVAILABLE**
WROTE "QX24982, GNR R. FAULKNER, 41ST FTD, GROVELY".

FLETCHER, JAMES HARDING, VX106571 (V39843), CORPORAL MID LEFT
DOB 21/2/12, NORTH FITZROY, VIC
ENLISTED 21/8/42, TINANA, QLD (HAWTHORN, VIC)
NOK, FLETCHER, T.
DISCHARGED 8/3/46, 1st ENTERTAINMENT UNIT
BAR CODE 6104832
WROTE "VX1039843, CPL J.H. FLETCHER, 3 DIV ENTERTAINMENT UNIT" PLUS HIS SIGNATURE, AND A DRAWING OF A SAXOPHONE IN A RECTANGLE. THIS SOLDIER HAS COMBINED HIS VX NUMBER AND HIS V NUMBER.

FLOYD, GEORGE ARTHUR, VX138481 (V195366), CORPORAL UPPER CENTRE
DOB 25/9/21, MELBOURNE, VIC
ENLISTED 30/3/43, IN THE FIELD, PAPUA (ABBOTSFORD, VIC)
NOK, FLOYD, MAVIS
DISCHARGED 13/12/45, 29/46th INFANTRY BATTALION
BAR CODE 6099439
WROTE "G. FLOYD, V195366, MELBOURNE".

THE DEPARTMENT OF DEFENCE RECORDS SECTION HAS VERIFIED THAT THIS SOLDIER'S *V* NUMBER (1077) ON THE NOMINAL ROLL IS INCORRECT. THE NATIONAL ARCHIVES RECORDS SECTION HAS CONFIRMED THE ABOVE IDENTIFICATION.

FRANCIS, LAWRENCE ARTHUR, QX33450, SAPPER MID RIGHT
DOB 11/3/21, MOREE, NSW
ENLISTED 1/9/42 BRISBANE, QLD, (GOONDIWINDI, QLD)
NOK, FRANCIS, MARGARET
DISCHARGED 12/3/46, 4th PORT OPERATING COMPANY
BAR CODE 4477203

WROTE "QX33450, PTE L.A. FRANCIS, GOONDIWINDI" IN A RECTANGLE. IT IS VERY HARD TO READ. LOCATED RIGHT OF MEEHAN. AN ATTEMPT WAS MADE TO ERASE THIS GRAFFITI.

First graffiti

FRANCIS, NORMAN, QX44671 (Q991), SERGEANT MID RIGHT
DOB 17/5/17, IPSWICH, QLD
ENLISTED 10/9/40, NAMBOUR, QLD (NAMBOUR, QLD)
NOK, FRANCIS, PAUL
DISCHARGED 15/8/46, 1st MULTI-CHANNEL WIRELESS TRANSMITTER SECTION
BAR CODE 4489419
WROTE "JUNE 3RD, SIG. NORMAN FRANCIS, Q991, GABBA," IN GRAFFITI STYLE, IN A SQUARE.

Second graffiti

FRANCIS, NORMAN, QX44671 (Q991), SERGEANT UPPER FAR RIGHT
WROTE "SIG. NORMAN, F, Q199" IN LARGE GRAFFITI-STYLE.

FREEBURY, RALPH DENNIS, WX9212, PRIVATE MID FAR RIGHT
DOB 12/6/20, NEWPORT, SOUTH WALES, UK
ENLISTED 30/10/40, CLAREMONT, WA (SOMERSET HILL, WA)
NOK, FREEBURY, EDWARD
DISCHARGED 7/2/46, 2/13th FIELD AMBULANCE
BAR CODE 6456912
WROTE "WX9212, PTE FREEBURY, R.D., SUBIACO, WA". UNDERLINED.

FREEMAN, GEORGE ANDREW, QX27266, PRIVATE LOWER FAR LEFT, BB
DOB 6/8/08, CORDALBA, QLD
ENLISTED 14/1/42 BUNDABERG, QLD (QUNABA, QLD)
NOK, FREEMAN, SARAH
DISCHARGED 24/4/45 3rd STATIONARY LAUNDRY
BAR CODE 4855229
WROTE "QX27266" ABOVE HARVATT.

FRIEND, ROBERT EMMET MARQUESS, QX44563 (Q109255), SERGEANT LOWER FAR LEFT
DOB 18/8/20, MAXWELTON, QLD
ENLISTED 7/1/41, SELLHEIM, QLD (RICHMOND, QLD)
NOK, FRIEND, JOHN

DISCHARGED 2/4/46, 31/51st INFANTRY BATTALION

BAR CODE 4489498 **DIGITAL COPY AVAILABLE**

WROTE "FRIEND R.E.M., THE GIFT TO THE FAIR SEX OF BRISBANE 109255, E. COMPANY, SELLHEIM". THIS QUOTE IS DIFFICULT TO READ. LOCATED ABOVE GUNALDA.

GLASSON, JOHN WILLIAM, V124208, PRIVATE MID CENTRE

DOB 27/1/21, MELBOURNE, VIC

ENLISTED 27/8/41, KEW, VIC (SEVILLE, VIC)

NOK, GLASSON

DISCHARGED 27/2/45, 46th INFANTRY BATTALION

BAR CODE 6276166

WROTE "J.W. GLASSON, HOME FORCES, MELBOURNE, ---?" IN A CIRCLE.

GOODWIN, FREDERICK JOHN, SX2109, PRIVATE LOWER CENTRE

DOB 3/4/17, MELBOURNE, VIC

ENLISTED 26/3/40, ADELAIDE, SA (URAIDLA, SA)

NOK, GOODWIN, ALICE

DISCHARGED 10/12/45, 2/12th INFANTRY BATTALION

BAR CODE 6663294

WROTE "SX2109, GOODWIN, F. J.". UNDERLINED.

GOSPER, ALFRED ANDREW, QX56500 (Q124650), SIGNALMAN MID RIGHT

DOB 23/5/23, NAMBOUR, QLD

ENLISTED 5/8/43, CAIRNS, QLD (EUMUNDI, QLD)

NOK, GOSPER, MELBA

DISCHARGED 29/1/46, SIGNALS FIXED DEFENCES

BAR CODE 4466406

WROTE "SIG A. GOSPER, Q124650, FORTRESS SIGS BRISBANE, FORT LYTTON" IN A RECTANGLE WITH A WAVY HERALDIC SYMBOL IN THE TOP RIGHT-HAND CORNER. IDENTIFICATION HAS BEEN VERIFIED BY THE NATIONAL ARCHIVES.

GRACE, JOHN JOSEPH**,** QX30501**,** PRIVATE MID CENTRE

DOB 2/4/05, NEWCASTLE, NSW

ENLISTED 17/3/42, BRISBANE, QLD (BLYTHDALE, QLD)

NOK, GRACE, MYRTLE

DISCHARGED 14/3/45, 1st PERSONNEL STAGING CAMP

BAR CODE 4915209

WROTE "QX30501, GRACE, J.J., NO. 2 CONV/U, COORPAROO".

GREENHALGH, GORDON RONALD, NX6170, PRIVATE LOWER LEFT

DOB 8/3/20, PARKES, NSW

ENLISTED 3/5/41, PADDINGTON, NSW (ST PETERS, NSW)

NOK, GREENHALGH, JOHN

DISCHARGED 20/9/45, 6th DIVISION, AUSTRALIAN ARMY SERVICE CORPS

BAR CODE 4922147 **DIGITAL COPY AVAILABLE**

WROTE "NX6170, DVR GREENHALGH, 6TH AUST. DIV. AASC AIF".

GULLIVER, RAYMOND ARTHUR, NX152644 (N217594), SAPPER MID LEFT

DOB, 18/11/20, CASINO, NSW

ENLISTED 13/5/41, WAVERLEY PARK, NSW (UNKNOWN)

NOK, GULLIVER, VIOLET

DISCHARGED 17/4/45, 18th FIELD COMPANY

BAR CODE 5636075

WROTE ORIGINALLY "SPR R. GULLIVER, 18TH AUS ARMY FIELD CO, FIRST AUS. ARMY HOME FORCES". THE ***SPR*** WAS THEN CHANGED TO ***SGT,*** WHICH WAS REVEALED BY BETTER PHOTOGRAPHIC TECHNIQUES. LOCATED IN AN OVAL UNDER THE O OF JACKSON.

BEST GUESS

GUTTERIDGE, PERCY OLIVER, N230758, PRIVATE MID FAR RIGHT

DOB 21/7/1909, GRAFTON, NSW

ENLISTED 9/5/42, KINGSFORD, NSW (KENSINGTON, NSW)

NOK, WARREN, ROSE

DISCHARGED 19/11/43, 34th LINES OF COMMUNICATION SALVAGE

BAR CODE 5566898

WROTE "P. GUTTERIDGE, 2/6 BATTALION, SYDNEY, OCT 42" IN AN OVAL, FAINT.

THIS IS THE ONLY P. GUTTERIDGE LISTED IN THE RECORDS.

HAM, JOHN ANDREW JOSEPH, QX25284, WARRANT OFFICER, CLASS 2 LOWER LEFT

DOB 23/7/13, GYMPIE, QLD

ENLISTED 27/11/41 BRISBANE, QLD (HENDRA, QLD)

NOK, HAM, AVRIL

DISCHARGED 9/1/46, NORTHERN TERRITORY FORCES CANTEENS

BAR CODE 4486134

WROTE "GNR J.A.J. HAM, 41ST FLD, GROVELY" LOCATED ABOVE AND TO THE LEFT OF PHIPPS.

HANCOCK, ALLAN, NX72930, PRIVATE MID RIGHT

DOB 9/12/1898, HILTON, SA

ENLISTED 15/4/41, PADDINGTON, NSW (BAULKHAM HILL, NSW)

NOK, SHOOTER, ANNIE

DISCHARGED 27/6/41, 1st TRAINING BATTALION

BAR CODE 4621123

WROTE "QLD, AMD 1, 31 LD? NX72930, 1ST BATT, 2/6/41, ALLAN HANCOCK". VERY FAINT, LOCATED ABOVE VEACH.

HANLEY, STUART WILLIAM, SX30974 (S36732), STAFF SERGEANT LOWER FAR RIGHT

DOB 13/4/22, GLADSTONE, SA

ENLISTED 7/1/43 PORT MORESBY, PAPUA NEW GUINEA (LAURA, SA)

NOK, HANLEY, RUTH

DISCHARGED 1/12/45, PAPUAN INFANTRY BATTALION

BAR CODE 6350586 **DIGITAL COPY AVAILABLE**

WROTE "S36732, SIG. HANLEY, S.W., AUSTRALIAN CORP OF SIGNALS, ATTACHED 11TH FIELD REG, GROVELY, ANOTHER SOUTH AUSTRALIAN".

HARRINGTON, EDWARD FREDERICK, VX56551, CRAFTSMAN UPPER RIGHT

DOB 17/4/21, CARLTON, VIC

ENLISTED 5/8/41, ROYAL PARK, VIC (NORTHCOTE, VIC)

NOK, HARRINGTON, EDITH

DISCHARGED 17/5/44, NEW GUINEA LINES OF COMMUNICATION AREA WORKSHOPS

BAR CODE 6110951 **DIGITAL COPY AVAILABLE**

WROTE "VX56551, PTE HARRINGTON". LOCATED ABOVE NEWMAN.

HARRIS, GUY, QX30204, DRIVER MID FAR LEFT

DOB 28/2/1915, TOOWOOMBA, QLD

ENLISTED 11/3/42, BRISBANE, QLD ("PINEVIEW" TARA, QLD)

NOK, HARRIS, DORIS

DISCHARGED 10/1/46, 2/96th TRANSPORT PLATOON.

BAR CODE 4915061

WROTE "QX30204, PTE G. HARRIS, PINEVIEW, TARA".

BEST GUESS

HARRISON, WILLIAM JOSEPH, VX144418, CORPORAL MID LEFT

DOB 5/8/18, BURNLEY, VIC

ENLISTED 5/9/43, IN THE FIELD, NEW GUINEA (RICHMOND, VIC)

NOK, HARRISON, CHARLES

DISCHARGED 8/10/46, 29/46th INFANTRY BATTALION

BAR CODE 6698063

WROTE "CPL W.J. HARRISON, 29 BN, V38579, CARRIERS".

THE NUMBER V38579 IS NOT LISTED IN THE NOMINAL ROLL RECORDS. THIS WOULD BE HIS CMF NUMBER. HE IS THE ONLY CORPORAL W.J. HARRISON LISTED AS BELONGING TO THE 29TH BATTALION.

First graffiti

HARVATT, CHARLES WILLIAM, QX20858, PRIVATE LOWER FAR LEFT, BB

DOB 31/12/09, SYDNEY, NSW

ENLISTED 2/4/41, BRISBANE, QLD (PETRIE TERRACE, QLD)

NOK, HARVATT, FREDERICK

DISCHARGED 15/1/46, 2/31st INFANTRY BATTALION

BAR CODE 4498129

WROTE "HARVATT, C., QX20858" ABOVE THE NAME BOWMAN, L.R., WHICH IS JUST VISIBLE.

Second graffiti

HARVATT, CHARLES WILLIAM, QX20858 MID RIGHT

WROTE "HARVATT, C.W., QX20858". VERY FAINT, DIFFICULT TO READ. LOCATED ABOVE BOWMAN AND BELOW LAWRENCE.

HATFIELD, GEORGE ALFRED, QX27336, CRAFTSMAN MID FAR RIGHT

DOB 10/3/12, MACKAY, QLD

ENLISTED 15/1/42, MACKAY, QLD (KOUMALA, QLD)

NOK, HATFIELD, MINNIE

DISCHARGED 1/6/45, HEADQUARTERS NORTHERN COMMAND ORDNANCE WORKSHOP

BAR CODE 4855491

WROTE "QX27336, HATFIELD, G.A., KOUMALA NCL" IN AN ORNATE FRAME.

HENSON, HENRY GEORGE, NX38826, SIGNALMAN MID FAR RIGHT

DOB 12/7/20, ORANGE, NSW

ENLISTED 15/7/41, PADDINGTON, NSW (CAMPBELLTOWN, NSW)

NOK, HENSON, WILLIAM

DISCHARGED 29/11/45, 2/3rd INDEPENDENT COMPANY

BAR CODE 4879630 **DIGITAL COPY AVAILABLE**

WROTE "NX38826, SIG. H.G. HENSON, 3RD AUS IND COY, AIF" WITH A DOUBLE DIAMOND HERALDIC SYMBOL. VERY FAINT. LOCATED NEAR FRAME UNDER FLATBUSH FLOOGIE.

HILL, JOHN, QX20524, PRIVATE MID FAR LEFT
DOB 17/6/12, BLUFF, QLD
ENLISTED 31/7/41, ROCKHAMPTON, QLD (KALKA, QLD)
NOK, HILL, MARSHALL
DISCHARGED 18/4/44, 31st EMPLOYMENT COMPANY
BAR CODE 4497803
WROTE "QX20524, HILL, J., LOST LEGION, REDBANK".

HOBBS, HERBERT ERIC MICHAEL, QX33460, CORPORAL UPPER LEFT
DOB 25/5/16, INGLEWOOD, QLD
ENLISTED 1/7/42, BRISBANE, QLD (INGLEWOOD, QLD)
NOK, HOBBS, DULCIE
DISCHARGED 14/3/46, 1st PARACHUTE MAINTENANCE PLATOON AAOC
BAR CODE 4477213
WROTE "PTE H.E.M. HOBBS, QX33460, AIF". FAINT, LOCATED ABOVE THE K OF JACKSON.

HODGE, ALFRED JAMES, NX38405, LANCE CORPORAL LOWER FAR RIGHT
DOB 28/10/13, HILLSTON, NSW
ENLISTED 10/7/41, PADDINGTON, NSW (GRIFFITH, NSW)
NOK, HODGE, CHARLES
DISCHARGED 27/2/46, 2/2nd COMMANDO SQUADRON
BAR CODE 4886698
WROTE "NX38405, GNR HODGE, A.J." UNDERLINED, LOCATED LEFT OF THE LARGE DRAWING OF A MAN'S HEAD.

HOWARD, SAMUEL CLARENCE, QX20501, PRIVATE LOWER FAR LEFT
DOB 13/11/12, ROCKHAMPTON, QLD
ENLISTED 17/7/41, ROCKHAMPTON, QLD (BOROREN, QLD)
NOK, HOWARD, MARGARET
DISCHARGED 2/1/46, 2/32nd INFANTRY BATTALION
BAR CODE 4497826
WROTE "S.C. HOWARD, QX20501". FAINT, LOCATED UNDER HILL.

HUGGONSON, WALTER SIDNEY, QX21599, CRAFTSMAN UPPER RIGHT
DOB 7/1/21, BIGGENDEN, QLD
ENLISTED 12/5/41, BRISBANE, QLD (PROSTON, QLD)
NOK, HUGGONSON, JAMES
DISCHARGED 24/11/44, 4TH ORDNANCE WORKSHOP COMPANY
BAR CODE 4490129

WROTE "W. HUGGONSON, QX21599, MURGON". UNDERLINED, VERY FAINT. MOST OF THE NAME HAS BEEN ERASED, BUT THE NUMBER IS LEGIBLE. LOCATED ABOVE NEWMAN.

HUGHES, RONALD WILLIAM, V39204, PRIVATE UPPER LEFT
DOB 1/3/19, CHELTENHAM, VIC
ENLISTED 12/1/40, PARKDALE, VIC (MOORABBIN, VIC)
NOK, HUGHES, WILLIAM
DISCHARGED 14/11/44, 46th INFANTRY BATTALION
BAR CODE 6290787
WROTE "R.W. HUGHES, 46 BATT, CHELTENHAM, VICTORIA". VERY FAINT, LOCATED RIGHT OF THE N IN JACKSON.

HUNTER, MERVYN ARTHUR, QX18847, PRIVATE UPPER FAR LEFT
DOB 25/12/21, MACKAY, QLD
ENLISTED 6/11/41 MACKAY, QLD (MACKAY, QLD)
NOK, HUNTER, ARTHUR
DISCHARGED 5/9/45, 23rd INFANTRY TRAINING BATTALION
BAR CODE 4494910
WROTE "-8847, HUNTER, M.A., ANTI TANK 41ST F T B, AIF, GROVELY".

INGRAM, CHARLES GAVIN, QX30341, SERGEANT LOWER LEFT
DOB 12/3/23, BRISBANE, QLD
ENLISTED 12/3/42, BRISBANE, QLD (PROSERPINE, QLD)
NOK, INGRAM, MARY
DISCHARGED 4/4/46, 114th LIGHT ANTI AIRCRAFT REGIMENT
BAR CODE 4915369
WROTE "QX30341, GNR. C.G. INGRAM, ---------? GROVELY, PROSERPINE".

JACKSON, ALAN CHARLES, QX18876, GUNNER UPPER LEFT
DOB 17/12/21, MACKAY, QLD
ENLISTED 27/11/41, MACKAY, QLD (ETON NORTH, QLD)
NOK, JACKSON, EDITH
DISCHARGED 2/1/46, 2/3rd A/A REGIMENT (COMPOSITE)
BAR CODE 4494941
WROTE "A.C. JACKSON, MACKAY" IN VERY LARGE LETTERS.

JACOBSON, HENRY IVAN, QX28868, PRIVATE LOWER CENTRE, BB
DOB 30/12/22, GYMPIE, QLD
ENLISTED 20/1/42, BRISBANE, QLD (GUNALDA, QLD)

NOK, JACOBSON, JOHN
DISCHARGED, 2/11/44, 2/9th INFANTRY BATTALION
BAR CODE 4485747 **DIGITAL COPY AVAILABLE**
WROTE "QX28868, PT H.I. JACOBSON, 2/8 PIONEERS, NO. 1 PLATOON, AIF, AUSTRALIA".

JOHNSTON, WILLIAM GEORGE, QX27406, PRIVATE MID LEFT
DOB 26/5/15 MILES, QLD
ENLISTED 17/2/42, BRISBANE, QLD (YULEBA, QLD)
NOK, JOHSTON, WILLIAM
DISCHARGED 8/1/46, 25th INFANTRY BATTALION
BAR CODE 4856023
WROTE "QX27406, W.G.JOHNSTON, RETURN MAN 101 CON DEPOT, COPOOROO".

FAINT WRITING, LOCATED ABOVE McNAUGHTON.

JONES, EARLE ALBERT, NX38209, PRIVATE MID FAR RIGHT
DOB 18/10/18, TUCABIA, NSW
ENLISTED 8/7/41, PADDINGTON, NSW (ULMARRA, NSW)
NOK, JONES, THELMA
DISCHARGED 16/11/45, 1st PARACHUTE BATTALION
BAR CODE 4886942 **DIGITAL COPY AVAILABLE**
WROTE "NX38209, GNR JONES, E.A., 2/1 AUST MED REGT, RAA". THE WRITING IS VERY DIFFICULT TO DECIPHER. LOCATED ABOVE RALPH BOLIO.

JORDON, CONRAD GEORGE, QX27905, GUNNER MID LEFT
DOB 28/6/22, FINCH HATTON, QLD
ENLISTED 18/2/42, BRISBANE, QLD (FINCH HATTON, QLD)
NOK, JORDON, GEORGE
DISCHARGED 23/7/46, 5th FIELD REGIMENT
BAR CODE 4485105
WROTE "QX27905, SIG. C. JORDON, AIF, GROVELY" IN A RECTANGLE.

First graffiti

JORGENSEN, CYRIL EDWARD, QX29624, GUNNER LOWER RIGHT
DOB 12/10/21, ESK, QLD
ENLISTED 27/12/41, BRISBANE, QLD (AVONDALE, QLD)
NOK, BRIX, HERMAN
DISCHARGED 7/3/44, 5th FIELD REGIMENT
BAR CODE 4920546 **DIGITAL COPY AVAILABLE**

WROTE “GUNNY CYRIL EDWARD JORGENSEN, QX29624, GROVELY, BUNDABERG”. VERY FAINT, LOCATED IN AN ELLIPSE JUST ABOVE THE BOARD AND LEFT OF VEACH.

Second graffiti

JORGENSEN, CYRIL EDWARD, QX29624, GUNNER LOWER LEFT
WROTE “CYRIL EDWARD JORGENSEN, QX29624, GROVELY” IN AN ELLIPSE.

THE GRAFFITI IS DAMAGED. LOCATED UNDER HARRISON JUST ABOVE THE BOARD.

KURKOWSKI, WILHELM KARL FRIEDRICK, QX30777, CRAFTSMAN LOWER RIGHT
DOB 23/9/07, HAMBURG, GERMANY
ENLISTED19/3/42, BRISBANE, QLD (CALEN, QLD)
NOK, KURKOWSKI, EVA
DISCHARGED 8/1/46, 1st INFANTRY TROOPS WORKSHOP
BAR CODE 4900638
WROTE “QX30777, PTE KURKOWSKI, CALEN, VIA MACKAY”. LOCATED JUST ABOVE THE BOARD.

LAWSON, ALVA ROYDON, QX25496, PRIVATE LOWER LEFT
DOB 17/8/20, MARYBOROUGH, QLD
ENLISTED 9/12/41, BRISBANE, QLD (MARYBOROUGH, QLD)
NOK, LAWSON, CHRISTINA
DISCHARGED 22/2/46, 1st PORT MAINTENANCE COMPANY
BAR CODE 4492662
WROTE “QX25496, GNR LAWSON, A.R., 41ST FLD BTY, AIF”. FAINT, LOCATED RIGHT OF LEE AND FRIEND AND UNDER HARRISON.

LEE, ARTHUR, Q64535, DRIVER LOWER FAR LEFT
DOB 9/5/20, TENTERFIELD, NSW
ENLISTED 7/7/40, SANDGATE, QLD (SANDGATE, QLD)
NOK, LEE, ARTHUR
DISCHARGED 5/5/45, 1st AUXILLARY HORSE TRANSPORT COMPANY AASC
BAR CODE 4899216
WROTE “A. LEE, QX27552, AUX H.TRANSPORT, ENOGGERA”. IN A RECTANGLE.

LEIGH, RICHARD ROY, QX27552, PRIVATE UPPER CENTRE/RIGHT
DOB 10/5/22, MACKAY, QLD
ENLISTED 11/2/42, BRISBANE, QLD, (CARMILA, QLD)
NOK, LEIGH, RICHARD
DISCHARGED 10/4/42, 101st CONVALESCENT DEPOT

BAR CODE 4856158

WROTE "R.R. LEIGH, QX27552, N.C.R." IN A RECTANGLE.

LENNANE, LESLIE EDWIN, VX81854 (V22657), LANCE CORPORAL UPPER RIGHT

DOB 7/5/18, TALLANGATTA, VIC

ENLISTED 28/7/42, IN THE FIELD, VIC (WANGARATTA, VIC)

NOK, LENNANE, MICHAEL

DISCHARGED 4/4/44, 8th CAVALRY REGIMENT

BAR CODE 6065311

WROTE "VX81854, TPR. LENNANE" IN A SQUARE.

LOVEDAY, ALFRED HENRY, QX34660 (Q191480), SERGEANT LOWER CENTRE

DOB 14/2/17, MARYBOROUGH, QLD

ENLISTED 21/5/40, LYTTON, QLD (MARYBOROUGH, QLD)

NOK, LOVEDAY, HEDWIG

DISCHARGED 11/3/46, 38th WIRELESS TASK SECTION

BAR CODE 4477467 **DIGITAL COPY AVAILABLE**

WROTE "A.H. LOVEDAY, QX34---, SIGS" IN CURSIVE SCRIPT.

MARSHALL, THOMAS HERBERT, QX29391, PRIVATE MID CENTRE

DOB 13/5/08, READING, ENGLAND

ENLISTED 16/12/41, BRISBANE CITY, QLD (GRANGE, QLD)

NOK, MARSHALL, MARJORY

DISCHARGED 27/10/44, 2/9th INFANTRY BATTALION

BAR CODE 4920296

WROTE "T.H. MARSHALL, QX29391, ATTD" IN A CIRCLE.

MARTIN, CHARLES CRAMMOND, QX14484, PRIVATE LOWER LEFT, BB

DOB 4/11/19, DUNDEE, SCOTLAND

ENLISTED 10/7/40, KELVIN GROVE, QLD (ASHGROVE, QLD)

NOK, MARTIN, CHARLES

DISCHARGED 6/2/42, 2/26th INFANTRY BATTALION

BAR CODE 4493060

WROTE "QX14484, C.C. MARTIN, 2/26 MALAYA" IN A CIRCLE.

McDERMID, SIDNEY WALLACE, QX26927, PRIVATE MID LEFT
DOB 29/7/22, CHINDERAH, NSW
ENLISTED 12/1/42, BRISBANE, QLD (WOOLLOONGABBA, QLD)
NOK, McDERMID, E.
DISCHARGED 3/6/46, 2/2nd MACHINE GUN BATTALION
BAR CODE 4486940
WROTE "QX26927, PTE S W MC DERMID, BIVOUAC 31st BTN SOUTHPORT".

BEST GUESS

McDONALD, JAMES REID, Q141524, SERGEANT MID CENTRE/RIGHT
DOB 15/7/1897, ABERDEENSHIRE, SCOTLAND
ENLISTED 9/5/42, BRISBANE, QLD (ASHGROVE, QLD)
NOK, MCDONALD, FLORENCE
DISCHARGED 29/4/46, CAPE RIVER MEATWORKS MAINTENANCE SECTION
BAR CODE 4463556
WROTE "J. McDONALD, 14 CHURCH LANE, INSCH, ABERDEENSHIRE, SCOTLAND". THE "J"IS PARTLY MISSING.

McDUFF, JOHN, QX29913, CRAFTSMAN LOWER FAR LEFT
DOB 12/6/17, MOUNT PERRY, QLD
ENLISTED 26/1/42, BUNDABERG, QLD (MOUNT PERRY, QLD)
NOK, McDUFF, JOYCE
DISCHARGED 20/12/45, 2/13th COMPOSITE ANTI AIRCRAFT REGIMENT WORKSHOP
BAR CODE 4920799
WROTE "QX29913, PTE J. McDUFF" IN AN OVAL. LOCATED BELOW BEUTEL.

McEWEN, THOMAS STEWART, QX27539, GUNNER MID LEFT
DOB 16/3/21, MACKAY, QLD
ENLISTED 11/2/42, BRISBANE, QLD (FINCH HATTON, QLD)
NOK, McEWEN, VALERIE
DISCHARGED 15/8/45, 141st HEAVY ANTI AIRCRAFT BATTERY, MOBILE
BAR CODE 4855463
WROTE "QX27539, GNR T.S. McEWEN, AIF, GROVELY".

McGILL, JAMES EDWARD, QX18836, BOMBARDIER UPPER FAR LEFT
DOB 17/10/21, MACKAY, QLD
ENLISTED 23/10/41, MACKAY, QLD (MACKAY, QLD)
NOK, McGILL, JAMES

DISCHARGED 1/4/46, 2/12th FIELD REGIMENT

BAR CODE 4494921 **DIGITAL COPY AVAILABLE**

WROTE "QX18836, GNR McGILL, J.E. 1ST TANK UNIT, AIF, GROVELY". LOCATED ABOVE WARNER.

McKENZIE, THOMAS, QX12245, PRIVATE LOWER RIGHT, BB

DOB 21/6/04, TOCAL, QLD

ENLISTED 7/7/40, ROCKHAMPTON, QLD (UNKNOWN)

NOK, McKENZIE, L.

DISCHARGED 23/12/43, 1st ANTI TANK REGIMENT (6 REINFORCEMENTS)

BAR CODE 4868600

WROTE "THE KID CHOCOLATE, QX12245" IN AN OVAL.

McKINNON, LEONARD FELIX, QX29278, PRIVATE UPPER CENTRE

DOB 25/11/21, TWEED HEADS, NSW

ENLISTED 5/1/42, CAIRNS, QLD (CAIRNS, QLD)

NOK, McKINNON, ANGUS

DISCHARGED 10/4/46, 2/3rd PORT OPERATING COMPANY

BAR CODE 4920169

WROTE "QX29278, PTE. L. McKINNON, C COY, 7 BTL, REDBANK". LOCATED LEFT OF LEIGH.

McLENNAN, WALTER DONALD, Q127861, PRIVATE LOWER CENTRE, BB

DOB 29/9/23, GRAFTON, NSW

ENLISTED 24/8/42, CHARLEVILLE, QLD (WARWICK, QLD)

NOK, McLENNAN, EMILY

DISCHARGED 1/7/46, 5th CARRIER COMPANY

BAR CODE 4451285

WROTE "Q127861, PTE. W. McLENNAN, WARWICK, 30.8.42" IN AN OVAL.

McLEOD, ERIC DANIEL, QX25321 (Q90195), PRIVATE LOWER LEFT

DOB 21/11/19, BRISBANE, QLD

ENLISTED 12/3/41, ALBION, QLD (PINKENBA, QLD)

NOK, McLEOD, ETHEL

DISCHARGED 29/11/45, 2/1st DOCKS OPERATING COMPANY

BAR CODE 4486157

WROTE "QX25321, GNR E.D. McLEOD, 41ST FLD TNG BTY, GROVELY, AIF". THE WRITING IS PARTIALLY DISFIGURED.

McLEOD, RODERICK DUNCAN, QX29336, PRIVATE UPPER RIGHT
DOB 5/7/20, BRISBANE, QLD
ENLISTED 10/1/42, TARA, QLD (UNDULLA CREEK, QLD)
NOK, McLEOD, JAMES
DISCHARGED 11/4/46, 2/7th INFANTRY BATTALION
BAR CODE 4920232
WROTE "PTE R.D. McLEOD, TARA" IN AN OVAL WITH THE WORD "MATES" AND THE NAME OF HIS MATE "PTE T.N.O. NEWMAN, TARA". THIS IS THE ONLY R.D. McLEOD FROM TARA.

McNAUGHTON, JOHN RICHARD, VX118736, (V38521), CORPORAL MID LEFT
ALSO KNOWN AS McNAUGHTAN, JACK RICHARD BREWENS
DOB 27/8/18, CARLTON, VIC
ENLISTED 5/1/40, MELBOURNE, VIC (COLLINGWOOD, VIC)
NOK, McNAUGHTON, LILIAN
DISCHARGED 22/5/46, 29/46th INFANTRY BATTALION
BAR CODE 6074152 (UNDER THE NAME OF JACK McNAUGHTAN)
WROTE "CPL J. McNAUGHTON, 29TH BN, V38521, CARRIERS".

MEEHAN, PHILLIP GEORGE, QX28971, SAPPER MID RIGHT
DOB 14/1/14, DALBY, QLD
ENLISTED 1/1/42, MACKAY, QLD (MACKAY, QLD)
NOK, MEEHAN, EDITH
DISCHARGED 2/10/45, 2/15th INFANTRY BATTALION
BAR CODE 4485877
WROTE "P.G. MEEHAN, QX28971, MACKAY, 22/2/1942" IN A RECTANGLE.

MELROSE, WILLIAM LUKE, QX40045 (Q15148), SAPPER MID RIGHT
DOB 13/7/22, QUIRINDI, NSW
ENLISTED 9/12/40, BRISBANE, QLD (CHERMSIDE, QLD)
NOK, MELROSE, ANNIE
DISCHARGED 8/3/45, 1st FIELD SURVEY COMPANY
BAR CODE 4903800
WROTE "SPR. W. MELROSE, GABBA" IN TWO SQUARES, GRAFITTI STYLE. THE TAIL OF THE "E" IS LONG AND CURLING. THIS IS THE ONLY SAPPER W. MELROSE IN THE NOMINAL ROLL.

MILLER, KEITH DOUGLAS, QX28788, PRIVATE UPPER FAR LEFT
DOB 9/11/21, DALBY, QLD
ENLISTED 3/1/42, BOONAH, QLD (MT ALFORD, QLD)

NOK, MILLER, ROSETTA
DISCHARGED 26/5/45, 2/25th FIELD PARK COMPANY
BAR CODE 4485332 **DIGITAL COPY AVAILABLE**
WROTE "-------R, K.D., ------8788, -----DALBY" IN A RECTANGLE NEXT TO THE FRAME. MOST OF THIS GRAFFITI IS COVERED IN PLASTER.

MILLER, RONALD ARTHUR, QX25320, PRIVATE LOWER RIGHT
DOB 23/11/17, BRISBANE, QLD
ENLISTED 2/12/41, BRISBANE, QLD (MOGGILL, QLD)
NOK, MILLER, BENJAMIN
DISCHARGED 28/1/44, 1st ARMOURED DIVISION PROVOST COMPANY
BAR CODE 4486158
WROTE "QX25320, PTE. R.A. MILLER, AIF, 1ST AUS ARMD DIV TPS COY AASC, DEAGON, SANDGATE" IN A RECTANGLE.

MILLGATE, ETHELBERT GEORGE, WX7004, PRIVATE MID FAR LEFT
DOB 18/1/06, KENT, ENGLAND
ENLISTED 30/7/40, CLAREMONT, WA (PERTH, WA)
NOK, MILLGATE, J.
DISCHARGED 14/12/45, 2/13th FIELD AMBULANCE
BAR CODE 6453121
WROTE "WX7004, 2/13 FD AMB, AIF". LOCATED ABOVE HARRIS.

MOIR, GEORGE LEO, SX27113 (S11225), PRIVATE LOWER RIGHT
DOB 27/4/20, LAUNCESTON, TAS
ENLISTED 10/11/42, PORT MORESBY, PAPUA/NG (COLONEL LIGHT GARDENS, SA)
NOK, MOIR, K
DISCHARGED 6/8/47, 13th FIELD REGIMENT
BAR CODE 6414175
WROTE "GNR. G.L. MOIR, SMX11225". THIS SOLDIER HAS CONFUSED HIS SX NUMBER AND HIS S NUMBER.

MORAN, GEORGE ALBERT, N346549, PRIVATE MID FAR RIGHT
DOB 17/10/23, PENRITH, NSW
ENLISTED 10/3/42, PENRITH, NSW (PENRITH, NSW)
NOK, MORAN, RUBY
DISCHARGED 27/1/43, 11th GYRO GUNSIGHT
BAR CODE 6173646
WROTE "NX346549, PTE G.A. MORAN, 35 UNION? RD, PENRITH, NSW" IN A SQUARE BELOW *W.* LAWRENCE. THE SOLDIER HAS USED NX INSTEAD OF N FOR HIS NUMBER.

MUDGE, EDWARD STANLEY, SX13434, PRIVATE LOWER FAR RIGHT
DOB 13/5/17, EDENHOPE, VIC
ENLISTED 28/6/41, WAYVILLE, SA (BARMERA, SA)
NOK, MUDGE, OLIVE
DISCHARGED 1/11/45, 13th FIELD REGIMENT
BAR CODE 6398269
WROTE "SX13434, E.S. MUDGE, BNE".

MUNRO, REGINALD DAVIS, QX32793, PRIVATE MID LEFT
DOB 26/5/23, CHARTERS TOWERS, QLD
ENLISTED 16/6/42, BRISBANE, QLD (CAIRNS, QLD)
NOK, MUNRO, MAVIS
DISCHARGED 12/3/46, 10th MOVEMENT CONTROL GROUP
BAR CODE 4473743
WROTE "QX32793, PTE MUNRO, R.D., HARRIS'S RANGERS, HUGHENDEN".

MURPHY, EDWARD JOFFRE, NX114918 (N266326), BOMBARDIER LOWER FAR RIGHT, BB
DOB, 26/2/15, NEWCASTLE, NSW
ENLISTED 11/9/42 SYDNEY, NSW (NORTH WOLLONGONG, NSW)
NOK, MURPHY, EUNICE
DISCHARGED 3/5/45, 32nd ANTI AIRCRAFT BATTERY
BAR CODE 5645596
WROTE "NX114918, GNR E.J. MURPHY" IN A RECTANGLE.

MYERS, GILBERT THOMAS, NX20608, PRIVATE TOP RIGHT-HAND CORNER OF MID CENTRE
DOB 4/4/16, BANGALOW, NSW
ENLISTED 6/6/40, PADDINGTON, NSW (MALLANGAREE, NSW)
NOK, MYERS, GILBERT
DISCHARGED 10/9/45, 26th FIELD BAKING PLATOON
BAR CODE 4642754 **DIGITAL COPY AVAILABLE**
WROTE "NX20608, PTE G.T. MYERS". VERY FAINT. LOCATED DIRECTLY BELOW LEIGH.

NEWMAN, THOMAS NEVILLE ORCHARD, QX29353, PRIVATE UPPER RIGHT
DOB 9/6/20, MUDGEE, NSW
ENLISTED 10/1/42, TARA, QLD ("TIBBEREENAH", TARA, QLD)
NOK, NEWMAN, MONICA
DISCHARGED 25/11/43, 2/7th INFANTRY BATTALION
BAR CODE 4920275 **DIGITAL COPY AVAILABLE**

WROTE "PTE T.N.O. NEWMAN, TARA" IN AN OVAL WITH THE WORD "MATES" AND THE NAME OF HIS MATE "PTE R.D. McLEOD, TARA". THIS IS THE ONLY T.N.O. NEWMAN IN THE RECORDS.

NIHILL, LAURENCE WILLIAM, VX107487 (V21084), SAPPER LOWER CENTRE
DOB 25/8/15, ABBOTSFORD, VIC
ENLISTED 11/7/42, MURRUMBA, QLD (HEIDELBERG, VIC)
NOK, NIHILL, MATTHEW
DISCHARGED 14/3/46, 21st FIELD COMPANY
BAR CODE 6106259
WROTE "SAPPER NIHELL, VX21084".
THIS SOLDIER HAS CONFUSED HIS V NUMBER WITH HIS VX NUMBER. LOCATED UNDER CHADWICK.

O'BRIEN, DERMOT FRANCIS, QX27641, PRIVATE MID CENTRE
DOB 28/10/04, CHARTERS TOWERS, QLD
ENLISTED 12/2/42, BRISBANE, QLD (CHARTERS TOWERS, QLD)
NOK, O'BRIEN, MICHAEL
DISCHARGED 16/2/45, 2/1st HEADQUARTERS GUARD BATTALION
BAR CODE 4855421
WROTE "QX27641, O'BRIEN, D.F.,-----BTN, BOGGABILLA" IN A RECTANGLE. VERY FAINT. SOME OF THE WRITING IS COVERED WITH PLASTER. LOCATED ABOVE MARSHALL.

OKEY, RONALD, VX70784, CORPORAL MID CENTRE/RIGHT
DOB 30/9/19, CLIFTON HILL, VIC
ENLISTED 5/1/42, CAULFIELD, VIC (CLIFTON HILL, VIC)
NOK, OKEY, ETHEL
DISCHARGED 24/1/46, 2/ 8th DOCKS OPERATING COMPANY
BAR CODE 6074793
WROTE "VX70784, SPR. R. OKEY" IN LARGE LETTERS.

OSBORNE, WILLIAM CHARLES, QX33458, PRIVATE MID LEFT/FAR LEFT
DOB 29/7/17, INGLEWOOD, QLD
ENLISTED 1/9/42, BRISBANE, QLD (INGLEWOOD, QLD)
NOK, OSBORNE, DAPHNE
DISCHARGED 26/2/44, 25th INFANTRY TRAINING BATTALION
BAR CODE 4477211
WROTE "PTE W.C. OSBORNE, QX33458, AIF" IN AN ELLIPSE. FAINT. RIGHT OF A IN JACKSON.

PARKINSON, ARTHUR EDWARD HENRY, QX27701, SAPPER MID LEFT
DOB 6/6/21, AYR, QLD
ENLISTED 25/2/42, BRISBANE, QLD (FINCH HATTON, QLD)
NOK, RHONDA, ELSIE
DISCHARGED 17/10/45, 2/1st MECHANICAL EQUIPMENT COMPANY
BAR CODE 4900949
WROTE "QX27701, SPR. A. PARKINSON, AIF GROVELY".

PASCOE, LIONEL BERT, PRIVATE, NX9389, PRIVATE LOWER LEFT
DOB 12/2/17, DENMAN, NSW
ENLISTED 22/12/39, PADDINGTON, NSW (DENMAN, NSW)
NOK, PASCOE, ROBERT
DISCHARGED 6/9/45, 6th DIVISION, AUSTRALIAN ARMY SERVICE CORPS
BAR CODE 4848849
WROTE "NX9389, DVR PASCOE, 6TH DIV, AASC, AIF" IN AN OVAL.

PEMBLE, REGINALD HENRY, N225195, PRIVATE UPPER FAR RIGHT
DOB 13/2/16, MURRUMBURRAH, NSW
ENLISTED 28/1/42, RANDWICK, NSW (BONDI JUNCTION, NSW)
NOK, PEMBLE, IRENE
DISCHARGED 1/11/45, 106th CASUALTY CLEARING STATION
BAR CODE 5577699
WROTE "R.H. PEMBLE, NX225195, 61 SPRING STREET, BONDI JUNCTION, NSW" IN A RECTANGLE. THIS SOLDIER HAS USED NX INSTEAD *OF* N IN HIS GRAFFITI.

PHIPPS, JOHN WILLIAM, VX77976, PRIVATE LOWER LEFT
DOB 7/10/19, GEELONG, VIC
ENLISTED 16/3/42, CAULFIELD, VIC (EAST GEELONG, VIC)
NOK, PHIPPS, A.
DISCHARGED 16/5/46, 2nd BASE ORDNANCE DEPOT
BAR CODE 6071252
WROTE "SAPPER J. PHIPPS, VX779--," IN A RECTANGLE JUST ABOVE THE BOARD.

BEST GUESS

PLYMIN, RONALD ALFRED, V35389, SIGNALMAN UPPER FAR LEFT
DOB 11/4/19, ABBOTSFORD, VIC
ENLISTED 5/1/40, PRESTON, VIC (CROXTON, VIC)
NOK, PLYMIN, HENRY
DISCHARGED 24/2/42, 3rd INFANTRY DIVISION SIGNALS

BAR CODE 6621340

WROTE "VX103935, R. PLYMIN, 3RD DIV, ENTERTAINMENT UNIT".

THIS VX NUMBER BELONGS TO ANOTHER SOLDIER. WHY IT WAS USED BY THIS SOLDIER IS UNKNOWN. THERE ARE ONLY TWO R. PLYMINS ON RECORD. THIS ONE IS IN THE 3RD DIVISION, WHICH WAS REFERRED TO IN THE GRAFFITI.

POPP, CECIL THOMAS, QX33457, PRIVATE MID LEFT/FAR LEFT

DOB 18/10/08, TEXAS, QLD

ENLISTED 1/9/42, BRISBANE, QLD (OMANAMA, QLD)

NOK, POPP, DULCIE

DISCHARGED 24/11/43, 2/1st ADVANCED WORKSHOP AEME

BAR CODE 4477210

WROTE "PTE C.T. POPP, QX33457, AIF" ABOVE THE M OF MACKAY.

RAMSDEN, HERBERT JAMES, QX32685, CRAFTSMAN LOWER RIGHT

DOB 22/5/18, ESK, QLD

ENLISTED 9/6/42, BRISBANE, QLD (KINGAROY, QLD)

NOK, RAMSDEN, MELANIE

DISCHARGED 29/1/46, 2/72nd LIGHT AVA DETACHMENT

BAR CODE 4488307

WROTE "QX32685, RAMSDEN, H". UNDERLINED. WRITTEN JUST ABOVE THE BOARD.

REID, JOHN, QX24899, CORPORAL MID FAR RIGHT

DOB 8/5/19, TOWNSVILLE, QLD

ENLISTED 1/1/42, TOWNSVILLE, QLD (TOWNSVILLE, QLD)

NOK, REID, ELDA (HOME ADDRESS, JARVIS FIELD, AYR, QLD)

DISCHARGED 6/12/45, 2/4th LIGHT ANTI AIRCRAFT WORKSHOPS AEME

BAR CODE 4483711 **DIGITAL COPY AVAILABLE**

WROTE "QX24899, J. REID, AYR, NQ" IN LARGE LETTERS.

BEST GUESS

RICE, RONALD FRANCIS STEPHENS, QX48705 (Q100784), SERGEANT MID FAR RIGHT

DOB 6/2/22, BRISBANE, QLD

ENLISTED 18/2/43, GOOMERI, QLD (CHERMSIDE, QLD)

NOK, RICE, ENID

DISCHARGED 27/3/46, 'Z' SPECIAL UNIT

BAR CODE 4487726 **DIGITAL COPY AVAILABLE**

WROTE "SIG R. RICE, GABBA" IN GRAFFITI STYLE ABOVE THE LARGE-LETTERED DAVIE. THIS IS THE ONLY R. RICE WHO WAS A SIGNALMAN.

RIEMAN, STANLEY ARTHUR, QX32592, PRIVATE LOWER FAR RIGHT
DOB 6/9/10, ROCKHAMPTON, QLD
ENLISTED 2/6/42, BRISBANE, QLD (CAPELLA, QLD)
NOK, RIEMAN, ELLEN
DISCHARGED 9/4/47, 2/16th INFANTRY BATTALION
BAR CODE 4915719
WROTE, "RIEMAN S.A., QX32592". UNDERLINED.

RITCHIE, THOMAS JOHN, QX31873, PRIVATE UPPER LEFT
DOB 26/6/18, WELLINGTON, NEW ZEALAND
ENLISTED 28/4/42, BILOELA, QLD (BILOELA, QLD)
NOK, RITCHIE, WILLIAM
DISCHARGED 21/6/46, 2/15th INFANTRY BATTALION
BAR CODE 4915542
WROTE "QX31873, PTE RITCHIE, T.J., BILOELA" IN A CIRCLE. FAINT. ABOVE THE N OF JACKSON.

ROBINSON, THOMAS, WX5641, CORPORAL LOWER RIGHT
DOB 25/5/06, NEWCASTLE, ENGLAND
ENLISTED 22/6/40, NORTHAM, WA (TAMBELLUP, WA)
NOK, ROBINSON, GERTRUDE
DISCHARGED 10/7/45, 2/16th INFANTRY BATTALION
BAR CODE 6457066
WROTE "WX5641, T. ROBINSON, 2/16 BATT, WEST AUS".

ROSS, JAMES, NX164097 (N346575) PRIVATE UPPER RIGHT
DOB 11/1/24, DUMFERMLINE, SCOTLAND
ENLISTED 9/6/43, DARLEY, VIC (KATOOMBA, NSW)
NOK, ROSS, MARY
DISCHARGED 30/4/46, 2/7th AUSTRALIAN GENERAL HOSPITAL
BAR CODE 5565565
WROTE "NX346575, J. ROSS, BRIXTON, CLARENCE ST, KATOOMBA, NSW" IN A RECTANGLE. THIS SOLDIER HAS CONFUSED HIS NX NUMBER AND HIS N NUMBER.

ROWE, GORDON JAMES, QX27007, PRIVATE MID LEFT
DOB 24/12/22, INNISFAIL, QLD
ENLISTED 1/1/42, TOWNSVILLE, QLD (CHARTERS TOWERS, QLD)

NOK, STEWART, JACK
DISCHARGED 7/7/45, 2/15th INFANTRY BATTALION
BAR CODE 4486980
WROTE "PTE G.J. ROWE, QX27007, HUGHENDEN" IN A CIRCLE. VERY FAINT. LOCATED ABOVE PARKINSON.

SANKEY, CHARLIE JOSEPH, Q149371, PRIVATE LOWER CENTRE
DOB 17/3/24, SANDGATE, QLD
ENLISTED 18/5/42, VALLEY, QLD (SANDGATE, QLD)
NOK, SANKEY, WALTER
DISCHARGED 15/4/44, LAND HEADQUARTERS
BAR CODE 4911478
WROTE "CHARLIE SANKEY, Q149371" IN A RECTANGLE.

SAXBY, HAROLD HENRY, SX5334, PRIVATE LOWER RIGHT
DOB 7/7/16, SYDNEY, NSW
ENLISTED 14/6/40, ADELAIDE, SA (EASTWOOD, SA)
NOK, SAXBY, EFFIE
DISCHARGED 18/11/44, 2/5th COMPANY AASC
BAR CODE 6643884 **DIGITAL COPY AVAILABLE**
WROTE "SX5334, H. SAXBY". FAINT. LOCATED UNDER VEACH.

SCOTT, GEORGE EARNSHAW, SX1150, SERGEANT MID FAR RIGHT
DOB 21/8/17, HOBART, TAS
ENLISTED 27/11/39, ADELAIDE, SA (ADELAIDE, SA)
NOK, SCOTT, CHARLES
DISCHARGED 31/7/45, 2/10th INFANTRY BATTALION
BAR CODE 6641836 **DIGITAL COPY AVAILABLE**
WROTE "SX1150, G.E.S". LOCATED ABOVE BEUTEL, NEXT TO THE FRAME.

SMITH, DONALD LINDSAY, QX29345, SAPPER MID LEFT
DOB 4/3/22, DALBY, QLD
ENLISTED 10/1/42, BRISBANE, QLD (TARA, QLD)
NOK, SMITH, LESLIE
DISCHARGED 12/3/45, 2/2nd DOCKS OPERATING COMPANY
BAR CODE 4920223
WROTE "QX29345, D.L. SMITH, ELDEREST? TARA, WITH LOVE XXXX". LOCATED LEFT OF PARKINSON.

SMITH, JOSHUA, Q135428, PRIVATE UPPER FAR RIGHT
DOB 22/1/22, BUNDABERG, QLD
ENLISTED 20/3/42, BIGGENDEN, QLD (BIGGENDEN, QLD)
NOK, SMITH, ELIZABETH
DISCHARGED 20/4/43, NORTHERN COMMAND ARMY TRADES TRAINING DEPOT
BAR CODE 4452326
WROTE "QX135428, J. SMITH". FAINT. LOCATED ABOVE BEINCKE. THIS SOLDIER HAS ADDED AN EXTRA X TO HIS NOMINAL ROLL MILITIA NUMBER.

SMITH, NEVILLE DAVID, NX106101 (21584), SERGEANT LOWER FAR RIGHT, BB
DOB 2/5/23, DELEGATE, NSW
ENLISTED 27/7/42, LONG BAY, NSW (DELEGATE, NSW)
NOK, SMITH, THOMAS
DISCHARGED 3/6/48, 32nd HEAVY ANTI AIRCRAFT BATTERY
BAR CODE NO RECORD
WROTE "NX106101, GNR N.D. SMITH" IN AN OVAL.

SNELL, VIVIAN EDDY, QX28872, PRIVATE LOWER FAR RIGHT, BB
DOB 16/11/14, NAMBOUR, QLD
ENLISTED 14/1/42, GYMPIE, QLD (GUNALDA, QLD)
NOK, SNELL, CHARLES
DISCHARGED 3/12/45, 2/7th INFANTRY BATTALION
BAR CODE 4485803
WROTE "QX28872, PTE V.E. SNELL, 2/8 PIONEER COY, NO. 1 PLATOON, AIF, GUNALDA, QUEENSLAND, AUSTRALIA" DIFFICULT TO READ.

SOLOMON, WILLIAM HENRY, VX69995, SAPPER LOWER FAR RIGHT
DOB 23/7/05, SEYMOUR, VIC
ENLISTED 29/12/41, CAULFIELD, VIC (ASCOT VALE, VIC)
NOK, SOLOMON, OLIVE
DISCHARGED 21/4/44, 2/11th FIELD COMPANY
BAR CODE 6115987
WROTE "HE WHO RITES ON SHIT HOUSE WALLS SHOULD ROLL HIM...? VX69995, W.H SOLOMON, AAOC, AIF, VICTORIA".

SPRY, EDWIN DIGBY, QX25106, PRIVATE MID LEFT
DOB 9/10/16, SYDNEY, NSW
ENLISTED 31/12/41, CAIRNS, QLD (KULARA, QLD)
NOK, SPRY, E
DISCHARGED 14/9/45, 62nd INFANTRY BATTALION

BAR CODE 4483924

WROTE "QX25106, PTE SPRY, E.D." IN AN ELLIPSE LOCATED ABOVE McEWEN.

STEVENS, FRANK STUART, QX18993, GUNNER LOWER CENTRE

DOB 25/1/20, MACKAY, QLD

ENLISTED 8/1/42, MACKAY, QLD (MACKAY, QLD)

NOK, STEVENS, MAY

DISCHARGED 12/11/45, 2/1st MEDIUM REGIMENT

BAR CODE 4495064

WROTE "GNR F.S. STEVENS, AIF, GROVELY". LOCATED ABOVE SANKEY. THIS IS THE ONLY GUNNER F. S. STEVENS ON RECORD.

STREET, CHARLES HAVENHAND, QX47166 (Q140313), SIGNALMAN MID CENTRE

DOB 21/1/24, BRISBANE, QLD

ENLISTED 2/3/42, BRISBANE, QLD (NEW FARM, QLD)

NOK, STREET, JOHN

DISCHARGED 13/6/46, 1st COMPOSITE SIGNALS SECTION

BAR CODE 4883636

WROTE "SIG C.H. STREET, Q140313, BNE FORTRESS SIGNALS, FORT LYTTON" IN A RECTANGLE WHICH ALSO INCLUDES A HERALDIC SYMBOL OF THREE CONCENTRIC SQUARES.

STREETER, MERVYN NEIL, QX23167, GUNNER MID FAR LEFT

DOB 12/9/22, BUNDABERG, QLD

ENLISTED 20/11/41, ROCKHAMPTON, QLD (UBOBO, QLD)

NOK, STREETER, WILLIAM

DISCHARGED 12/4/44, 56th COMPOSITE ANTI AIRCRAFT REGIMENT

BAR CODE 4484129 **DIGITAL COPY AVAILABLE**

WROTE "QX23167, PTE M. N. STREETER, UBOBO, B.V. LINE" (BOYNE VALLEY LINE) IN A WAVY ELLIPSE.

TARBUCK, JOSEPH BERNARD, QX12821, PRIVATE LOWER FAR RIGHT

DOB 15/1/08, WALSALL, ENGLAND

ENLISTED 21/3/41, BRISBANE, QLD (BRISBANE, QLD)

NOK, TARBUCK, WINNIFRED

DISCHARGED 25/10/45, 2/31st INFANTRY BATTALION, 7 REINFORCEMENTS

BAR CODE 4499910

WROTE "QX12821, PTE J.B. TARBUCK, 2/31 BTN, AIF" IN A SQUARE IN THE CORNER.

TAYLOR, LESLIE RAYMOND, QX27588, SAPPER LOWER/MID CENTRE
DOB 19/11/1917, MACKSVILLE, NSW
ENLISTED 14/2/42, BRISBANE, QLD (WEST KEMPSEY, NSW)
NOK, TAYLOR, NORBERT
DISCHARGED 9/4/46, OPERATING COMPANY AATNC
BAR CODE 4862666
WROTE "L.R. TAYLOR, WEST KEMPSEY, NSW". VERY FAINT. LOCATED ABOVE CHADWICK

NOTE: SAPPER TAYLOR'S RESIDENCE AT THE TIME OF HIS ENLISTMENT HAS BEEN INCORRECTLY RECORDED ON THE NOMINAL ROLL AS KEMPLEY INSTEAD OF KEMPSEY.

TAYLOR, WILLIAM FRANK, QX32683, DRIVER LOWER FAR RIGHT
DOB 30/10/13, COLEFORD, ENGLAND
ENLISTED 9/6/42, BRISBANE, QLD (MONICA MAINE, QLD)
NOK, TAYLOR, LOUISA
DISCHARGED 13/8/46, AUSTRALIAN-NEW GUINEA ADMINISTRATIVE UNIT
BAR CODE 4488305
WROTE "QX32683, TAYLOR, W.F." WRITTEN JUST ABOVE THE BOARD.

BEST GUESS

VALLIS, ALEXANDER ROBERT, QX48378 (Q138563), PRIVATE LOWER FAR LEFT
ALSO RAAF 425787, AIRCRAFTMAN 2
DOB 29/7/22, ROCKHAMPTON, QLD
NOK, VALLIS, VERA
ENLISTED **AIF** 30/3/42, GLADSTONE, QLD (GLADSTONE, QLD)
ENLISTED **RAAF** 26/4/42, BRISBANE, QLD (GLADSTONE, QLD)
DISCHARGED **RAAF** 6/7/42, No. 3 INITIAL TRAINING SCHOOL
DISCHARGED **AIF** 15/3/46, 3rd FIELD BUTCHERY PLATOON
BAR CODE **AIF** 4487522, **RAAF** 5529954
WROTE "L.A.C. VALLIS, GOONDOON ST, GLADSTONE, QLD". THE DEPARTMENT OF VETERANS' AFFAIRS HAS CONFIRMED THAT THIS SOLDIER WAS LIVING IN GOONDOON STREET, GLADSTONE, AT THE TIME OF HIS ENLISTMENT.

BEST GUESS

VEIGEL, JAMES HENRY, NX128104 (N265714), PRIVATE MID LEFT
DOB 5/7/20, WOONOONA, NSW
ENLISTED 20/8/42, DAPTO, NSW (WOLLONGONG, NSW)
NOK, VEIGEL, CHARLES

DISCHARGED 8/6/45, 3rd INFANTRY DIVISION, MOBILE LAUNDRY & FIELD DECONTAMINATION UNIT

BAR CODE 5616422

WROTE "J. VEIGEL, 34, AIB, WOLLONGONG". VERY FAINT. LOCATED LEFT OF PARKINSON. IDENTIFICATION IS BASED ON INITIALS, SURNAME AND LOCALITY UPON ENLISTMENT.

VIQUERAT, RUSSELL MATTHEW, NX59337, GUNNER — UPPER RIGHT

DOB 25/1/19, PENSHURST, NSW

ENLISTED 15/7/40, PADDINGTON, NSW (LIDCOMBE, NSW)

NOK, VIQUERAT, REGINALD

DISCHARGED 12/3/46, 2/1st SURVEY REGIMENT RAA

BAR CODE 4653296

WROTE "NX59337, GNR R.M. VIQUERAT, D----? 2/1 SURVEY REGT, AIF". LOCATED RIGHT OF LEIGH.

WALLACE, HENRY, QX23005, PRIVATE — LOWER FAR LEFT

DOB 27/9/18, ROCKHAMPTON, QLD

ENLISTED 7/8/41, ROCKHAMPTON, QLD (YEPPOON, QLD)

NOK, WALLACE, IRENE

DISCHARGED 11/6/42, 101st ANTI TANK TRAINING BATTERY

BAR CODE 4490992

WROTE "QX23005, GNR WALLACE, H, 2/10 41ST FTB, GROVELY".

WARNER, ALLAN FREDERICK, QX31247, PRIVATE — UPPER FAR LEFT

DOB 11/12/22, ROMA, QLD

ENLISTED 7/4/42, BRISBANE, QLD (ALLANDALE, QLD)

NOK, WARNER, ALFRED

DISCHARGED 5/8/42, 101st CONVALESCENT DEPOT

BAR CODE 4873707

WROTE "QX31247, A.F. WARNER, ROMA" IN AN ELLIPSE. TEXT IS PARTIALLY MISSING.

WERNER, ALLAN EDWARD, QX24293, CORPORAL — UPPER FAR RIGHT

DOB 1/6/22, ROSEWOOD, QLD

ENLISTED 23/10/41, BRISBANE, QLD (AUCHENFLOWER, QLD)

NOK, WERNER, EDWARD

DISCHARGED 22/8/46, 2/9th FIELD REGIMENT

BAR CODE 4483129 — **DIGITAL COPY AVAILABLE**

WROTE "GNR A WERNER, GROVELY, QX" ALONG WITH HIS MATE'S NAME "GNR H. DREW". VERY FAINT. LOCATED LEFT OF PEMBLE. THIS SOLDIER IS THE ONLY A.

WERNER WITH A QX NUMBER. HIS NATIONAL ARCHIVES SERVICE RECORDS CONFIRM HIS IDENTITY.

WESTON, GEORGE HENRY, QX25322, (Q90210), CORPORAL LOWER LEFT

DOB 27/7/15, BRISBANE, QLD

ENLISTED 23/8/40, ANNERLEY, QLD (ANNERLEY, QLD)

NOK, WESTON ,GEORGE

DISCHARGED 15/1/46, 2/10th DOCKS OPERATING COMPANY

BAR CODE 4486156 **DIGITAL COPY AVAILABLE**

WROTE "QX25322, GNR. G.H. WESTON, 41ST FLD. TNG BTY, GROVELY, AIF".

WHEBELL, FREDERICK, QX32526, CORPORAL MID RIGHT

DOB 25/6/14, TOWNSVILLE, QLD

ENLISTED 25/5/42, BRISBANE, QLD (SOUTH TOWNSVILLE, QLD)

NOK, WHEBELL, GERTRUDE

DISCHARGED 8/9/45, QUEENSLAND LINES OF COMMUNICATION, ATTD

BAR CODE 4915647

WROTE "QX32526, PTE WHEBELL, F., 1.M.D, ATTD, WOOLLOONGABBA" IN A RECTANGLE WITH "AUST" IN TOP RIGHT-HAND CORNER. "1 MD" REFERS TO THE 1ST MILITARY DISTRICT, WHICH IS QUEENSLAND.

WRIGHT, JOHN WILLIAM, QX565 (QX26108), PRIVATE MID CENTRE

DOB 29/10/15, BRISBANE, QLD

ENLISTED 22/10/39, BRISBANE, QLD (COOPERS PLAINS, QLD)

NOK, WRIGHT, JAMES

DISCHARGED 16/5/43, 101st CONVALESCENT DEPOT

BAR CODE 4257836

WROTE "QX26108, WRIGHT, J. W." IN A CIRCLE. THE WRITING HAS BEEN PARTIALLY DISFIGURED.

WYATT, WILLIAM ARTHUR, NX144940 (N204140), DRIVER LOWER FAR LEFT

DOB 6/8/08, ALBURY, NSW

ENLISTED 19/12/42, 121st QLD IN THE FIELD (NARRANDERA, NSW)

NOK, WYATT, MARIE

DISCHARGED 10/2/46, 131st GENERAL TRANSPORT COMPANY

BAR CODE 5631266

WROTE "W.A. WYATT, 131 GTC, LATE OF NARRANDERA". SOME OF THE WRITING HAS BEEN DAMAGED.

UNIDENTIFIED SOLDIERS

In the future, with improved photographic techniques, more comprehensive data bases and additional information from the public, some of these men may be identified.

"LIEUT. R. GALLEN", UNDERLINED. LOCATED MID RIGHT, UNDER EDWARDS.

THERE IS NO MENTION OF THIS OFFICER IN THE NOMINAL ROLL. THERE ARE HOWEVER TWO RAAF FLIGHT LIEUTENANTS, R. GOLLAN, LISTED — 424784 AND 283196.

"**W. LAWRENCE**, AIF, GROVELY" WRITTEN IN LARGE LETTERS UPPER RIGHT/ FAR RIGHT

NO MORE INFORMATION IS PROVIDED. THERE ARE 66 W. LAWRENCES ON THE NOMINAL ROLL OF WHICH 46 ARE IN THE ARMY.

"**GUNALDA BOYS**". ANONYMOUS CONTRIBUTORS LOWER FAR LEFT, BB

PRIVATE JACOBSON AND PRIVATE SNELL ARE THE ONLY TWO MEN SO FAR IDENTIFIED WHO HAVE ANY CONNECTION TO THE TOWN OF GUNALDA. THIS MOST PROBABLY REFERS TO THEM.

"PTE J. O'CONNOR, BRISBANE". UPPER FAR LEFT

LOCATED NEAR THE FRAME. NO MORE INFORMATION IS PROVIDED. THERE ARE 162 J. O'CONNORS LISTED IN THE ARMY ON THE NOMINAL ROLL.

ANONYMOUS "NO 1 FITTERS, NO ACTION? LOST LEGION, WOLLONGABBA". BADLY DAMAGED, WRITTEN IN AN OVAL. MID LEFT

ANONYMOUS "DIRTY DEMPSEY". LOWER FAR LEFT

"C.S. WAL-----? 3 AUST DIV--------ONSER? 17.9.42". UPPER LEFT

MOST OF THIS SIGNATURE IS UNDER PLASTER AND TOO DIFFICULT TO READ. LOCATED RIGHT OF WARNER, ABOVE THE A OF JACKSON.

"**DON G. REIKER**". NAME ONLY MID CENTRE

THERE ARE NO RECORDS OF D. G. REIKER IN THE NOMINAL ROLL. LOCATED UNDER AND RIGHT OF MARSHALL. THIS MAY BE A CIVILIAN.

"GNR R (OR 'K') E. M----------? 41st FLD TNG BTY, GROVELY" LOWER LEFT

THE NAME IS BADLY DAMAGED. IT IS LOCATED JUST ABOVE THE BOARD LEFT OF PHIPPS, CLOSE TO SEVERAL OTHER SOLDIERS FROM THE 41ST FIELD TRAINING BATTERY, AIF, GROVELY.

"**R. SMITH,** C/O ML AND FD UNIT, LIVERPOOL". MID LEFT

LOCATED TO THR RIGHT OF PARKINSON. ML AND FD UNIT REFERS TO MOBILE LAUNDRY AND FIELD DECONTAMINATION UNIT. THERE ARE FOUR POSSIBLE R. SMITHS IN THE NOMINAL ROLL WITH CONNECTIONS TO LIVERPOOL. THESE ARE:

RAYMOND GLEN SMITH	N375711
RONALD GEORGE SMITH	NX167238 (N25290)
REGINALD ROSS SMITH	NX168088 (N436852)
ROBERT JOHN SMITH	NX149837 (450272)

AMERICAN VISITORS

"**C.J.EARL?** U.S.A". LOWER FAR LEFT

IN LARGE CURSIVE AMERICAN SCRIPT, FAINT, VERY DIFFICULT TO READ.

"**RALPH PIECK**, RUTHVEN, IOWA" MID CENTRE

WRITTEN IN A RECTANGLE. NO EXTRA INFORMATION HAS BEEN PROVIDED.

"**DANIEL HARRIS**, TAMPA, FLORIDA, USA." MID RIGHT

WRITTEN IN A RECTANGLE. NO EXTRA INFORMATION HAS BEEN PROVIDED.

"**PVT. RALPH BOLIO**. SCPC. LONG ISLAND, NY. AUGUST 22/42". LOWER FAR RIGHT

WRITTEN IN A DOUBLE RECTANGLE.

"**GEORGE R. McCALL**, ---------W, FLORIDA, 6/2/42" MID FAR LEFT

FAINT. THE TOWN'S NAME IS ILLEGIBLE.

"**A.W. VEACH**, *USS TULSA*, DETROIT MICHI, BUD" MID RIGHT

WRITTEN IN A LARGE CIRCLE.

A DRAWING OF THE HEAD OF A US SOLDIER MARKED **E.D.H.** LOWER FAR RIGHT

NO EXTRA INFORMATION PROVIDED. LOCATED BELOW RALPH BOLIO.

"**FORT MONMOUTH, NEW JERSEY"** LOWER FAR RIGHT

WITH A DRAWING OF A HEAD WEARING A TOP HAT. COULD THIS BE *UNCLE SAM*? FORT MONMOUTH WAS AN ARMY INSTALLATION IN NEW JERSEY.

"**FLATBUSH FLOOGIE**" MID FAR RIGHT

PROBABLY WRITTEN BY A US CITIZEN. FLATBUSH IS AN AREA IN NEW YORK. *FLOOGIE* (ALSO KNOWN AS *FLOOSIE*) IS COLLOQUIAL FOR A FEMALE OF INDISCRIMINATE MORALS.

APPENDIX 2

LIST OF LOCATIONS

QUEENSLAND	BORN	ENLISTED	RESIDENCE
IN THE FIELD		3	

BRISBANE AREA	10	56	3
ALBION		1	
ANNERLEY		1	1
ASHGROVE			2
AUCHENFLOWER			1
CHERMSIDE			2
COOPERS PLAINS			1
GORDON PARK			1
GRANGE			1
HENDRA			1
KALINGA			1
KELVIN GROVE		1	
LYTTON		2	
MOGGILL			1
NEW FARM			2
PETRIE TERRACE			1
PINKENBA			1
ROSALIE			1
SANDGATE	1	1	2
VALLEY		1	
WOOLLOONGABBA			1
TOTAL	11	66	23

AREAS OUTSIDE OF BRISBANE			
AJUKAN			1
ALLANDALE			1
AVONDALE			2
AYR	1		1
BARALBA			1
BEAUDESERT		1	1
BIGGENDEN	1	1	1
BILOELA		1	1
BLUFF	1		
BLYTHDALE			1

	BORN	ENLISTED	RESIDENCE
BOONAH		2	
BOROREN			1
BUNDABERG	5	2	
CAIRNS	1	3	2
CALEN			1
CAPELLA	1		1
CARMILA			1
CHARLEVILLE	1	1	
CHARTERS TOWERS	2		2
CLERMONT			1
COOROY	1		
CORDALBA	1		
DALBY	4		
ESK	3		
ETON NORTH			1
EUMUNDI			1
FERNVALE			1
FINCH HATTON	1		3
FOREST HILL			1
GLADSTONE	1	1	1
GOOMERI		1	
GOONDIWINDI			1
GUNALDA			2
GYMPIE	2	1	
HARRISVILLE	1		1
INGLEWOOD	2		2
INNISFAIL	1		
IPSWICH	2		1
KALKA			1
KINGAROY			1
KOUMALA			1
KULARA			1
KURILDALA	1		
LOWOOD	1		
MACKAY	11	8	5
MARYBOROUGH	2	2	2
MAXWELTON	1		
MILES	1		
MIRANI	1		

	BORN	ENLISTED	RESIDENCE
MIRIAM			1
MITCHELL	1		1
MOUNT ALFORD			1
MOUNT MARTIN			1
MOUNT MORGAN	1		
MOUNT PERRY	2		2
MURGON			1
MURRUMBA		1	
NAMBOUR	3	1	1
NORTH KOLAN			1
OMANAMA			1
PROSERPINE	1		2
PROSTON			1
QUNABA			1
RICHMOND			1
ROADVALE	1		1
ROCKHAMPTON	4	5	
ROMA	1		
ROSEWOOD	1		
SARINA			1
SELLHEIM		1	
SPRINGSURE	2	1	2
TARA		2	4
TEXAS	1		
THURSDAY ISLAND		1	
TINANA		1	
TOCAL	1		
TOOWOOMBA	1	1	1
TOWNSVILLE	3	3	2
UBOBO			1
UNDALLA CREEK			1
WALLANGARRA			1
WARWICK		1	1
WINTON			1
YALBOROO			1
YANDARAN			1
YEPPOON			1
YULEBA			1
TOTAL	73	42	80

	BORN	ENLISTED	RESIDENCE
NEW SOUTH WALES			
IN THE FIELD		0	
SYDNEY AREA	3	1	
BAULKHAM HILL			1
BLACKTOWN	1		1
KENSINGTON			1
KINGSFORD		1	
BONDI JUNCTION			1
CAMPBELLTOWN			1
LONG BAY			1
PADDINGTON		9	
PENSHURST	1		
RANDWICK			1
ST PETERS			1
WAVERLEY PARK		1	
TOTAL	5	15	6
AREAS OUTSIDE OF SYDNEY			
ALBURY	1		
BANGALOW	1		
BEGA			1
CANDELO	1		
CASINO	1		
CHINDERAH	1		
DAPTO			1
DELEGATE	1		1
DENMAN	1		1
GRAFTON	2		
GRIFFITH			1
HILLSTON	1		
INVERELL	1		
KATOOMBA			1
LIDCOMBE			1
LIVERPOOL			1
MACKSVILLE	1		
MALLANGAREE			1
MOREE	1		

	BORN	ENLISTED	RESIDENCE
MUDGEE	1		
MUNGINDI	1		
MURRUMBURRAH	1		
NARRANDERA			1
NEWCASTLE	2		
ORANGE	1		
PARKES	1		
PENRITH	1	1	1
QUIRINDI	1		
TENTERFIELD	2		
TUCABIA	1		
TWEED HEADS	1		
ULMARRA			1
WEST KEMPSEY			1
WOLLONGONG			2
WOONOONA	1		
TOTAL	27	2	14

VICTORIA			
IN THE FIELD		3	

MELBOURNE AREA	3	1	
ABBOTSFORD	2		1
ASCOT VALE			1
BURNLEY	1		
CARLTON	2		
CARNEGIE			1
CAULFIELD	1	3	
CHELTENHAM	1		1
CLIFTON HILL	1		1
COLLINGWOOD			1
CROXTON			1
EAST ST KILDA			1
HAMPTON			2
HAWTHORN			1
HEIDELBERG			1
IVANHOE	1		
KEW		1	

	BORN	ENLISTED	RESIDENCE
MOORABBIN			1
NORTH FITZROY	1		
NORTHCOTE			1
OAKLEIGH	1		
PARKDALE		1	
PRESTON		1	
RICHMOND			1
ROYAL PARK		1	
TOTAL	14	12	14
AREAS OUTSIDE OF MELBOURNE			
BENDIGO	1		
DARLEY		1	
EDENHOPE	1		
GEELONG	1		1
MITTA MITTA			1
SEVILLE			1
SEYMOUR	1		
TALLANGATTA	2		
TANDARA			1
WANGARATTA			1
TOTAL	6	1	5
SOUTH AUSTRALIA			
IN THE FIELD		0	
ADELAIDE AREA		3	1
COLONEL LIGHT GARDENS			1
EASTWOOD			1
HILTON	1		
STIRLING NORTH			1
URAIDLA			1
WAYVILLE		2	
TOTAL	1	5	5
AREAS OUTSIDE OF ADELAIDE			
BARMERA			1

	BORN	ENLISTED	RESIDENCE
GLADSTONE	1		
LAURA			1
PORT LINCOLN	1		
TOTAL	2	0	2
WESTERN AUSTRALIA			
IN THE FIELD		0	
PERTH AREA			1
AREAS OUTSIDE OF PERTH			
CLAREMONT		2	
GUILFORD	1		
NORTHAM		2	
SOMERSET HILL			1
TAMBELLUP			1
YOTING			1
TOTAL	1	4	3
TASMANIA			
IN THE FIELD		0	
HOBART	1		
LAUNCESTON	1		
UNKNOWN	1	2	7
BORN OVERSEAS			
NEW ZEALAND			
WELLINGTON	1		
ENGLAND			
COLEFORD	1		
KENT	1		
LEEDS	1		
NEWCASTLE	1		

	BORN	ENLISTED	RESIDENCE
READING	1		
WALSALL	1		
SCOTLAND			
ABERDEENSHIRE (INSCH)	1		
DUMFERMLINE	1		
DUNDEE	1		
WALES			
NEWPORT	1		
GERMANY			
HAMBURG	1		
PAPUA/NEW GUINEA (ENLISTMENTS)			
IN THE FIELD	2		
PORT MORESBY	4		
UNITED STATES (RESIDENCE)			
DETROIT, MICHIGAN	1		
FLATBUSH, NEW YORK	1		
FLORIDA	1		
FORT MONMOUTH, NEW YORK	1		
LONG ISLAND, NEW YORK	1		
RUTHVEN, IOWA	1		
TAMPA, FLORIDA	1		
UNKNOWN	2		

APPENDIX 3

ARMY MEDICAL CLASSIFICATIONS

This list is supplied courtesy of the Department of Veterans' Affairs *May 2006 Repatriation Handbook.*

Army Medical Classifications – World War II

Class 1	Fit for active service with field formations
Class 11A	Fit for specified duties in any unit in which the particular disability was no bar
Class 11B	Fit for any duty other than with field formations
Class 111	Labour Units, CMF, Temporarily Unfit, Unfit

From 7th August 1942, the classifications were:

A1	Medically fit for all active service duties
A2	Medically fit for all active service for which the particular disability is not a bar
B1	Medically fit for active service, except with field formations
B2	Medically fit for sedentary duties only
B3	Fit for service in labour units only
C	Temporarily unfit
D	Permanently unfit for military service

These classifications were later replaced by:

A1	Medically fit for all duties
A2	Medically fit for all duties for which the particular disability is not a bar
B	Medically fit to carry out certain duties which require only restricted medical fitness. These duties will be shown in war establishments.
C	Temporarily medically unfit
D	Medically unfit for military service

LIST OF APPRECIATION

The Right Honourable the Lord Mayor of Brisbane
Councillor Graham Quirk

Australian Department of Defence

Australian Department of Veterans' Affairs

Australian War Memorial

Brisbane City Council

John Oxley Library (State Library of Queensland)

National Archives of Australia

SPECIAL APPRECIATION

Dr Jonathon Ford
Brisbane City Council Heritage Unit

Graham Mckenzie-Smith
Military Historian, Researcher and Author

Karen Nunan
American History Researcher
Macarthur Museum

Major (Retd) Patrick O'Keeffe, OAM
Battle for Australia Commemoration National Council

Dr Andrew Richardson
Army History Unit
Department Of Defence

Professor Dennis Shanks
Army Malaria Institute
Department Of Defence

VETERAN CONTRIBUTORS

Archer, Ron, AIF, 1941-1946

Dulley, Richard Charles, AIF, 1940-1945

Huggonson, Walter Sidney, AIF 1941-1944, Wall Signatory

Hughes, Ronald William, AIF 1940-1944, Wall Signatory

Lahanas, Peter, AIF, 1942-1944

Watson, Bertram Francis, AIF, 1943-1946

Several World War II veterans wished to remain anonymous

WALL SIGNATORY CONTRIBUTORS

Beutel, L.R.

Cross, J.E.

Davie, M.T.J.

Davy, C.

Dixon, A.J.S.

Dull, H.A.

Edwards, G. L.

Faulkner, R.

Friend, R.E.M.

Greenhalgh, G.R.

Hanley, S.W.

Harrington, E.F.

Henson, H.G.

Huggonson, W. S.

Hughes, R. W.

Jacobson, H.I.

Jones, E.A.

Jorgensen, C.E.

Loveday, A.H.

McGill, J.E

Miller, K.D.

Myers, G.T.

Newman, T.N.O.

Reid, J.

Rice, R.F.S.

Saxby, H.H.

Scott, G.E.

Streeter, M.

Werner, A.E.

Weston, G.H.

SPECIAL THANKS

To the relatives of the World War II veterans including wall signatories, family and friends, co-workers, members of the public and the many staff members from various government agencies that have been so helpful with the production of this book.

Arkell, Robert

Astin, Heidi

Bate, Edna

Bittner, Susan

Black, Dianne

Blyth, Madeline *née* Eagar

Bourne, Alan

Brosnan, Gloria *née* Sherriff

Calam, Sidney

Calos, Penelope *née* Lahanas

Calos, Peter

Calvert, Judith *née* Loveday

Campbell, Kimberleigh *née* Bacon

Carmichael, Bill

Carpenter, Ronald

Culbert, Ron

Daniel, Terence

Denham, Peter

Dixon, Melissa

Dull, Rebecca

Dulley, John

Dulley, Joyce

Edwards, Thomas

Fletcher, Melissa

Gott, Rosemary

Gough, Brian

Grant, Judith *née* Weston

Griffin, Jeanie *née* Turnbull

Hawley, Kevin

Hogan, Beverley

Hornery, Cherrie

Huggonson, David

Hughes, Florence *née* Keir

Iliff, Sally

Jacobson, Gladys

Kastrissios, Irene

Klazema, John

Londos, George

Louwrens, Karin

Mavronickolas, Jim

Middleton, Jenny *née* Coop

Mifsud, Tim

Mitchell, Gregory

Newlands, Ros *née* Dulley

Noffke, Robert

O'Shea, Myra *née* Harris

Oberoi, Karan

Ogden, Brian

Phillips, Kaye *née* Saxby

Rammerath, Ann *née* Kastrissios

Rammerath, Robert

Savage, Beryl

Stephensen, Robyn *née* Edwards

Townend, Olga

Tucker, Viv

Veigel, Iris

Viles, Ronald

Wagland, David

Watson, Darren

Weston, Gary

Weston, Heather

Weston, Ronald

Winterton, Paul

Woolley, Marjory

Woolley, Roy

Several contributors wished to remain anonymous.

WITH SPECIAL THANKS TO THE GENERAL PUBLIC WHO HAVE PROVIDED SO MUCH INTERESTING AND HELPFUL INFORMATION

INTERNET SOURCES

Australian Government – Department of Defence
http://www.defence.gov.au
Defence Honours and Awards

Australian Government – Department of Veterans' Affairs
http://www.dva.gov.au
http://www.ww2.roll.gov.au
World War II Nominal Roll

Australian War Memorial
http://www.awm.gov.au
Official Histories of World War II
War Diaries of World War II

John Oxley Library
(State Library of Queensland)
http://www.slq.qld.gov.au
One Search

National Archives of Australia
http://www.naa.gov.au
RecordSearch

http://trove.nla.gov.au
Trove Newspapers

Wikipedia

RECOMMENDED READING

- Beaumont, Joan, *Australian Defence: Sources and Statistics*, Oxford University Press, 2001
- Clark, Chris, *Encyclopaedia of Australia's Battles*, Allen & Unwin, 2010
- Coates, John, *An Atlas of Australia's Wars*, Oxford University Press, Second Edition, 2006
- Dennis, Peter and Grey, Jeffrey (eds.), *The Oxford Companion to Australian Military History*, Oxford University Press , Second Edition, 2008
- Grey, Jeffrey, *A Military History of Australia*, Cambridge University Press, Third Edition, 2008
- Long, Gavin, *The Six Years War: a concise history of Australia in the 1939-45 War*, Australian War Memorial, 1973
- McKenzie-Smith, Graham, *The Unit Guide: The Australian Army 1939-1945.*
    - Volume 1 – Index to Unit Types, Unit Index, Location Index, Bibliography and Selected Orders of Battle
    - Volume 2 – HQs, Infantry, Cavalry, Armoured and Intelligence Units
    - Volume 3 – Artillery, Air Defence and Engineer Units
    - Volume 4 – Medical and Signals Units
    - Volume 5 – Supply, Transport, Ordnance and Workshop Units
    - Volume 6 – Women's Services, Volunteer Defence Corps, Survey, Labour, Provost, Training, Dental, Veterinary, Bath, Transit, Amenities, Graves, Pay, Records and Postal Units.

  To be published by the Army History Unit by Big Sky Publications, Newport, NSW (In print, 2014)
- Smith, Neil, *They Came Unseen – The Men and Women of Z Special Unit*, Mostly Unsung Publications, First Edition, 2010

ABOUT THE AUTHOR

Lyris Mitchell graduated in Arts from the University of Queensland with majors in History and Psychology. She initially began writing military biographies from World War I and later included soldiers from World War II. While working as a Tour Guide at Brisbane's City Hall, she became familiar with the Heritage listed Soldiers' Signature Wall and was immediately aware of its potential. She began identifying the signatories and researching the backgrounds of the men. After providing the identifications to the Brisbane City Council for its website, she was awarded a Commendation by the former Lord Mayor, Campbell Newman. Since then, many of the soldiers' relatives have contacted City Hall and provided information about the men. Lyris has appeared on several documentaries concerning the wall, including *The Soul of Brisbane* for Channel 9 and the Brisbane City Council and *Time Walks* with Tony Robinson for the History Channel. She is currently pursuing her favourite pastime writing military biographies.